Hands-on ML Projects with OpenCV

Master Computer Vision and Machine Learning using OpenCV and Python.

by

Mugesh S.

www.orangeava.com

Copyright © 2023, Orange Education Pvt Ltd, AVA™

All rights reserved. No part of this book may be reproduced, stored in a retrieval system, or transmitted in any form or by any means, without the prior written permission of the publisher, except in the case of brief quotations embedded in critical articles or reviews.

Every effort has been made in the preparation of this book to ensure the accuracy of the information presented. However, the information contained in this book is sold without warranty, either express or implied. Neither the author nor Orange Education Pvt Ltd. or its dealers and distributors, will be held liable for any damages caused or alleged to have been caused directly or indirectly by this book.

Orange Education Pvt Ltd. has endeavored to provide trademark information about all of the companies and products mentioned in this book by the appropriate use of capital. However, Orange Education Pvt Ltd. cannot guarantee the accuracy of this information.

First published: August 2023
Published by: Orange Education Pvt Ltd, AVA™
Address: 9, Daryaganj, Delhi, 110002

ISBN: 978-93-88590-87-7

www.orangeava.com

Dedicated to

My loving family, supportive friends, and inspiring teachers:

S. Mallika (amma)
V. Sudalai Raja (appa)

&

My special thanks to
C. Subramanian & C. Thangaraja

Who supported my education and keep motivating me during my tough times.

About the Author

This is **Mugesh S.** I am working as a Data Scientist at Infosys, with a passion for leveraging data-driven insights to tackle complex challenges and drive business success. I am an engineering graduate who completed the PG program in Data Science and Engineering as well as a Master's in Mathematics and Data Science, to deepen my understanding of the intricacies of data analytics.

I have over 7 years of hands-on experience in SQL, Python, ETL projects, and machine learning projects, including time series forecasting, Chabot, people face detection, face recognition, Statistical Data Analysis, Computer vision, NLP, and SQL/No SQL. I possess a good Knowledge of version control systems and cloud computing systems. In addition, I have an excellent work ethic and am an influential team member.

I have been an instrumental force in delivering successful data-driven projects across diverse industries, earning accolades for my ability to translate raw data into meaningful business intelligence. My commitment to professional growth is evident through my prestigious certifications, including the esteemed Infosys- certified AI professional and Infosys- certified Automation professional certifications.

These credentials underscore my dedication to staying at the forefront of advancements in the ever-evolving data science landscape. With an insatiable curiosity and an analytical mindset, I am known for my meticulous approach to problem-solving and my proficiency in designing cutting-edge machine learning models.

My collaborative nature has made me a valuable team player, effectively collaborating with colleagues and stakeholders to drive innovation and achieve project milestones. Beyond my technical expertise, my passion for data science lies in its potential to create a positive societal impact. I am driven by the belief that data-driven insights hold the key to solving complex challenges and improving the lives of people worldwide. In my spare time, I enjoy exploring new avenues in data science, experimenting with emerging technologies, and sharing my knowledge through mentorship and educational initiatives.

Technical Reviewer

Jalem Raj Rohit is an ML and Data Science professional with over 8 years in the field. He currently works as a Lead Data Scientist in a heal care-tech company. He has written books on Serverless Engineering and Julia programming language and is actively involved in the data science community of India. He has diverse experience in the fields of data engineering, data science, MLOps, and backed engineering, and has led teams that built data science stacks of several product companies from the ground-up.

LinkedIn profile:

http://linkedin.com/in/jalemrajrohita

Acknowledgments

I would like to express my deepest gratitude to all those who have contributed to the creation of this book. First and foremost, I would like to thank my family and friends for their unwavering support and encouragement throughout this journey.

To my teachers, past and present, I am grateful for your guidance, knowledge, and expertise. Your passion for teaching and dedication to helping students succeed has been instrumental in shaping my understanding of machine learning and OpenCV. I extend my appreciation to the reviewers and technical editors who have dedicated their time and expertise to ensure the accuracy and quality of the content.

Lastly, I am grateful to the developers and contributors of the OpenCV library, whose dedication and hard work have made it possible for us to explore the exciting world of computer vision and machine learning.

This book would not have been possible without the collective efforts and contributions of all those mentioned above. Thank you for your immense support and belief in this project.

Preface

Welcome to "Hands-on ML Projects with OpenCV." In today's world, machine learning has become an essential tool for solving complex problems and making intelligent decisions. OpenCV, a popular computer vision library, combined with the power of Python, provides a robust platform for implementing machine learning algorithms in real-world applications.

This book is designed to be a practical guide that takes you on a journey to explore the exciting field of machine learning using OpenCV. Whether you are a beginner or an experienced developer, this book will equip you with the knowledge and skills to leverage the capabilities of OpenCV for machine-learning tasks.

Throughout this book, we will cover a wide range of topics, starting with the basics of machine learning and its applications in computer vision. We will dive into the fundamentals of OpenCV and Python, exploring key concepts and techniques that form the foundation of machine learning with OpenCV.

You will learn how to preprocess and transform data, create and train machine learning models, and evaluate their performance. We will explore popular algorithms in neural networks which is CNN and see how they can be implemented using OpenCV.

Moreover, we will delve into advanced topics, including deep learning, transfer learning, and model optimization. You will gain hands-on experience by working on real-world projects and datasets, enabling you to apply the concepts and techniques learned in practical scenarios.

By the end of this book, you will have a strong understanding of machine learning principles and the ability to apply them using OpenCV and Python. You will be ready to tackle complex machine-learning tasks and contribute to cutting-edge applications in computer vision.

We divided this book into 11 chapters. So, let's embark on this exciting journey into the world of practical machine learning with OpenCV. Get ready to unlock the potential of machine learning and discover the endless possibilities it offers. Let's dive in and explore the fascinating world of intelligent machines.

Happy learning and coding!
Mugesh

Chapter 1
In this chapter, you will be introduced to the basics of OpenCV (Open Source Computer Vision Library) and learn how to set up your development environment. You will explore the core functionalities of OpenCV, such as reading and displaying images and videos and understanding the color representation of images. This chapter serves as a foundation for the subsequent chapters, providing you with the necessary knowledge to start working with OpenCV.

Chapter 2
In this chapter, you will dive deeper into image and video analytics using OpenCV. You will learn how to perform basic operations on images, such as read, write, and show Images and videos. You will also explore techniques for video analysis, including extracting frames, playing videos, and capturing video from a webcam.

Chapter 3
In this chapter, we focus on image processing techniques using OpenCV. You will learn how to apply various filters and transformations to images, including Bitwise Operations, Resizing, and rotating and Remove background. By the end of this chapter, you will have a solid understanding of different image processing techniques and their applications.

Chapter 4
In this chapter, we focus on image processing techniques using OpenCV. You will learn how to apply various filters and transformations to images, including Smoothing Images Blurring Images OpenCV Image Gradients, and Edge Detection. By the end of this chapter, you will have a solid understanding of different image processing techniques and their applications.

Chapter 5
In this chapter, we focus specifically on thresholding and contour techniques in image processing using OpenCV. You will learn different thresholding methods to convert images into binary form and extract relevant information. Additionally, you will explore contour detection algorithms to identify and extract shapes and objects from images.

Chapter 6
In this chapter, we focus on the concepts of corner detection and road lane detection using OpenCV. You will learn how to identify and locate corners in images using techniques like Harris corner detection and Shi-Tomasi corner detection. Furthermore, you will explore methods for detecting and tracking road lanes in images or video streams. These techniques are fundamental for applications

such as object tracking, Feature matching with FLANN, and Background subtraction methods in OpenCV.

Chapter 7
In this chapter, we focus on motion detection and object tracking using OpenCV. You will learn how to detect and track moving objects in videos or webcam feeds using techniques like object detection and object tracking using HSV color space. Additionally, you will explore algorithms for object tracking, including methods like MeanShift and CamShift.

Chapter 8
In this chapter, we focus on image segmentation techniques and face detection using OpenCV. You will learn about segmentation algorithms like watershed segmentation, QR code detection, and Optical character recognition using OpenCV. Additionally, you will explore techniques for detecting and recognizing faces in images and videos using Haar cascades and deep learning-based models.

Chapter 9
In this chapter, we focus on the introduction to deep learning and its application in computer vision using OpenCV. You will learn the basics of neural networks, deep learning frameworks, and how to train deep learning models for image classification and object detection. You will also explore pre-trained deep-learning models and learn how to use them for various computer vision tasks. This chapter lays the foundation for advanced deep-learning projects in the following chapter.

Chapter 10
In this chapter, we focus on advanced deep-learning projects using OpenCV. You will explore advanced topics such as Introduction to YOLO detection, YOLO v3 object detection, and YOLO v5 custom dataset. You will implement projects like Face recognition, Real-time age prediction, and Emotion detection using TensorFlow using deep learning techniques. This chapter equips you with the skills to tackle complex and cutting-edge deep-learning projects.

Chapter 11
In the final chapter, you will learn about the deployment of OpenCV projects. You will explore different techniques for optimizing and deploying OpenCV applications, including Integrating OpenCV projects with web applications using Flask. This chapter provides you with the knowledge and tools to take your OpenCV projects from development to production.

Downloading the code bundles and colored images

Please follow the link to download the
Code Bundles of the book:

https://github.com/OrangeAVA/Hands-on-ML-Projects-with-OpenCV

The code bundles and images of the book are also hosted on
https://rebrand.ly/0087d4

In case there's an update to the code, it will be updated on the existing GitHub repository.

Errata

We take immense pride in our work at Orange Education Pvt Ltd and follow best practices to ensure the accuracy of our content to provide an indulging reading experience to our subscribers. Our readers are our mirrors, and we use their inputs to reflect and improve upon human errors, if any, that may have occurred during the publishing processes involved. To let us maintain the quality and help us reach out to any readers who might be having difficulties due to any unforeseen errors, please write to us at :

errata@orangeava.com

Your support, suggestions, and feedback are highly appreciated.

DID YOU KNOW

Did you know that Orange Education Pvt Ltd offers eBook versions of every book published, with PDF and ePub files available? You can upgrade to the eBook version at www.orangeava.com and as a print book customer, you are entitled to a discount on the eBook copy. Get in touch with us at: **info@orangeava.com** for more details.

At **www.orangeava.com**, you can also read a collection of free technical articles, sign up for a range of free newsletters, and receive exclusive discounts and offers on AVA™ Books and eBooks.

Piracy

If you come across any illegal copies of our works in any form on the internet, we would be grateful if you would provide us with the location address or website name. Please contact us at **info@orangeava.com** with a link to the material.

Are you interested in authoring with us?

If there is a topic that you have expertise in, and you are interested in either writing or contributing to a book, please write to us at **business@orangeava.com**. We are on a journey to help developers and tech professionals to gain insights on the present technological advancements and innovations happening across the globe and build a community that believes Knowledge is best acquired by sharing and learning with others. Please reach out to us to learn what our audience demands and how you can be part of this educational reform. We also welcome ideas from tech experts and help them build learning and development content for their domains.

Reviews

Please leave a review. Once you have read and used this book, why not leave a review on the site that you purchased it from? Potential readers can then see and use your unbiased opinion to make purchase decisions. We at Orange Education would love to know what you think about our products, and our authors can learn from your feedback. Thank you!

For more information about Orange Education, please visit **www.orangeava.com**.

Table of Contents

1. **Getting Started With OpenCV** 1
   Introduction 1
   Structure 1
   Introduction to Computer Vision 1
   Introduction to OpenCV 2
   Benefits of Learning OpenCV 3
   OpenCV Real-time Applications in Computer Vision 4
   OpenCV Architecture and Explanation 5
   Features of OpenCV Library 6
   Python Code Editors for OpenCV 7
   Downloading and Installing OpenCV for Windows 8
   Downloading and Installing OpenCV for MacOS 10
   Google Colab for OpenCV 11
   Conclusion 13
   Points to Remember 13
   References 14
   Questions/MCQs 14

2. **Basic Image and Video Analytics in OpenCV** 15
   Introduction 15
   Structure 15
   Read, Write, and Show Images in OpenCV 15
   Covert Color in Images Using OpenCV 17
   Read, Write, and Show Videos from a Camera in OpenCV 18
   Covert color in Video Using OpenCV 21
   Draw Geometric Ahapes on Images Using OpenCV 23
   Setting Camera Parameters in OpenCV 28
   Show the Date and Time on Videos Using OpenCV 29
   Show Text on Videos Using OpenCV 31
   Basic Mouse Events Using OpenCV 33
   Conclusion 36
   Points to Remember 36
   References 36

3. **Image Processing 1 Using OpenCV** 37
   Introduction 37
   Structure 37
   Basic Image Processing Techniques 37
      Image wait function 38
      Image cropping 39
      Image resizing 40
      Image rotation 40
      Grayscaling 42
      Image split 42
      Merging image 43
      Adding two images 45
      Blend two images with different weights 46
      Region of interest (ROI) 47
      Background Removal 48
   Reshaping the Video Frame 50
   Pausing the Video Frame 52
   More Mouse Event Examples 53
      Extract the color of a pixel on the image using the mouse 53
      Extract the X, and Y values and pixel color on the image using the left and right mouse buttons, respectively 55
      Draw the rectangle and curve using the left-click button mouse 58
   Bitwise Operations 60
   Binding a Trackbar 63
   Image Trackbar 65
   Conclusion 67
   Points to Remember 67
   References 67

4. **Image Processing 2 using OpenCV** 69
   Introduction 69
   Structure 69
   Matplotlib with OpenCV 69
   Morphological Transformations Using OpenCV 72
   Smoothing and Blurring Images Using OpenCV 76
   Image Gradients Using OpenCV 80
   Image Pyramids with OpenCV 83

Image Blending Using OpenCV	85
Edge Detection Using OpenCV	90
Sobel Operator Using OpenCV	90
Laplacian of Gaussian (LoG) Filter Using OpenCV	92
Canny Edge Detection Using OpenCV	93
Conclusion	96
Points to Remember	96
References	96

5. Thresholding and Contour Techniques Using OpenCV 97

Introduction	97
Structure	97
Image Thresholding using OpenCV	97
Simple thresholding	97
Adaptive thresholding	99
Otsu's thresholding	100
Binary thresholding	101
Inverted thresholding	103
Finding and Drawing Contours with OpenCV	104
Detecting Simple Geometric Shapes Using OpenCV	107
Understanding Image Histograms Using OpenCV	110
Template Matching Using OpenCV	113
Hough Line Transform Theory in OpenCV	117
Standard Hough line transform using OpenCV	119
Probabilistic Hough Transform Using OpenCV	121
Circle Detection Using OpenCV Hough Circle Transform	123
Camera Calibration Using OpenCV	125
Conclusion	129
Points to Remember	129
References	129

6. Detect Corners and Road Lane Using OpenCV 131

Introduction	131
Structure	131
Road Lane Line Detection Using OpenCV	131
Detecting Corners in OpenCV	137
Types of Detect Corners in OpenCV	139

        Harris Corner Detector 139
        Shi Tomasi Corner Detector 141
        FAST corner detection 143
        Blob Detection 144
        Scale-invariant feature transform 147
    Feature Matching with FLANN 148
    Background Subtraction Methods in OpenCV 151
    Types of Background Subtraction Methods in OpenCV 152
        BackgroundSubtractorMOG2 152
        BackgroundSubtractorKNN 154
    Conclusion 156
    Points to Remember 156
    References 156

7. Object And Motion Detection Using Opencv 157
    Introduction 157
    Structure 157
    HSV Color Space 157
    Object Detection Using HSV Color Space 159
    Object Tracking Using HSV Color Space 161
    Motion Detection and Tracking Using OpenCV 164
    Mean Shift Object Tracking Using OpenCV 165
    Camshift Object Tracking Method Using OpenCV 168
    Augmented Reality in OpenCV 171
    Conclusion 176
    Points to Remember 176
    Questions 176
    References 176

8. Image Segmentation and Detecting Faces Using OpenCV 177
    Introduction 177
    Structure 177
    Image Segmentation Using OpenCV 177
    Introduction to Haar Cascade Classifiers 180
    Face Detection Using Haar Cascade Classifiers 181
    Eye Detection Haar Feature-based Cascade Classifiers 185
    Smile Detection Haar Feature-based Cascade Classifiers 189

QR Code Detection Using OpenCV	193
Optical Character Recognition Using OpenCV	197
Conclusion	201
Points to Remember	202
References	202

9. Introduction to Deep Learning with OpenCV 203

Introduction	203
Structure	203
Introduction to Machine Learning	203
Types of machine learning	204
Introduction to Deep Learning	206
Artificial Neural Networks	207
Types of neural networks	207
Neural network architecture	211
Activation functions	211
Neural networks optimization techniques	213
Steps for training neural networks	214
Deep learning frameworks	215
Deep learning applications	216
Introduction to Deep Learning in OpenCV	217
Neural networks in the image and video analytics	217
Image classification with deep neural networks	218
Object detection with neural networks	219
Face detection and recognition with neural networks	221
Semantic segmentation in neural networks	222
Generative adversarial networks	223
Integration of OpenCV with Robotics	224
Iris Dataset in TensorFlow	225
Fashion-MNIST in TensorFlow	228
Digit Recognition Training Using TensorFlow	232
Testing Digit Recognition Model Using OpenCV	236
Dog Versus Cat Classification in TensorFlow with OpenCV	238
Dog versus cat classification with OpenCV	241
Conclusion	244
Points to Remember	244
References	244

10. Advance Deep Learning Projects with OpenCV 245
Introduction 245
Structure 245
Introduction to YOLO 245
YOLO Versions 249
YOLO v3 Object Detection Using TensorFlow 250
YOLO v5 and Custom Dataset Using TensorFlow 254
Face Recognition Using TensorFlow with OpenCV 261
FaceNet Architecture 262
Real-time Age Prediction Using TensorFlow and RESNET 50_CNN 269
RESNET 50_CNN 269
Facial Expression Recognition Using TensorFlow 276
    Emotion detection methods 276
Content-based Image Retrieval Using TensorFlow 288
Conclusion 297
Points to Remember 297
References 297

11. Deployment of OpenCV Projects 299
Introduction 299
Structure 299
Introduction to Deploying OpenCV Projects 299
    Deploying OpenCV projects in Azure 301
    Deploying OpenCV projects in Azure 303
Integrating OpenCV with web applications 306
    Integrating dog vs. cat classification project and flask 307
Conclusion 311
Points to Remember 311
References 311

Index 312

CHAPTER 1

Getting Started With OpenCV

Introduction

This chapter will cover a detailed introduction to computer vision and OpenCV and their practical application in real-time, and then finally a complete explanation of installation procedures.

Structure

In this chapter, we will cover the following topics:

- Introduction to Computer Vision
- Introduction to OpenCV
- Benefits of learning OpenCV
- OpenCV real-time applications in computer vision
- OpenCV architecture and explanation
- Features of OpenCV Library
- Python Code Editors for OpenCV
- Downloading and Installing OpenCV
  - Windows
  - Mac
- Google colab for OpenCV

Introduction to Computer Vision

Computer vision is a field of computer science that uses artificial intelligence and machine learning algorithms to process digital images and videos. It is a subset of artificial intelligence that focuses on giving computers the ability to understand and interpret the visual world. Computer vision algorithms can be used to detect objects, identify faces, recognize patterns, classify images, segment images into meaningful parts, and more.

Computer vision is used in many fields such as robotics, medical imaging, driverless cars, facial recognition, and industrial inspection. By applying computer vision algorithms to digital images and videos, machines can gain an understanding of the content of the image or video. This understanding can then be used to make decisions or guide actions.

Computer vision algorithms can be divided into two categories:

- **Low-level algorithms:** It is focused on analyzing the pixels of an image to detect basic shapes and patterns, such as lines and curves.
- **High-level algorithms:** It is used to identify objects or recognize complex structures.

The process of computer vision usually starts with a set of images or videos as input. The images or videos are then pre-processed to improve the quality of the data. This is followed by feature extraction, which involves extracting meaningful information from images or videos. Finally, the extracted features are used to train the computer vision algorithms.

Computer vision has been widely used in many applications such as medical imaging, robotics, surveillance, facial recognition, and augmented reality. In medical imaging, computer vision algorithms are used to detect tumors, diagnose diseases, and measure vital signs. In robotics, computer vision algorithms are used to recognize objects and navigate around obstacles.

In surveillance, computer vision algorithms are used to detect suspicious activities. In facial recognition, computer vision algorithms are used to identify and classify people. In augmented reality, computer vision algorithms are used to display virtual objects in real-world environments.

Introduction to OpenCV

OpenCV (Open-Source Computer Vision Library) is an open-source computer vision library. It was originally developed by Intel Corporation in 1999 and later became a collaborative effort of several companies and universities. It is written in C++ and supports many programming languages.

OpenCV is an open-source computer vision and machine learning software library, and its main goal is real-time computer vision applications. It was built to provide a good infrastructure for computer vision applications and to improve the use of machine vision in commercial products.

OpenCV library has more than 2500 optimized algorithms and has a modular structure, which means that the package includes several shared or static libraries, and developers can pick and choose which parts they wish to use. For example, OpenCV includes numerous features, such as pattern recognition, motion detection, and object identification. OpenCV can be used in a wide variety of applications and platforms, including embedded systems, robotics, mobile phones, video surveillance, and computer vision. Its code is portable, and it is suitable for real-time applications. OpenCV is also available as a library of optimized functions in various programming languages.

OpenCV has become the go-to library for computer vision and machine learning. It is being used in many industries, such as medical, automotive, retail, and robotics, to develop applications that can recognize objects, analyze images, and extract useful data from them. This can be used in 3D point clouds from stereo cameras, stitch images together to produce a high-resolution image of an entire scene, find similar images from an image database, and much more.

OpenCV is open-source and free to use, so developers can access and modify its source code according to their needs. The library is constantly updated with new algorithms and features, making it a powerful and constantly evolving library.

Benefits of Learning OpenCV

Learning OpenCV can have tremendous benefits for a wide variety of users. OpenCV is a powerful open-source library providing easy access to both basic and advanced computer vision techniques, allowing developers to create applications quickly and easily. This can be used to create several different applications, from simple games to complex AI-driven applications.

OpenCV is the vast number of resources available to the user. OpenCV has an extensive library of tools and tutorials that can help new developers become comfortable with the language, and advanced users quickly create complex applications. OpenCV also has a wide range of example projects, which can serve as great starting points for learning.

Let us discuss the major benefits of learning OpenCV Library:

- **Versatility:** OpenCV can be used for a wide variety of tasks, such as object tracking, facial recognition, motion detection, and more. This is extremely valuable, as it allows developers to create a wide range of applications without having to learn multiple languages and frameworks.
- **Compatibility:** OpenCV can be used with a wide variety of languages and frameworks, such as Python, C++, Java, and even the popular .NET Framework. This is extremely useful, as it allows developers to interact with different platforms quickly and easily, without having to learn multiple languages.
- **Deep learning:** OpenCV has many tools and APIs that make it easy to integrate deep learning algorithms into applications. This can be used

to create AI-driven applications that can harness the power of machine learning, such as facial recognition, object detection, and so on.

- **Scalability:** OpenCV is designed to work with large amounts of data and can easily handle large datasets, allowing developers to quickly and easily develop applications that can quickly and accurately process huge amounts of data.

- **Opportunities for developers:** OpenCV is a very popular language, and there is a wide range of jobs that require knowledge of OpenCV. Many companies are looking for developers with OpenCV skills, and these jobs can be quite lucrative.

In summary, learning OpenCV can have tremendous benefits for a wide variety of users. OpenCV is a powerful open-source library providing easy access to both basic and advanced computer vision techniques, allowing developers to create applications.

Furthermore, OpenCV is versatile, compatible, supports deep learning, and is extremely scalable. Finally, learning OpenCV can open up a world of opportunities for developers, as knowledge of OpenCV is highly valued in the job market.

OpenCV Real-time Applications in Computer Vision

OpenCV is an open-source computer vision library that provides real-time applications for vision-based operations. OpenCV provides several powerful tools for image processing and computer vision research, including a feature detection and tracking library, a real-time gesture recognition system, and a computer vision-enabled language recognition library.

OpenCV offers high speed and accuracy for identifying objects in photographs, videos, and other digital images. It can detect faces, identify features and characteristics, read text from images, and recognize objects. Let us now discuss examples of real-time applications in computer vision using OpenCV Library:

- **Image and video processing:** OpenCV provides a wide range of functions for image and video processing, such as image filtering, segmentation, and feature extraction.

- **Medical imaging:** OpenCV can be used to analyze medical images, such as X-rays and MRI scans, to assist with diagnosis and treatment.

- **Object detection and recognition:** OpenCV provides tools for detecting and recognizing objects in images and videos, including face detection, pedestrian detection, and object recognition.

- **Video surveillance:** OpenCV can be used to develop video surveillance systems, including motion detection and tracking.
- **Augmented reality:** OpenCV can be used to create augmented reality applications that overlay virtual objects onto the real world.
- **Robotics:** OpenCV can be used to develop algorithms for robots to navigate and interact with their environment, including obstacle detection and avoidance.
- **Autonomous vehicles:** OpenCV can be used to develop algorithms for autonomous vehicles, such as lane detection and object detection. It is also used to build similar products like Google street view and helps compete in challenges like the DARPA.
- **Gaming:** OpenCV can be used to create interactive games that use gestures and facial expressions as input.
- **Space:** OpenCV has been used for some of the most high-profile projects like space exploration. It was used in the Curiosity rover mission to Mars to help the rover navigate and avoid obstacles. The rover used a combination of stereo cameras and OpenCV algorithms to create 3D maps of the terrain and identify potential hazards.

These are just a few examples of the many applications of OpenCV. With its wide range of functions and algorithms, OpenCV is a powerful tool for developing computer vision and machine learning applications.

OpenCV Architecture and Explanation

OpenCV architecture is divided into several components that work together to provide a comprehensive framework for image and video processing. Here are the main components of the OpenCV architecture:

- **Core Functionality:** This is the core of the OpenCV library and includes basic data structures, mathematical functions, and algorithms for image processing. It provides support for basic image operations such as image conversion, filtering, and morphological operations.
- **High-Level GUI:** This component provides high-level graphical user interface functionality and includes functions for creating windows, displaying images, and handling mouse and keyboard events.
- **Video I/O:** This component provides support for reading and writing video files in various formats. It also provides functions for capturing video from cameras and other sources.
- **Image Processing:** This component includes a wide range of image processing algorithms, such as edge detection, image segmentation,

object detection, and feature detection. It also provides support for image transformations, such as scaling, rotation, and affine transformations.

- **Feature Detection and Description:** This component provides functions for detecting and describing image features, such as corners, blobs, and edges. It also includes algorithms for matching features between images, which are useful for tasks such as object recognition and tracking.
- **Object Detection and Recognition:** This component provides support for object detection and recognition, using techniques such as Haar cascades, HOG features, and deep learning-based methods.
- **Machine Learning:** OpenCV includes several machine learning algorithms, such as decision trees, support vector machines, and neural networks. These algorithms can be used for tasks such as classification, regression, and clustering.
- **Miscellaneous:** This component includes various other functions and algorithms, such as camera calibration, stereo vision, optical flow, and 3D reconstruction.

Overall, the OpenCV architecture provides a comprehensive framework for image and video processing and includes a wide range of functions and algorithms that can be used for a variety of applications.

Features of OpenCV Library

OpenCV is a powerful library for image and video processing, and it comes with a wide range of features that make it a popular choice for developers and researchers. Here are some of the key features of OpenCV:

- **Cross-platform:** OpenCV is available on multiple platforms, including Windows, Linux, Mac OS, and Android.
- **Efficient:** OpenCV is optimized for performance, with functions that are written in C/C++ for speed and efficiency.
- **Large collection of functions:** OpenCV includes a large collection of functions and algorithms for image and video processing, including basic image operations, feature detection, object recognition, machine learning, and more.
- **Support for multiple programming languages:** OpenCV supports multiple programming languages, including Python, C/C++, Java, and MATLAB.

- **High-level GUI:** OpenCV provides a high-level graphical user interface (GUI) for displaying images and videos, creating windows, and handling user input.
- **Camera calibration:** OpenCV includes functions for camera calibration, which is important for tasks such as 3D reconstruction and stereo vision.
- **Support for multiple file formats:** OpenCV supports multiple file formats for reading and writing images and videos, including JPEG, PNG, TIFF, AVI, and MP4.
- **Open source:** OpenCV is an open-source library, which means that developers can use, modify, and redistribute the code without restriction.

Overall, the features of OpenCV make it a powerful tool for image and video processing, and it is widely used in research, industry, and education.

Python Code Editors for OpenCV

There are many Python code editors available that can be used for developing OpenCV applications. Here are some popular ones:

- Visual Studio Code: Visual Studio Code is a lightweight code editor that is highly extensible through plugins. This includes support for Python development and has several plugins available for OpenCV development. It includes features such as syntax highlighting, code completion, and an integrated Terminal.
- **Jupyter Notebook:** Jupyter Notebook is a web-based interactive environment for running Python code, and it includes support for OpenCV development. It provides an easy way to experiment with OpenCV code and visualize the output in real-time. It also allows for the creation of interactive documents that can be shared with others.
- **PyCharm:** PyCharm is a powerful IDE for Python development, and it includes features specifically designed for OpenCV development. It includes an interactive debugger, a code editor with syntax highlighting and autocomplete, and integration with Git for version control. PyCharm also provides support for Jupyter notebooks, which can be used for experimenting with OpenCV code.
- **Spyder:** Spyder is an open-source IDE for scientific Python development that includes a code editor, interactive console, and several other tools for data analysis and visualization. It also includes support for OpenCV

development through the use of the QtConsole, which provides a graphical interface for running Python code and displaying OpenCV output.
- **Sublime Text:** Sublime Text is a lightweight code editor that is highly customizable and extensible through plugins. This includes support for Python development and has several plugins available for OpenCV development. It includes features such as syntax highlighting, code completion, and an integrated Terminal.

These are just a few examples of the many code editors available for developing OpenCV applications in Python. The choice of editor depends on personal preference, project requirements, and development style.

Downloading and Installing OpenCV for Windows

Here are the steps to download and install Anaconda on Windows and open Jupyter Notebook:

Download Anaconda: Go to the Anaconda website at https://www.anaconda.com/products/individual and scroll down to the bottom of the page and download the latest version of Anaconda for Windows.

Choose the version that matches your system architecture (32-bit or 64-bit) and your version of Python.

The following figure represents the available Anaconda versions for all operating systems:

Anaconda Installers

Windows	MacOS	Linux
Python 3.9	Python 3.9	Python 3.9
64-Bit Graphical Installer (621 MB)	64-Bit Graphical Installer (688 MB)	64-Bit (x86) Installer (737 MB)
	64-Bit Command Line Installer (681 MB)	64-Bit (PowerR and Power9) Installer (360 MB)
	64-Bit (M1) Graphical Installer (484 MB)	
	64-Bit (M1) Command Line Installer (472 MB)	64-Bit (AWS Graviton2 / ARM64) Installer (534 MB)
		64-bit (Linux on IBM Z & LinuxONE) Installer (282 MB)

Figure 1.1: Available Anaconda versions

Install Anaconda: Double-click on the downloaded Anaconda installer and follow the instructions to install Anaconda on your system. You can accept the default settings unless you have a specific reason to change them.

Getting Started With OpenCV

Open Jupyter Notebook: Once Anaconda is installed, open the Anaconda Navigator application. You should be able to find it in the Start menu or by searching for **Anaconda Navigator** in the Windows search bar. The following figure is an example of the Anaconda Navigator page:

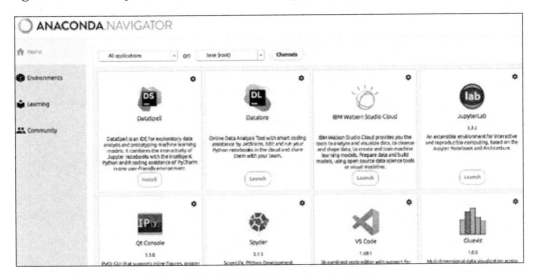

Figure 1.2: *Available IDE in Anaconda Navigator*

Launch Jupyter Notebook: In the Anaconda Navigator, click on the **Launch** button under the Jupyter Notebook icon. This will open a new tab in your default web browser with the Jupyter Notebook interface.

Create a new notebook: To create a new notebook, click the **New** button on the right-hand side of the Jupyter Notebook interface and select **Python 3** (or another kernel, if you prefer). This will create a new notebook with an empty code cell. Refer to the image below:

Figure 1.3: *New Jupyter Notebook interface*

Type in the following command and press *Shift + Enter*:

```
! pip install opencv-python
```

Refer to the following figure for the new notebook page:

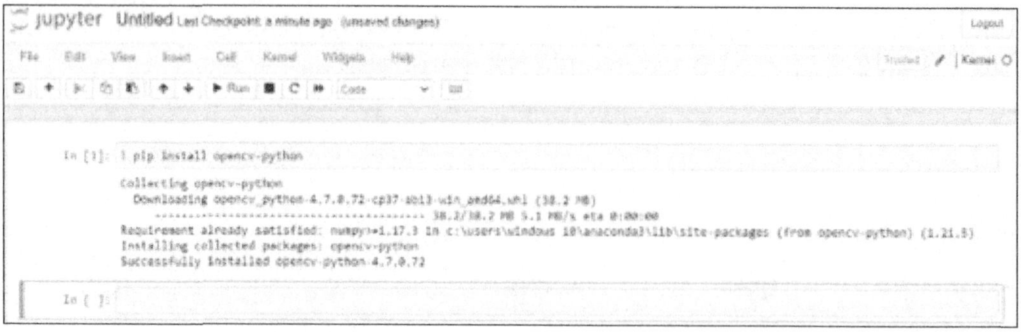

Figure 1.4: Installation of OpenCV in Jupyter Notebook

Import OpenCV: To import OpenCV into your notebook, enter the following code in a new cell and run it:

```
import cv2
print(cv2.__version__)
```

Refer to the following figure to check the Version of OpenCV:

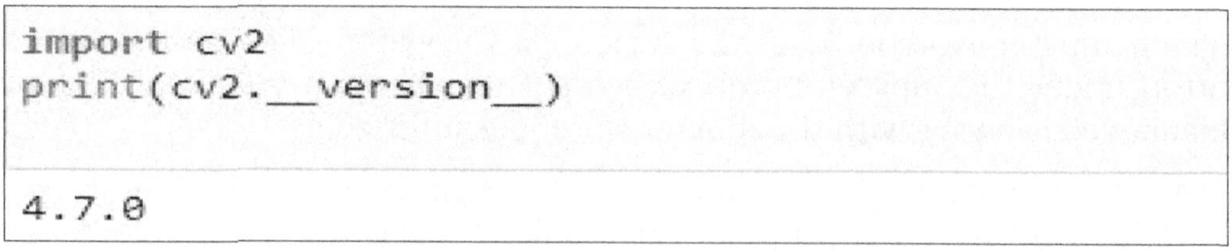

Figure 1.5: OpenCV successfully installed

This should display the version of OpenCV that you have installed.

You have successfully installed Anaconda on your Windows system and are ready to start using Jupyter Notebook to write and run OpenCV code.

Downloading and Installing OpenCV for MacOS

Here are the steps to download and install Anaconda on macOS and open Jupyter Notebook:

Download Anaconda: Go to the Anaconda website at https://www.anaconda.com/products/individual and download the latest version of Anaconda for macOS.

Choose the version that matches your system architecture (32-bit or 64-bit) and your version of Python. (Refer to *Figure 1.1*):

1. **Install Anaconda:** Double-click on the downloaded Anaconda installer and follow the instructions to install Anaconda on your system. You can accept the default settings unless you have a specific reason to change them.
2. **Open Terminal:** To open the Terminal app, go to the `Applications` folder, then to the `Utilities` folder, and click `Terminal`.
3. **Launch Jupyter Notebook:** In the Terminal window, type the following command and press Enter: (Refer to *Figure 1.3*):

    `jupyter notebook`

This will start the Jupyter Notebook server and open a new tab in your default web browser with the Jupyter Notebook interface.

1. **Create a new notebook:** To create a new notebook, click the "New" button on the right-hand side of the Jupyter Notebook interface and select "Python 3" (or another kernel, if you prefer). This will create a new notebook with an empty code cell.
2. Type in the following command and press *Shift + Enter*: (Refer to *Figure 1.4*):

    `! pip install opencv-python`

Import OpenCV: To import OpenCV into your notebook, enter the following code in a new cell and run it: (Refer to *Figure 1.5*)

```
import cv2
print(cv2.__version__)
```

This should display the version of OpenCV that you have installed.

You have successfully installed your macOS system and are ready to start using Jupyter Notebook to write and run OpenCV code.

Google Colab for OpenCV

Google Colab is a free cloud-based platform that provides a Jupyter Notebook environment to run Python code. It has the advantage of providing free access to high-performance computing resources.

Google Colab provides a powerful platform for developing OpenCV applications, and it can be used for a wide range of tasks, such as image and video processing, object detection, and machine learning.

To use Google Colab for OpenCV, follow these steps:

1. **Open Google Colab:** Go to https://colab.research.google.com/ and sign in with your Google account.

2. **Create a new notebook:** Click on **New Notebook** to create a new notebook. You can choose to create a blank notebook or use one of the available templates. Refer to the following *Figure 1.6*:

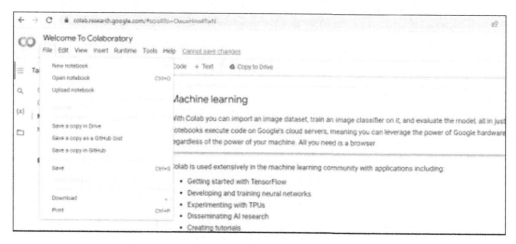

Figure 1.6: *Home page for Google colab*

3. **Install OpenCV:** To install OpenCV, run the following command in a new code cell:

   ```
   !pip install opencv-python
   ```

   The following figure represents the new Colab notebook:

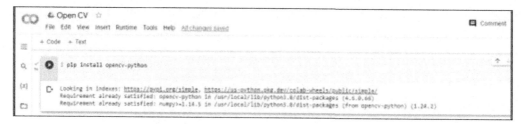

Figure 1.7: *Installation of OpenCV in Google colab*

This will download and install the latest version of OpenCV.

4. **Upload images or videos:** If you want to work with images or videos, you can upload them to Google Colab by clicking on the **Files** tab in

the left panel and selecting **Upload**. You can then access the uploaded files in your code using the appropriate file path. Refer to the following *Figure 1.8*:

Figure 1.8: *Upload image/File/video using the upload button*

5. **Write your OpenCV code:** In a new code cell, write your OpenCV code using the appropriate functions and methods. You can use the standard OpenCV syntax for Python.

6. **Run your code:** To run your code, click on the **Play** button in the code cell or use the shortcut *Shift + Enter*. You can view the output of your code in the cell below.

Conclusion

In this chapter, we have discussed Computer Vision in the Artificial Intelligence field and the Open CV library's contribution to the computer vision field. Further, we discussed the benefits of learning OpenCV and its structure. Finally, we learnt the detailed procedure for installation in the different Operating systems.

In the next chapter, we will discuss how to do basic image and video analytics in OpenCV using image and video files and their basic exercises in OpenCV using Python as a programming language.

Points to Remember

Always import the OpenCV library as CV2 (import cv2).

References

Anaconda Windows installation: https://docs.anaconda.com/anaconda/install/windows/

Anaconda Mac OS installation: https://docs.anaconda.com/anaconda/install/mac-os/

Questions/MCQs

1. What is Computer Vision in the artificial intelligence field?
2. What is OpenCV and what are its real-time applications?

CHAPTER 2

Basic Image and Video Analytics in OpenCV

Introduction

This chapter will cover the basic exercise on image and Video analytics including drawing geometric shapes and handling mouse events using OpenCV and Python programming language.

Structure

In this chapter, we will cover the following topics:

- Read, Write, and Show Images in OpenCV
- Covert color in Images using OpenCV
- Read, Write, and Show Videos from a Camera in OpenCV
- Covert color in Video using OpenCV
- Draw geometric shapes on images using OpenCV
- Setting Camera Parameters in OpenCV
- Show the Date and Time on Videos using OpenCV
- Show Text on Videos using OpenCV
- Basic Mouse Events in OpenCV

Read, Write, and Show Images in OpenCV

In OpenCV, you can easily read, write, and show images using the `cv2.imread()`, `cv2.imwrite()`, and `cv2.imshow()` functions respectively. Here is how to use these functions:

Read Images: To read an image in OpenCV, use the `cv2.imread()` function.

This function takes the path of the image as input and returns a NumPy array representing the image:

```
import cv2
img = cv2.imread('image.jpg')
```

Write Images: To write an image in OpenCV, use the `cv2.imwrite()` function. This function takes the path of the image and the image data as input and saves the image to disk.

```
import cv2
img = cv2.imread('image.jpg')
cv2.imwrite('output.jpg', img)
```

Show Images: To show an image in OpenCV, use the `cv2.imshow()` function. This function takes the window name and the image data as input and displays the image in a window.

```
import cv2
img = cv2.imread('image.jpg')
cv2.imshow('Image', img)
#close the function
cv2.waitKey(0)
cv2.destroyAllWindows()
```

Refer to the following figure for reading and showing images in OpenCV:

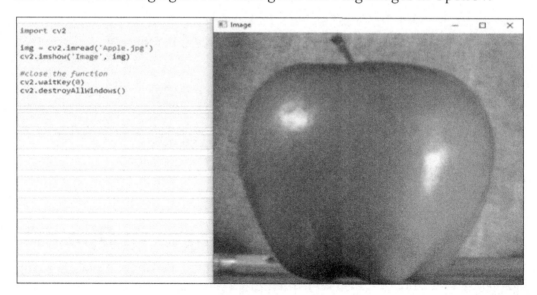

Figure 2.1: *Display the Images*

NOTE: **Press the 'q' button to exit the code.**

In the preceding code, **cv2.waitKey(0)** waits for a keyboard event and **cv2.destroyAllWindows()** closes all open windows.

Covert Color in Images Using OpenCV

When you use cv2.imread() to read an image, it returns a NumPy array in BGR format (Blue-Green-Red), which is the opposite of the standard RGB (Red-Green-Blue) format. Therefore, you need to convert the image to RGB format before displaying it using **cv2.imshow()** or any other library that expects RGB images.

To do this, you can use the **cv2.cvtColor()** function, as follows:

```
import cv2

img = cv2.imread('image.jpg')
img_rgb = cv2.cvtColor(img, cv2.COLOR_BGR2RGB)
cv2.imshow('Image', img_rgb)
cv2.waitKey(0)
cv2.destroyAllWindows()
```

Refer to the following figure for covert color in OpenCV:

Figure 2.2: *Covert color of Images*

Read, Write, and Show Videos from a Camera in OpenCV

In OpenCV, you can easily read, write, and show videos using the `cv2.VideoCapture()`, `cv2.VideoWriter()`, and `cv2.imshow()` functions respectively. Here is how to use these functions:

Read and Show Videos: To read a video in OpenCV, use the `cv2.VideoCapture()` function. This function takes the path of the video as input and returns a VideoCapture object.

```
import cv2

cap = cv2.VideoCapture('video.mp4')
while True:
    ret, frame = cap.read()
    if not ret:
        break
    cv2.imshow('Video', frame)

#break the loop - Press Q button
    if cv2.waitKey(1) == ord('q'):
        break
cap.release()
cv2.destroyAllWindows()
```

Refer to the following figure for covert color in OpenCV:

***Figure 2.3**: Read and show videos*

> **NOTE:** In the preceding code, replace the video file path with zero (VideoCapture(0)) to get the real-time video feed to the code.

```
import cv2

cap = cv2.VideoCapture(0)
while True:
    ret, frame = cap.read()
    if not ret:
        break
    cv2.imshow('Video', frame)

#break the loop - Press 'q' button

    if cv2.waitKey(1) == ord('q'):
        break
cap.release()
cv2.destroyAllWindows()
```

In the preceding code, **cv2.VideoCapture()** returns a **VideoCapture** object, which you can use to read frames from the video using the **cap.read()** function.

The function returns two values, ret and frame. ret is a Boolean value that indicates whether a frame was successfully read, and the frame is a NumPy array representing the image frame.

The code loops through all the frames in the video and displays them in a window using **cv2.imshow()**. The code also waits for a keyboard event using **cv2.waitKey(1)** and breaks the loop if the 'q' key is pressed. Finally, the **cap.release()** function releases the video capture object and **cv2.destroyAllWindows()** closes all open windows.

Write Videos: To write a video in OpenCV, use the **cv2.VideoWriter()** function. This function takes the path of the output video, the fourCC code for the video codec, the frames per second (FPS), and the frame size as input, and returns a **VideoWriter** object.

```
import cv2

cap = cv2.VideoCapture('video.mp4')
fourcc = cv2.VideoWriter_fourcc(*'XVID')

out = cv2.VideoWriter('output.avi', fourcc, 25, (640, 480))
```

```
    while True:
        ret, frame = cap.read()
        if not ret:
            break
        out.write(frame)
        cv2.imshow('Video', frame)
        if cv2.waitKey(1) == ord('q'):
            Break

    cap.release()
    out.release()
    cv2.destroyAllWindows()
```

> **NOTE: In the preceding code, replace the video file path with zero to get the real-time video feed to the code and save the video into the local folder.**

```
    import cv2

    cap = cv2.VideoCapture('video.mp4')
    fourcc = cv2.VideoWriter_fourcc(*'XVID')
    out = cv2.VideoWriter('output.avi', fourcc, 25, (640, 480))
    while True:
        ret, frame = cap.read()
        if not ret:
            break
        out.write(frame)
        cv2.imshow('Video', frame)

     #break the loop - Press 'q' button
        if cv2.waitKey(1) == ord('q'):
            break
    cap.release()
    out.release()
    cv2.destroyAllWindows()
```

In the preceding code, **cv2.VideoWriter()** returns a **VideoWriter** object, which you can use to write frames to the output video using the **out.write()** function. The code also displays the frames in a window using **cv2.imshow()**.

Refer to the following figure for displaying the output using OpenCV:

Figure 2.4: *Display the output*

The code waits for a keyboard event using `cv2.waitKey(1)` and breaks the loop if the '`q`' key is pressed. Finally, the `cap.release()` and `out.release()` functions release the video capture and video writer objects respectively, and `cv2.destroyAllWindows()` closes all open windows.

> **NOTE:** The fourCC code is a four-byte code that identifies the video codec. The code 'XVID' is used for the MPEG-4 codec. You can find the fourCC codes for other codecs on the OpenCV documentation website.

Covert color in Video Using OpenCV

When you use `cv2.imread()` to read an image, it returns a NumPy array in BGR format (Blue-Green-Red), which is the opposite of the standard RGB (Red-Green-Blue) format. Therefore, you need to convert the image to RGB format before displaying it using `cv2.imshow()` or any other library that expects RGB images.

To do this, you can use the **cv2.cvtColor()** function, as follows:

```
#importing libraries
import cv2

#Capture the real-time input
cap = cv2.VideoCapture(0)

# read the frame
while True:
    ret, frame = cap.read()
    if not ret:
        break

    frame = cv2.cvtColor(frame, cv2.COLOR_BGR2GRAY)
    cv2.imshow('Video', frame)

    #break the loop - Press Q button
    if cv2.waitKey(1) == ord('q'):
        break

cap.release()
cv2.destroyAllWindows()
```

Refer to the following figure for covert color in videos using OpenCV:

Figure 2.5: *Covert color in videos using OpenCV*

Draw Geometric Ahapes on Images Using OpenCV

In OpenCV, you can easily draw geometric shapes on images using various functions such as `cv2.line()`, `cv2.rectangle()`, `cv2.circle()`, and `cv2.putText()`. Here is how to use these functions to draw shapes on images:

Draw a Line: To draw a line on an image in OpenCV, use the `cv2.line()` function. This function takes the image, the starting and ending points of the line, the color of the line, the thickness of the line, and the line type as input:

```
import cv2
import numpy as np

img = np.zeros((512, 512, 3), np.uint8)
cv2.line(img, (0, 0), (511, 511), (255, 0, 0), 5)
cv2.imshow('Image', img)
cv2.waitKey(0)
cv2.destroyAllWindows()
```

Refer to the following figure to draw a line in images:

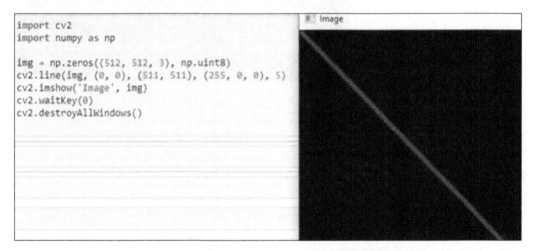

Figure 2.6: *Draw lines in images using OpenCV*

We create a black image using the `np.zeros()` function in the preceding code. We then draw a blue line on the image using the `cv2.line()` function. The line starts at point (0, 0) and ends at point (511, 511). The color of the line is blue (255, 0, 0), and the thickness of the line is 5 pixels.

Draw an Arrow Line: To draw an arrow line on an image in OpenCV, use the `cv2.arrowedLine()` function. This function takes the image, the starting and ending points of the line, the color of the line, the thickness of the line, and the line type as input.

```
import cv2
import numpy as np

img = np.zeros((512, 512, 3), np.uint8)
cv2.arrowedLine(img, (500,255) , (255,255) , (255,0,0) , 5)
cv2.imshow('Image', img)
cv2.waitKey(0)
cv2.destroyAllWindows()
```

Refer to the following figure to draw an arrow line in images:

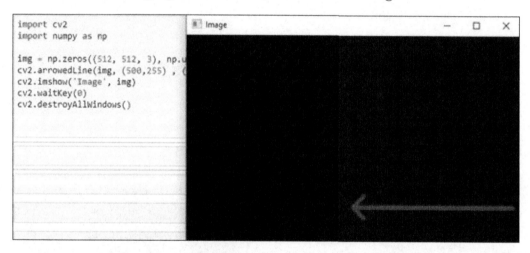

Figure 2.7: Draw an arrow line in images using OpenCV

We create a black image using the `np.zeros()` function in the preceding code. We then draw a blue line on the image using the `cv2.arrowedLine()` function. The line starts at point (500, 255) and ends at point (255, 255). The color of the line is blue (255, 0, 0), and the thickness of the line is 5 pixels.

Draw a Rectangle: To draw a rectangle on an image in OpenCV, use the `cv2.rectangle()` function. This function takes the image, the top-left and bottom-right corners of the rectangle, the color of the rectangle, the thickness of the rectangle, and the line type as input. (Refer to *Figure 2.7*):

```
import cv2
import numpy as np

img = np.zeros((512, 512, 3), np.uint8)
cv2.rectangle(img, (100, 100), (400, 400), (0, 255, 0), 3)
cv2.imshow('Image', img)
```

```
cv2.waitKey(0)
cv2.destroyAllWindows()
```

We create a black image using the **np.zeros()** function in the preceding code. We then draw a green rectangle on the image using the **cv2.rectangle()** function. The top-left corner of the rectangle is at the point (100, 100), and the bottom-right corner is at the point (400, 400). The color of the rectangle is green (0, 255, 0), and the thickness of the rectangle is 3 pixels.

Draw a Circle: To draw a circle on an image in OpenCV, use the **cv2.circle()** function. This function takes the image, the center of the circle, the radius of the circle, the color of the circle, the thickness of the circle, and the line type as input. (Refer to *Figure* 2.7):

```
import cv2
import numpy as np

img = np.zeros((512, 512, 3), np.uint8)
cv2.circle(img, (256, 256), 100, (0, 0, 255), 2)
cv2.imshow('Image', img)
cv2.waitKey(0)
cv2.destroyAllWindows()
```

We create a black image using the **np.zeros()** function in the preceding code. We then draw a red circle on the image using the **cv2.circle()** function. The center of the circle is at the point (256, 256), and the radius of the circle is 100 pixels. The color of the circle is red (0, 0, 255), and the thickness of the circle is 2 pixels

Draw an Ellipse: To draw an ellipse on an image in OpenCV, use the **cv2.ellipse()** function. This function takes the image, the center of the ellipse, the major and minor axis lengths, the angle of rotation of the ellipse, the start and end angles of the ellipse arc, the color of the ellipse, the thickness of the ellipse, and the line type as input. (Refer to *Figure* 2.8):

```
import cv2
import numpy as np

img = np.zeros((512, 512, 3), np.uint8)
cv2.ellipse(img, (256, 256), (100, 50), 0, 0, 360, (255, 0, 0), 2)
cv2.imshow('Image', img)
cv2.waitKey(0)
cv2.destroyAllWindows()
```

We create a black image using the **np.zeros()** function in the preceding code. We then draw a blue ellipse on the image using the **cv2.ellipse()** function. The center of the ellipse is at the point (256, 256), and the major and minor axis lengths are 100 and 50 pixels, respectively. The angle of rotation of the ellipse is 0 degrees, and the start and end angles of the ellipse arc are 0 and 360 degrees, respectively. The color of the ellipse is blue (255, 0, 0), and the thickness of the ellipse is 2 pixels.

Draw Polylines: To draw a set of connected line segments (polylines) on an image in OpenCV, use the `cv2.polylines()` function. This function takes the image, the coordinates of the vertices of the polyline, a flag indicating whether the polyline is closed or open, the color of the polyline, the thickness of the polyline, and the line type as input. (Refer to *Figure 2.8*):

```
import cv2
import numpy as np

img = np.zeros((512, 512, 3), np.uint8)
pts = np.array([[100, 100], [200, 300], [400, 200], [300, 100]], np.int32)
cv2.polylines(img, [pts], True, (0, 255, 0), 3)
cv2.imshow('Image', img)
cv2.waitKey(0)
cv2.destroyAllWindows()
```

We create a black image using the `np.zeros()` function in the preceding code. We then define the coordinates of the vertices of a polyline and store them in the pts array. We draw a green closed polyline on the image using the `cv2.polylines()` function.

The coordinates of the vertices of the polyline are passed as a list of arrays, and the flag indicating that the polyline is closed is set to `True`. The color of the polyline is green (0, 255, 0), and the thickness of the polyline is 3 pixels.

Refer to the following figure to draw geometric shapes in images:

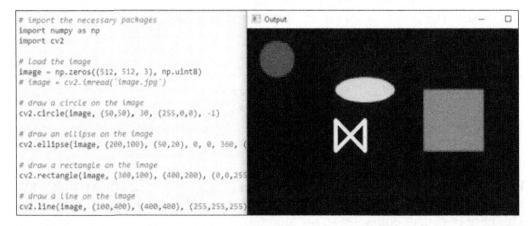

Figure 2.8: *Geometric shapes in images using OpenCV*

Draw Text: To draw text on an image in OpenCV, use the `cv2.putText()` function. This function takes the image, the text to be written, the position of the text, the font type, the font scale, the color of the text, the thickness of the text, and the line type as input:

```
import cv2
import numpy as np

# Create a black image
img = np.zeros((512, 512, 3), np.uint8)

# Write some text on the image
font = cv2.FONT_HERSHEY_SIMPLEX
cv2.putText(img, 'OpenCV', (200, 300), font, 2, (255, 255, 255), 2, cv2.LINE_AA)
# Show the image
cv2.imshow('Image', img)
cv2.waitKey(0)
cv2.destroyAllWindows()
```

In the preceding code, we first create a black image using the `np.zeros()` function. Then, we define the font type (`cv2.FONT_HERSHEY_SIMPLEX`), the text to be written ('OpenCV'), the position of the text (200, 300) (where (0, 0) is the top-left corner of the image), the font scale (2), the color of the text ((255, 255, 255) for white), the thickness of the text (2), and the line type (`cv2.LINE_AA` for anti-aliased line). Finally, we use the `cv2.imshow()` function to show the image on the screen.

Refer to the following figure to write text in images.

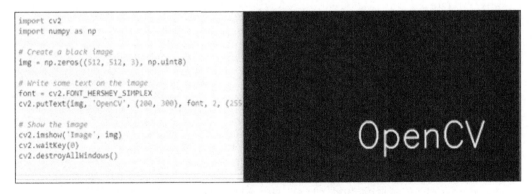

Figure 2.9: Write the text in images using OpenCV

Setting Camera Parameters in OpenCV

In OpenCV Python, you can set the camera parameters such as resolution, frame rate, brightness, contrast, and so on, using the **cv2.VideoCapture()** function. Here's an example code that shows how to set camera parameters:

```python
import cv2

# Open the default camera (index 0)
cap = cv2.VideoCapture(0)

# Set the camera resolution to 640x480
cap.set(cv2.CAP_PROP_FRAME_WIDTH, 640)
cap.set(cv2.CAP_PROP_FRAME_HEIGHT, 480)

# Set the camera brightness to 50 (range: 0 to 100)
cap.set(cv2.CAP_PROP_BRIGHTNESS, 50)

# print the values
print("Width:", cap.get(cv2.CAP_PROP_FRAME_WIDTH))
print("Height:",cap.get(cv2.CAP_PROP_FRAME_HEIGHT))
print("Brightness:",cap.get(cv2.CAP_PROP_BRIGHTNESS))
print("Sharpness:",cap.get(cv2.CAP_PROP_SHARPNESS))

# Set the camera contrast to 50 (range: 0 to 100)
cap.set(cv2.CAP_PROP_CONTRAST, 50)

# Loop through the frames
while True:
    # Capture frame-by-frame
    ret, frame = cap.read()

    # Display the resulting frame
    cv2.imshow('frame', frame)

    # Exit if 'q' is pressed
    if cv2.waitKey(1) & 0xFF == ord('q'):
        break

# Release the camera and close the window
cap.release()
cv2.destroyAllWindows()
```

Refer to the following figure to print the camera parameters:

Figure 2.10: Print camera parameters using OpenCV

In the code above, we first open the default camera using the `cv2.VideoCapture()` function. We then use the `cap.set()` function to set the camera resolution to 640x480, brightness to 50, and contrast to 50. After that, we loop through the frames using a while loop, capturing each frame using the `cap.read()` function. We then display the resulting frame using the `cv2.imshow()` function. Finally, we release the camera and close the window using the `cap.release()` and `cv2.destroyAllWindows()` functions, respectively.

You can adjust the camera parameters as per your requirements by modifying the values passed to the `cap.set()` function. The available camera properties that can be set using the `cap.set()` function include `cv2.CAP_PROP_FRAME_WIDTH`, `cv2.CAP_PROP_FRAME_HEIGHT`, `cv2.CAP_PROP_BRIGHTNESS`, `cv2.CAP_PROP_CONTRAST`, `cv2.CAP_PROP_FPS`, and many more.

Show the Date and Time on Videos Using OpenCV

To show the date and time of videos using OpenCV Python, you can use the `cv2.putText()` function to put the text on each frame of the video. Here's an example code that shows how to do this:

```
import cv2
import datetime

# Open the video file
cap = cv2.VideoCapture('video.mp4')
```

```python
# Get the width and height of the video frames
width = int(cap.get(cv2.CAP_PROP_FRAME_WIDTH))
height = int(cap.get(cv2.CAP_PROP_FRAME_HEIGHT))

# Define the codec and create VideoWriter object
fourcc = cv2.VideoWriter_fourcc(*'mp4v')
out = cv2.VideoWriter('output.mp4', fourcc, 30, (width, height))

# Loop through the frames
while cap.isOpened():
    # Read the current frame
    ret, frame = cap.read()

    # If the frame was read successfully
    if ret:
        # Get the current date and time
        now = datetime.datetime.now()
        date_time = now.strftime("%d-%m-%Y %H:%M:%S")

        # Put the date and time on the frame
        font = cv2.FONT_HERSHEY_SIMPLEX
        cv2.putText(frame, date_time, (10, 50), font, 1, (0, 255,
        255), 2, cv2.LINE_AA)

        # Write the frame to the output video
        out.write(frame)

        # Display the resulting frame
        cv2.imshow('frame', frame)

        # Exit if 'q' is pressed
        if cv2.waitKey(1) & 0xFF == ord('q'):
            break
    else:
        break

# Release everything
cap.release()
out.release()
cv2.destroyAllWindows()
```

> **NOTE:** In the preceding code, replace the video file path with zero (cv2.VideoCapture(0)) to get the real-time video feed to the code.

Refer to the following figure to show data and time in Videos:

Figure 2.11: *Print date and time using OpenCV*

In the preceding code, we first open the video file using `cv2.VideoCapture()` function. We then get the width and height of the video frames using the `cap.get()` function. After that, we define the codec and create a `cv2.VideoWriter()` object to write the output video.

We then loop through the frames using a while loop, capturing each frame using the `cap.read()` function. For each frame, we get the current date and time using the `datetime.datetime.now()` function, and then use the `cv2.putText()` function to put the date and time on the frame.

We then write the frame to the output video using the `out.write()` function and display the resulting frame using the `cv2.imshow()` function. Finally, we release the video and output objects, and close the window using the `cap.release()`, `out.release()`, and `cv2.destroyAllWindows()` functions, respectively.

You can customize the date and time format, font type, font size, text color, text position, and other parameters as per your requirements by modifying the values passed to the `now.strftime()` and `cv2.putText()` functions.

Show Text on Videos Using OpenCV

To show text on videos using OpenCV in Python, you can use the `cv2.putText()` function to put the text on each frame of the video.

Here's an example code that shows how to do this:

```python
import cv2

# Open the video file
cap = cv2.VideoCapture('video.mp4')

# Get the width and height of the video frames
width = int(cap.get(cv2.CAP_PROP_FRAME_WIDTH))
height = int(cap.get(cv2.CAP_PROP_FRAME_HEIGHT))

# Define the codec and create VideoWriter object
fourcc = cv2.VideoWriter_fourcc(*'mp4v')
out = cv2.VideoWriter('output.mp4', fourcc, 30, (width, height))

# Loop through the frames
while cap.isOpened():
    # Read the current frame
    ret, frame = cap.read()

    # If the frame was read successfully
    if ret:
        # Put the text on the frame
        font = cv2.FONT_HERSHEY_SIMPLEX
        cv2.putText(frame, 'Sample Text', (10, 50), font, 1, (0, 255, 255), 2, cv2.LINE_AA)

        # Write the frame to the output video
        out.write(frame)

        # Display the resulting frame
        cv2.imshow('frame', frame)

        # Exit if 'q' is pressed
        if cv2.waitKey(1) & 0xFF == ord('q'):
            break
    else:
        break

# Release everything
cap.release()
```

```
out.release()
cv2.destroyAllWindows()
```

Refer to the following figure to show text on videos:

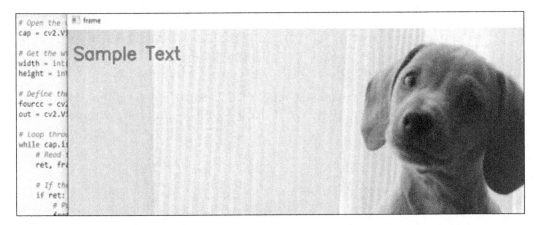

Figure 2.12: Print Text in videos using OpenCV

> **NOTE:** In the preceding code, replace the video file path with zero (cv2.VideoCapture(0)) to get the real-time video feed to the code

In the code above, we first open the video file using the `cv2.VideoCapture()` function. We then get the width and height of the video frames using the `cap.get()` function. After that, we define the codec and create a `cv2.VideoWriter()` object to write the output video.

We then loop through the frames using a while loop, capturing each frame using the `cap.read()` function. For each frame, we use the `cv2.putText()` function to put the text on the frame. We then write the frame to the output video using the `out.write()` function and display the resulting frame using the `cv2.imshow()` function.

Finally, we release the video and output objects, and close the window using the `cap.release()`, `out.release()`, and `cv2.destroyAllWindows()` functions, respectively.

You can customize the text, font type, font size, text color, text position, and other parameters as per your requirements by modifying the values passed to the `cv2.putText()` function.

Basic Mouse Events Using OpenCV

OpenCV provides several mouse events that can be used to interact with images and video streams in real time.

Here are some basic mouse events that can be used:

- **Mouse click event:** This event is triggered when the user clicks the mouse button. It can be used to select a region of interest (ROI) in an image or to trigger an action.
- **Mouse move event:** This event is triggered when the user moves the mouse. It can be used to track the movement of an object in an image or to display information about the current pixel under the mouse cursor.

You can use the `cv2.setMouseCallback()` function to set a callback function that will be called when a mouse event occurs on the specified window:

```python
import cv2
import numpy as np

# Define the callback function
def mouse_callback(event, x, y, flags, param):
    if event == cv2.EVENT_LBUTTONDOWN:
        print('Left button clicked at (%d, %d)' % (x, y))
    elif event == cv2.EVENT_RBUTTONDOWN:
        print('Right button clicked at (%d, %d)' % (x, y))
    elif event == cv2.EVENT_MOUSEMOVE:
        print('Mouse moved at (%d, %d)' % (x, y))

# Create a window and set the callback function
cv2.namedWindow('image')
cv2.setMouseCallback('image', mouse_callback)

#create a blank image
img =np.zeros((512,512, 3), np.uint8)

# Load and display the image
# img = cv2.imread('image.jpg')
cv2.imshow('image', img)

# Wait for a key press and exit
cv2.waitKey(0)
cv2.destroyAllWindows()
```

Basic Image and Video Analytics in OpenCV

Refer to the following figure for handling mouse movement using OpenCV:

```
# Load and display the image
img = np.zeros((512,512, 3), np.uin
img.fill(255)
#img = cv2.imread('image.jpg')
cv2.imshow('image', img)

# Wait for a key press and exit
cv2.waitKey(0)
cv2.destroyAllWindows()
```

```
Mouse moved at (118, 121)
Mouse moved at (113, 117)
Mouse moved at (108, 116)
Mouse moved at (106, 114)
Mouse moved at (103, 113)
Mouse moved at (102, 112)
Mouse moved at (102, 111)
Mouse moved at (101, 111)
Right button clicked at (101, 111)
Mouse moved at (101, 111)
Left button clicked at (101, 111)
Mouse moved at (101, 111)
Mouse moved at (108, 111)
Mouse moved at (125, 112)
Mouse moved at (143, 115)
Mouse moved at (164, 119)
Mouse moved at (186, 125)
```

Figure 2.13: *Print handling mouse movement using OpenCV*

The callback function takes four arguments: the event type, the *x* and *y* coordinates of the mouse pointer, and some additional data.

Here's an example code that demonstrates how to handle mouse events in OpenCV Python:

In the code above, we define a callback function called `mouse_callback()` that prints a message to the console when a left-click button, right-click button, or mouse move event occurs. We then create a window using the `cv2.namedWindow()` function and set the mouse callback function using the `cv2.setMouseCallback()` function.

We then load and display an image using the `cv2.imread()` and `cv2.imshow()` functions. Finally, we wait for a key press using the `cv2.waitKey()` function and close the window using the `cv2.destroyAllWindows()` function.

You can modify the callback function to perform any custom action you want when a mouse event occurs. The flags and param arguments can be used to pass additional data to the callback function if needed.

Conclusion

In this chapter, we have discussed basic image and video analytics using OpenCV and python programming language. Which is to draw the geometric shapes on the images and set and get the camera parameters value from the video using the OpenCV library. Furthermore, we discussed how to set the text, date, and time values in videos and get the pixel value of images using mouse events.

In the next chapter, we will discuss the details of image processing techniques and more mouse events and their functionality with OpenCV and Python.

Points to Remember

Replace the video file path with zero (cv2.VideoCapture(0)) to get the real-time video feed to the code.

Place the image or video file in the same folder where the Jupyter notebook exists to read the file. Else, copy the file path and place it inside the function.

Example: cv2.imread('folder1/folder2/image.jpg') or cv2.VideoCapture('folder1/folder2/vid.mp4')

References

Draw functions in OpenCV: https://docs.opencv.org/3.4/dc/da5/tutorial_py_drawing_functions.html

CHAPTER 3

Image Processing 1 Using OpenCV

Introduction

This chapter will cover the basic image processing techniques such as cropping, resizing, rotating, background removal, and bitwise operations. Besides more mouse events, trackbar control using OpenCV & python programming language.

Structure

In this chapter, we will cover the following topics in OpenCV:

- Basic image processing techniques
- Reshaping the video frame
- Pausing the video frame
- More Mouse Event Examples
- Bitwise Operations
- Binding a trackbar
- Image Trackbar

Basic Image Processing Techniques

Image processing techniques can be used to process and analyze images. Here are some commonly used images processing techniques in OpenCV:

- **Image Filtering:** This technique is used to smoothen or sharpen an image. OpenCV provides various image filtering algorithms, such as Gaussian, Median, and Bilateral.
- **Image Thresholding:** This technique is used to create binary images from grayscale images by setting all pixel values below a certain threshold to zero and all pixel values above the threshold to 255.

- **Edge Detection:** This technique is used to identify the edges of objects in an image. OpenCV provides various edge detection algorithms, such as Canny, Sobel, and Laplacian.
- **Morphological Operations:** These operations are used to manipulate the shape and size of objects in an image. OpenCV provides morphological operations, such as dilation, erosion, opening, and closing.
- **Feature Detection and Extraction:** These techniques are used to identify and extract important features from an image. OpenCV provides various feature detection and extraction algorithms, such as SIFT, SURF, and ORB.
- **Object Detection:** This technique is used to identify specific objects in an image. OpenCV provides object detection algorithms such as Haar Cascade and Histogram of Oriented Gradients (HOG).
- **Image Segmentation:** This technique is used to partition an image into multiple segments or regions based on similar characteristics such as color, texture, or intensity. OpenCV provides various image segmentation algorithms such as watershed and GrabCut.

These are just a few examples of the image processing techniques available in OpenCV. Depending on the specific application, different combinations of these techniques can be used to achieve the desired result.

Basic code in OpenCV for performing the following image processing operations:

Image wait function

The image `waitKey()` function is used to wait for a keyboard event for a specified amount of time. In the example `waitKey(5000)`, the function is called with a parameter of 5000, which means it will wait for 5000 milliseconds (or 5 seconds) for a keyboard event before continuing the execution of the program:

```
import cv2

# Load image
img = cv2.imread('image.jpg')

# Display image
cv2.imshow('Image', img)

# Wait for 5 seconds
cv2.waitKey(5000)
```

```
# Close all windows
cv2.destroyAllWindows()
```

Image cropping

Image cropping is the process of selecting a rectangular portion of an image and discarding the remaining parts. This operation is useful when we want to focus on a specific part of an image or remove unwanted parts. In OpenCV, we can perform image cropping using NumPy array slicing:

```
import cv2

# Read an image
img = cv2.imread('apple.jpg')

# Crop the image
crop_img = img[100:400, 200:500]

# Display the processed images
cv2.imshow('Cropped Image', crop_img)

# Wait for a key press and then close the windows
cv2.waitKey(0)
cv2.destroyAllWindows()
```

Refer to the following figure for image cropping in OpenCV:

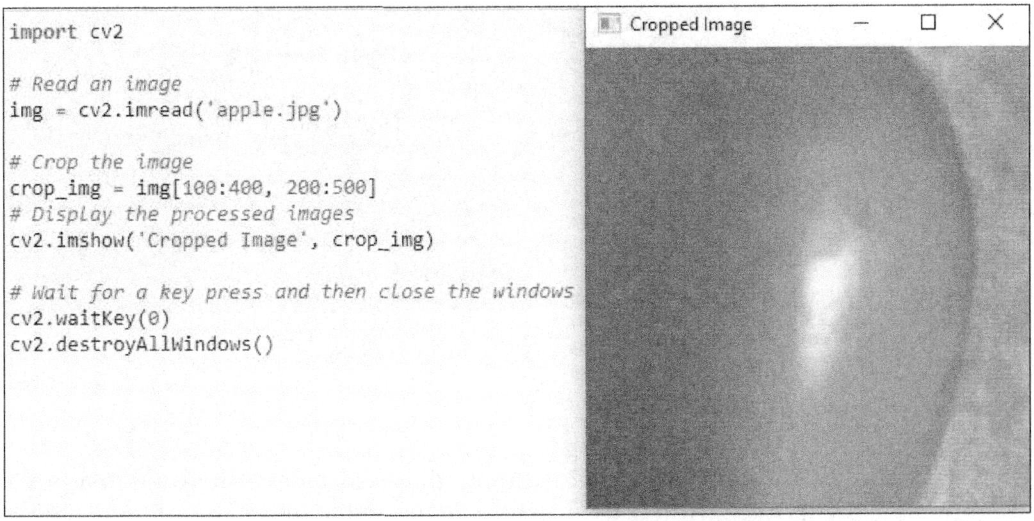

Figure 3.1: *Display the image cropping*

Image resizing

Image resizing is the process of changing the dimensions of an image. This operation is useful when we want to change the resolution of an image or when we need to resize an image to fit a specific display or device. In OpenCV, we can perform image resizing using the `cv2.resize()` function:

```
import cv2

# Read an image
img = cv2.imread('apple.jpg')

# Resize the image
resized_img = cv2.resize(img, (640, 480))

# Display the processed images
cv2.imshow('Resized Image', resized_img)

# Wait for a key press and then close the windows
cv2.waitKey(0)
cv2.destroyAllWindows()
```

Refer to the following figure for image resizing in OpenCV:

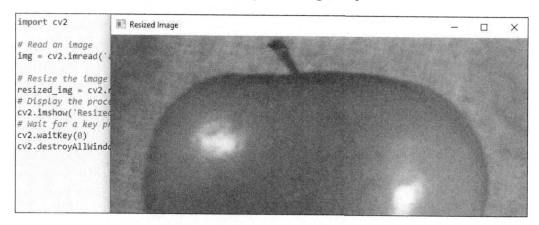

Figure 3.2: Display the image resizing

Image rotation

Image rotation is the process of rotating an image by a certain angle around a specific point. This operation is useful when we need to align an image or when we want to view an image from a different angle. In OpenCV, we can perform image rotation using the `cv2.getRotationMatrix2D()` and `cv2.warpAffine()` functions.

getRotationMatrix2D: which takes the centre of rotation (specified as (cols/2, rows/2)), the angle of rotation (theta), and the scaling factor (1).

- **warpAffine:** it is used to perform affine transformations on images. An affine transformation is a linear mapping that preserves parallel lines and ratios of distances. It can be used to perform operations such as rotation, translation, scaling, and shearing on an image:

```
import cv2

# Read an image
img = cv2.imread('apple.jpg')

# Rotate the image
(rows, cols) = img.shape[:2]
M = cv2.getRotationMatrix2D((cols/2, rows/2), 45, 1)
rotated_img = cv2.warpAffine(img, M, (cols, rows))

# Display the processed images
cv2.imshow('Rotated Image', rotated_img)

# Wait for a key press and then close the windows
cv2.waitKey(0)
cv2.destroyAllWindows()
```

Refer to the following figure for image rotation in OpenCV:

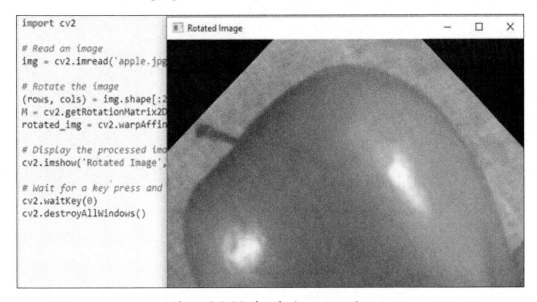

Figure 3.3: Display the image rotation

Grayscaling

Grayscaling is the process of converting an image from its original color space to a grayscale color space. This operation is useful when we want to simplify an image or when we want to remove the color information from an image. In OpenCV, we can perform gray scaling using the **cv2.cvtColor()** function:

```
import cv2

# Read an image
img = cv2.imread('apple.jpg')

# Convert the image to grayscale
gray_img = cv2.cvtColor(img, cv2.COLOR_BGR2GRAY)

# Display the processed images
cv2.imshow('Grayscale Image', gray_img)

# Wait for a key press and then close the windows
cv2.waitKey(0)
cv2.destroyAllWindows()
```

Refer to the following figure for image grayscaling in OpenCV:

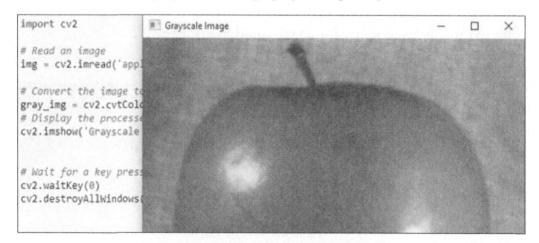

Figure 3.4: Display the image grayscaling

Image split

Image split is the process of splitting into its individual color channels and can be useful for a variety of image processing tasks, such as color correction, histogram equalization, and feature extraction. The function takes a single argument - the input image - and returns a tuple containing the individual color channels as separate grayscale images.

The order of the channels in the output tuple is blue, green, and red (BGR), which is the default color order in OpenCV. In OpenCV, we can perform Splitting an image using the `cv2.split()` function:

```
import cv2
import numpy as np

# load an image as a 3-channel color image
img = cv2.imread("apple.jpg")

# split the image into its color channels
b, g, r = cv2.split(img)

# display the individual color channels
cv2.imshow("Blue Channel", b)
cv2.imshow("Green Channel", g)
cv2.imshow("Red Channel", r)

# wait for a key press and then close the windows
cv2.waitKey(0)
cv2.destroyAllWindows()
```

Refer to the following figure for image splitting in OpenCV:

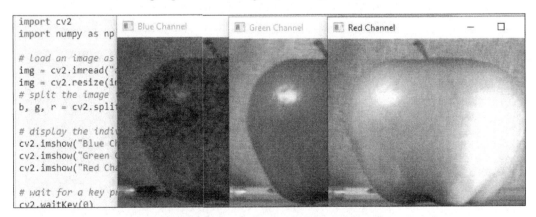

Figure 3.5: *Display the image splitting*

Merging image

Merging image is the process of merging multiple grayscale or color channels into a single multi-channel image. The function takes a tuple of individual grayscale or color channels as separate images and returns a single multi-channel image. The order of the channels in the input tuple should be the same as the desired output order. In OpenCV, we can perform merging images using the **cv2.merge()** function:

```
import cv2

# Read an image
img = cv2.imread('messi5.jpg')

# Merge the image
img =cv2.merge((b,g,r))
ball = img[280:340, 330:390]
img[273:333, 100:160] = ball

# Display the processed images
cv2.imshow('img', img)

# Wait for a key press and then close the windows
cv2.waitKey(0)
cv2.destroyAllWindows()
```

In the preceding code, we first created three grayscale images with different pixel values using NumPy: img1 is all black, img2 is a mid-gray color, and img3 is all white.

Refer to the following figure for image merging in OpenCV:

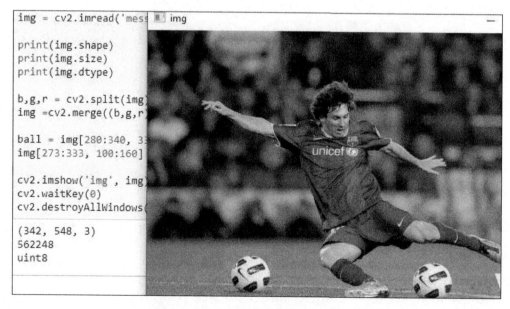

Figure 3.6: *Display the image merging*

Adding two images

Adding two images or a scalar value to an image can be useful for a variety of image processing tasks, such as brightness and contrast adjustment, blending images, and image thresholding.

The function takes two arguments: the first argument is the source image or scalar value, and the second argument is the image or scalar value to be added to the source image. The two arguments must have the same size and type, or the second argument can be a scalar value. In OpenCV, we can perform merging images using the **cv2.add()** function:

```
import cv2

# Read an image
img = cv2.imread('messi5.jpg')
img2 = cv2.imread('opencv-logo.png')

# add 2 images
img = cv2.resize(img, (512,512))
img2 = cv2.resize(img2 , (512,512))
add = cv2.add(img2, img)

# Display the processed images
cv2.imshow('img', add )

# Wait for a key press and then close the windows
cv2.waitKey(0)
cv2.destroyAllWindows()
```

Refer to the following figure to adding two images in OpenCV:

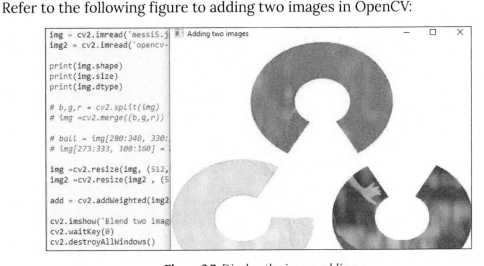

Figure 3.7: *Display the image adding*

Blend two images with different weights

Blending two images with different weights can be useful for a variety of image processing tasks, such as image masking, image filtering, and image enhancement.

The function performs a weighted addition of the two input arrays or images, with the resulting pixel values calculated as follows:

output = src1 * alpha + src2 * beta + gamma

where **src1** is the first input array or image, **alpha** is the weight of the first image, **src2** is the second input array or image, **beta** is the weight of the second image, **gamma** is a scalar added to each sum, and output is the resulting output array or image. In OpenCV, we can perform Merging images using the **cv2.addWeighted()** function:

```
import cv2

# Read an image
img = cv2.imread('messi5.jpg')
img2 = cv2.imread('opencv-logo.png')

# blend 2 images with weight
img = cv2.resize(img, (512,512))
img2 = cv2.resize(img2 , (512,512))
add = cv2.addWeighted(img2,.3, img, .7, 0)

# Display the processed images
cv2.imshow('img', add )

# Wait for a key press and then close the windows
cv2.waitKey(0)
cv2.destroyAllWindows()
```

Refer to the following figure for image blending in OpenCV:

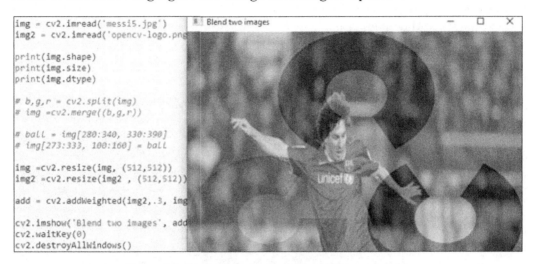

Figure 3.8: Display the image adding different weights

Region of interest (ROI)

Selecting a rectangular ROI from an image can be useful for a variety of image processing tasks, such as object detection, object tracking, and region-based image analysis. The function takes a single argument, which is the input image. It then displays the input image in a new window and allows the user to select a rectangular region of interest by clicking and dragging the mouse. Once the user has selected the desired ROI, they can press the *Enter* key to confirm the selection, or the *Esc* key to cancel it.

The function returns a tuple containing the x and y coordinates of the top-left corner of the selected ROI, as well as its width and height. The returned values can be used to crop the input image to the selected ROI using NumPy array slicing:

```
import cv2

# load an image
img = cv2.imread("apple.jpg")

# display the image and select a ROI
x, y, w, h = cv2.selectROI(img)

# crop the image to the selected ROI
roi = img[y:y+h, x:x+w]

# display the cropped ROI
cv2.imshow("ROI", roi)
```

```
# wait for a key press and then close the window
cv2.waitKey(0)
cv2.destroyAllWindows()
```

Refer to the following figure for image ROI in OpenCV:

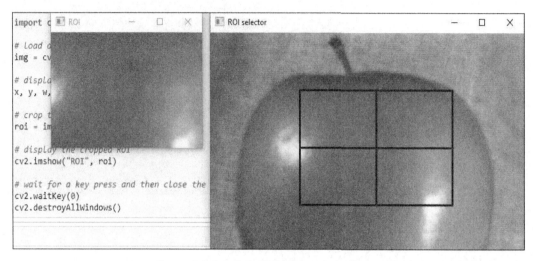

Figure 3.9: *Display the ROI using the image*

Background Removal

Background removal is removing the background from an image. This operation is useful when we want to isolate the foreground object from the background or when we want to remove noise from an image.

In OpenCV, we can perform background removal using a combination of thresholding, erosion, dilation, and bitwise operations, as shown in the example code I provided earlier:

```
import cv2

# Read an image
img = cv2.imread('apple.jpg')

# Convert the image to grayscale
gray_img = cv2.cvtColor(img, cv2.COLOR_BGR2GRAY)

# Remove the background using a threshold

# median filter is applied to reduce noise in the image
gray_img = cv2.medianBlur(gray_img, 5)
```

Image Processing 1 Using OpenCV

```python
# A binary threshold is applied to the grayscale image using a
threshold
ret, thresh = cv2.threshold(gray_img, 150, 255, cv2.THRESH_BINARY_
INV)

# The binary image is eroded to remove small objects and fill in
small gaps using erode
mask = cv2.erode(thresh, None, iterations=2)

# The binary image is dilated to expand the remaining foreground
objects # and fill in gaps using dilate
mask = cv2.dilate(mask, None, iterations=2)

# The original input image is combined with the binary mask using
bitwise_and
background_removed_img = cv2.bitwise_and(img, img, mask=mask)

# Display the processed images
cv2.imshow('Background Removed Image', background_removed_img)

# Wait for a key press and then close the windows
cv2.waitKey(0)
cv2.destroyAllWindows()
```

For background removal using **rembg** library, install rembg using **! pip install rembg** in Jupyter notebook, then follow this code to remove the background from the image:

```python
from rembg import remove
import cv2

#input path for image
input_path = 'apple.jpg'
output_path = 'output.png'

#read the image
input = cv2.imread(input_path)
output = remove(input)

# save the image
cv2.imwrite(output_path, output)

# Display the processed images
img = cv2.imread('output.png')
```

```
cv2.imshow('Background Removed Image', img)

# Wait for a key press and then close the windows
cv2.waitKey(0)
cv2.destroyAllWindows()
```
Refer to the following figure for image background removal in OpenCV:

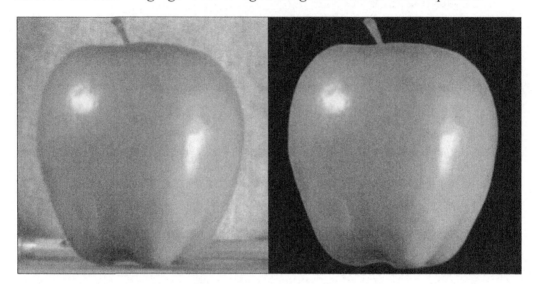

Figure 3.10: *Display the background image removal*

Reshaping the Video Frame

You can reshape an OpenCV video frame in Python using the `cv2.resize()` function.

This function takes in the frame as the first argument and the desired output size as the second argument.

Here's an example:

```
import cv2

# Open the video capture device
cap = cv2.VideoCapture(0)

while True:
    # Read a frame from the video capture device
    ret, frame = cap.read()
```

Image Processing 1 Using OpenCV

```
        # Reshape the frame to a new size
        resized = cv2.resize(frame, (640, 480))

        # Display the original and resized frames
        cv2.imshow('Original Frame', frame)
        cv2.imshow('Resized Frame', resized)

        # Exit the loop if the 'q' key is pressed
        if cv2.waitKey(1) & 0xFF == ord('q'):
            Break

    # Release the video capture device and close all windows
    cap.release()
    cv2.destroyAllWindows()
```

In this example, we open a video capture device using OpenCV's `VideoCapture()` function.

We then loop through each frame of the video capture device using a `while` loop.

For each frame, we use the `cv2.resize()` function to reshape the frame to a new size of 640x480.

Refer to the following figure for video resizing in OpenCV:

Figure 3.11: *Display the video resizing*

We then display the original and resized frames using OpenCV's `imshow()` function.

Finally, we exit the loop if the 'q' key is pressed, release the video capture device and close all windows.

Pausing the Video Frame

You can use the `time.sleep()` with `cv2.VideoCapture()` functions for a variety of video processing tasks, such as creating video visualizations or applying real-time processing to each frame. The `time.sleep()` function in Python can be used with OpenCV's `cv2.VideoCapture()` function to pause the video capture for a specified amount of time:

```python
import cv2
import time

# create a video capture object
cap = cv2.VideoCapture(0)

# loop over frames from the video capture
while True:
    # read a frame from the video capture
    ret, frame = cap.read()

    # check if the frame was successfully read
    if not ret:
        break

    # display the frame
    cv2.imshow("Frame", frame)

    # pause for 5 second
    time.sleep(5)

    # check if the user pressed the 'q' key to exit
    key = cv2.waitKey(1) & 0xFF
    if key == ord('q'):
        break

# release the video capture object and close all windows
cap.release()
cv2.destroyAllWindows()
```

In the preceding code, we first create a video capture object cap using `cv2.VideoCapture()`. We then loop over frames from the video capture using a while loop, reading each frame with `cap.read()` and displaying it using `cv2.imshow()`.

Refer to the following figure for video pausing in OpenCV:

We also use `time.sleep(5)` to pause the video capture for 5 seconds between each frame. This can be useful for slowing down the video playback or creating a time delay for processing each frame.

More Mouse Event Examples

Extract the color of a pixel on the image using the mouse

In this example, we define a callback function `get_pixel_color()` that is called when a left-click button-down event occurs on the window. The function extracts the BGR color value of the pixel at the mouse position and prints it to the console:

```
import cv2

# Define the callback function
```

```python
def get_pixel_color(event, x, y, flags, param):
    """ A callback function to get the color of a pixel in an image using mouse events.
    Parameters:
        event (int): The type of mouse event that occurred.
        x (int): The x-coordinate of the mouse cursor.
        y (int): The y-coordinate of the mouse cursor.
        flags (int): Any special flags associated with the mouse event.
        param (object): Optional parameters passed to the mouse callback.
        Returns: None.

    Side Effects: Prints the BGR and RGB values of the pixel at the given coordinates in the image. """

    if event == cv2.EVENT_LBUTTONDOWN:
        bgr_color = img[y, x]
        print('BGR color:', bgr_color)
        rgb_color = tuple(reversed(bgr_color))
        print('RGB color:', rgb_color)

# Load the image and create a window
img = cv2.imread('image.jpg')
cv2.namedWindow('image')

# Set the mouse callback function
cv2.setMouseCallback('image', get_pixel_color)

# Display the image and wait for a keypress
while True:
    cv2.imshow('image', img)
    if cv2.waitKey(1) == ord('q'):
        break

# Cleanup
cv2.destroyAllWindows()
```

Refer to the following figure to extract the color of a pixel:

Figure 3.12: Extract the color of the pixel using OpenCV

It also calculates the RGB color value by reversing the order of the BGR values and prints it to the console as well. Finally, we load the image, create a window, set the mouse callback function, display the image, and wait for a key press. These are just a couple of examples of how to handle mouse events in OpenCV Python. You can customize the callback function to perform any action you want based on the type of mouse event that occurs.

Extract the X, and Y values and pixel color on the image using the left and right mouse buttons, respectively

In this example, we define a callback function `click_event()` that is called when the left and the right-click button-down event occurs on the window. The function extracts the *x* and *y* coordinates of the mouse pointer using the left-click button clicked and gets the color of the pixel using the right-click button clicked.

The callback function takes four arguments: the event type, the *x* and *y* coordinates of the mouse pointer, and some additional data. Here's an example code that demonstrates how to handle mouse events in OpenCV Python:

```python
import cv2
def click_event(event, x, y, flags, param):
    """
    A callback function for handling mouse click events in an OpenCV
    window.

    Parameters:
        event (int): The type of mouse event that occurred.
        x (int): The x-coordinate of the mouse cursor.
        y (int): The y-coordinate of the mouse cursor.
        flags (int): Any special flags associated with the mouse
        event.
        param (object): Optional parameters passed to the mouse
        callback.

    Returns:
        None.

    Side Effects:
        Depending on the type of mouse event, this function may
        display text on the image window.

    """
    if event == cv2.EVENT_LBUTTONDOWN:
        # Handle left button-down event
        print('Left button clicked at (%d, %d)' % (x, y))

        # Add text to the image window displaying the coordinates of
        the click
        font = cv2.FONT_HERSHEY_SCRIPT_SIMPLEX
        strxy = str(x) + ', ' + str(y)
        cv2.putText(img, strxy, (x, y), font, 1, (255, 255, 0), 2)

        # Update the image window with the new text
        cv2.imshow('image', img)

    if event == cv2.EVENT_RBUTTONDOWN:
        # Handle right button down event
        blue = img[x, y, 0]
        green = img[x, y, 1]
        red = img[x, y, 2]
```

Image Processing 1 Using OpenCV

```
        # Add text to the image window displaying the BGR color
        values of the pixel
        font = cv2.FONT_HERSHEY_SCRIPT_SIMPLEX
        strBGR = str(blue) + ', ' + str(green) + ', ' + str(red)
        cv2.putText(img, strBGR, (x, y), font, 1, (0, 255, 255), 2)

        # Update the image window with the new text
        cv2.imshow('image', img)

# Display the image
img = cv2.imread('image.jpg', 1)
cv2.imshow('image', img)

cv2.setMouseCallback('image', click_event )

cv2.waitKey(0)
cv2.destroyAllWindows()
```

Refer to the following figure to extract X, and Y values and pixel color on the image:

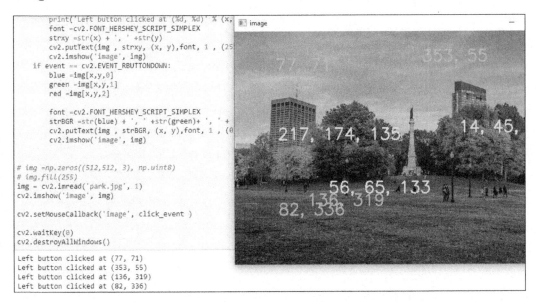

Figure 3.13: *Extract X, and Y values and pixel color using OpenCV*

The X and Y coordinate value will be displayed on the screen while clicking the left mouse button and the Color of the pixel will be displayed on the screen while clicking the right mouse button.

Draw the rectangle and curve using the left-click button mouse

In this example, we define a callback function `draw_curve()` that is called when the left-click button-down event occurs on the window. The function has two modes, which are rectangles and curves using the left-click button. To change the mode of the drawing, press the M button on the keyboard.

The callback function takes four arguments: the event type, the x and y coordinates of the mouse pointer, and some additional data. Here is an example code that demonstrates how to draw rectangles and curves using handle mouse events in OpenCV Python:

```
import numpy as np
import cv2

drawing = False # true if mouse is pressed
mode = True # if True, draw a rectangle. Press 'm' to toggle to curve
ix,iy = -1,-1

# mouse callback function
def draw_curve(event,x,y,flags,param):

    """
    Input parameters:
    - event: An event that is triggered when a mouse action occurs on the image.
    - x: The x-coordinate of the mouse pointer on the image.
    - y: The y-coordinate of the mouse pointer on the image.
    - flags: Flags associated with the mouse event.
    - param: Optional parameter for the function.

    Output:
    This function does not return any output.

    Global variables used:
    - ix: The x-coordinate of the starting point of the curve.
    - iy: The y-coordinate of the starting point of the curve.
    - drawing: A boolean flag indicating whether the user is currently drawing or not.
    - mode: A boolean flag indicating whether the user has chosen to
```

draw a rectangle or a circle.

If the left button of the mouse is pressed down, the function sets the drawing flag to True and records the starting point of the curve. If the mouse moves while the drawing flag is True, the function draws a rectangle or a circle depending on the mode chosen by the user. If the left button is released, the drawing flag is set to False and the function draws a rectangle or a circle depending on the mode chosen by the user.
"""

```
    global ix,iy, drawing, mode
    if event == cv2.EVENT_LBUTTONDOWN:
        drawing = True
        ix,iy = x,y
    elif event == cv2.EVENT_MOUSEMOVE:
        if drawing == True:
            if mode == True:
                cv2.rectangle(img,(ix,iy),(x,y),(0,255,0),-1)
            else:
                cv2.circle(img,(x,y),3,(0,0,255),-1)
    elif event == cv2.EVENT_LBUTTONUP:
        drawing = False
        if mode == True:
            cv2.rectangle(img,(ix,iy),(x,y),(0,255,0),-1)
        else:
            cv2.circle(img,(x,y),5,(0,0,255),-1)

img = np.zeros((512,512,3), np.uint8)
cv2.namedWindow('image')
cv2.setMouseCallback('image',draw_curve)

while True:
    cv2.imshow('image',img)
    k = cv2.waitKey(1) & 0xFF
    if k == ord('m'):
        mode = not mode

    # press the Q button to exit
    elif k == ord('q'):
```

```
        break
cv2.destroyAllWindows()
```

Refer to the following figure to draw the rectangle and curve using the left-click button mouse:

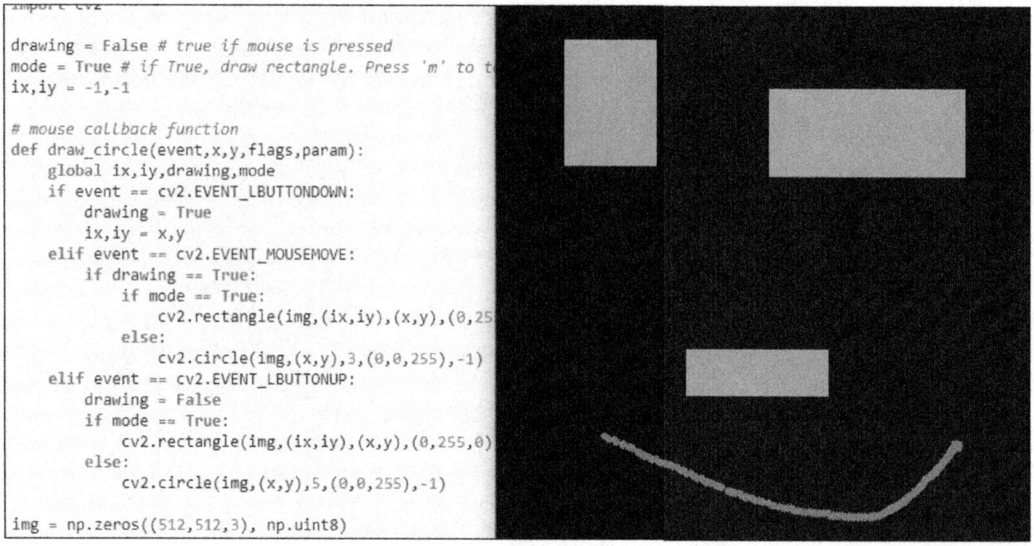

Figure 3.14: *Draw the rectangle and curve*

A blank black screen will be created using the **namedwindow()** function, then the rectangle and curve can be drawn using the left-click button. Finally, click the q button to exit the function.

Bitwise Operations

Bitwise operations are fundamental operations used in image processing to manipulate the pixel values of an image. OpenCV provides several bitwise operations that we can use to perform operations such as AND, OR, NOT, and XOR on images. Here's an example of how to perform bitwise operations using OpenCV in Python:

```
import cv2
import numpy as np

# Load two images
img1 = cv2.imread('image1.jpg')
img2 = cv2.imread('image2.jpg')
```

```python
# Resize the images to the same size
img1 = cv2.resize(img1, (300, 300))
img2 = cv2.resize(img2, (300, 300))

# Create a mask by thresholding the first image
gray_img1 = cv2.cvtColor(img1, cv2.COLOR_BGR2GRAY)
ret, mask = cv2.threshold(gray_img1, 100, 255, cv2.THRESH_BINARY)
mask = cv2.bitwise_not(mask)

# Perform a bitwise AND operation on the images
bitwise_and = cv2.bitwise_and(img1, img2, mask=mask)

# Perform a bitwise OR operation on the images
bitwise_or = cv2.bitwise_or(img1, img2, mask=mask)

# Perform a bitwise XOR operation on the images
bitwise_xor = cv2.bitwise_xor(img1, img2, mask=mask)

# Perform a bitwise NOT operation on the mask
bitwise_not = cv2.bitwise_not(mask)

# Display the results
cv2.imshow('Image 1', img1)
cv2.imshow('Image 2', img2)
cv2.imshow('Mask', mask)
cv2.imshow('Bitwise AND', bitwise_and)
cv2.imshow('Bitwise OR', bitwise_or)
cv2.imshow('Bitwise XOR', bitwise_xor)
cv2.imshow('Bitwise NOT', bitwise_not)
cv2.waitKey(0)
cv2.destroyAllWindows()
```

In the preceding code, we first load two images and resize them to the same size. We then create a mask by thresholding the first image, inverting the mask using the **cv2.bitwise_not()** function, and using the mask to extract the background from the second image using the **cv2.bitwise_and()** function. We also use the mask to extract the foreground from the first image using the same **cv2.bitwise_and()** function.

Refer to the following figure for bitwise operations in OpenCV:

Figure 3.15: Display the image 1 and 2

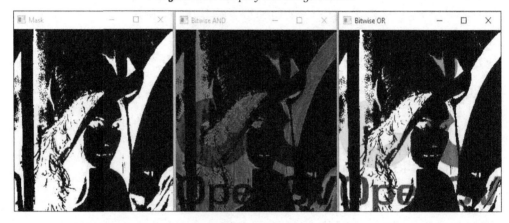

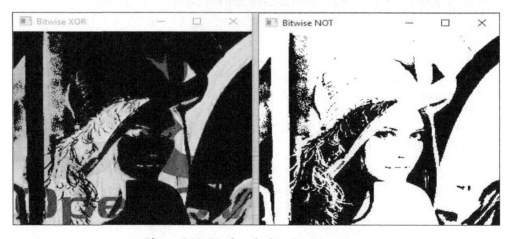

Figure 3.16: Display the bitwise operations

We then combine the foreground and background images using the bitwise OR operator (`cv2.bitwise_or()`) and display the result. This operation allows us to overlay the foreground image on top of the background image.

In this example, we load two images using OpenCV's `imread()` function and resize them to the same size using the `cv2.resize()` function. We then create a mask by thresholding the first image. We perform a bitwise AND operation on the images using the `cv2.bitwise_and()` function and the mask we created. We also perform bitwise OR and XOR operations using `cv2.bitwise_or()` and `cv2.bitwise_xor()` functions, respectively.

Finally, we perform a bitwise NOT operation on the mask using the `cv2.bitwise_not()` function. We display all the results using the `cv2.imshow()` function. Note that the mask used in the bitwise operations should have the same size as the images. Also, the values in the mask should be either 0 or 255.

Overall, bitwise operations are a powerful tool for manipulating the pixel values of images and can be used in a wide range of image processing tasks.

Binding a Trackbar

In OpenCV, we can use trackbars to dynamically adjust the values of various parameters in real time, which is especially useful when we want to fine-tune the results of image processing operations. Here's an example of how to bind a trackbar to an image using OpenCV in Python:

```python
import cv2
import numpy as np

# Create a black image
img = np.zeros((300, 512, 3), np.uint8)

# Create a window to display the image
cv2.namedWindow('image')

# Create a function to handle trackbar changes
def trackbar_callback(x):
    pass

# Create trackbars for each color channel
cv2.createTrackbar('R', 'image', 0, 255, trackbar_callback)
cv2.createTrackbar('G', 'image', 0, 255, trackbar_callback)
cv2.createTrackbar('B', 'image', 0, 255, trackbar_callback)
```

```python
while True:
    # Display the image
    cv2.imshow('image', img)

    # Get the current position of the trackbars
    r = cv2.getTrackbarPos('R', 'image')
    g = cv2.getTrackbarPos('G', 'image')
    b = cv2.getTrackbarPos('B', 'image')

    # Set the color of the image based on the trackbar positions
    img[:] = [b, g, r]

    # Check for user input
    key = cv2.waitKey(1) & 0xFF
    if key == ord('q'):
        break

# Clean up
cv2.destroyAllWindows()
```

In the preceding code, we first create a black image and a window to display the image. We then create a function to handle trackbar changes (in this case, the function does not do anything), and we create three trackbars for the red, green, and blue color channels using the **cv2.createTrackbar()** function.

Refer to the following figure for trackbar operations in OpenCV:

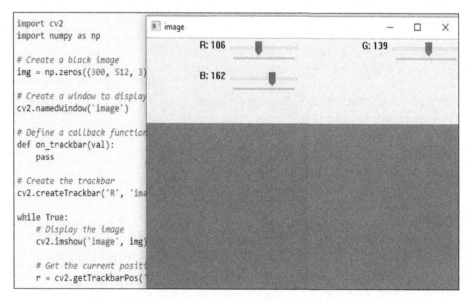

Figure 3.17: *Display the bind the trackbar using OpenCV*

We then enter a loop where we continuously display the image and update its color based on the current positions of the trackbars using the `cv2.getTrackbarPos()` function. Finally, we check for user input and exit the loop if the user presses the *q* key.

Overall, this code demonstrates how to create and bind trackbars to an image using OpenCV in Python. This technique can be used in a wide range of image-processing applications, where we need to adjust the values of various parameters in real-time.

Image Trackbar

Trackbars are a useful feature in OpenCV that allows us to dynamically adjust the values of various parameters in real time. In Python, we can use OpenCV's `cv2.createTrackbar()` function to create trackbars, and the `cv2.getTrackbarPos()` function to retrieve their current positions. Here's an example of how to use trackbars in OpenCV with Python:

```
import cv2
import numpy as np

# read the image
img = cv2.imread('lena.jpg')
cv2.namedWindow('image')
#create nothing
def nothing(x):
    print(x)

# create trackbar
cv2.createTrackbar('cp', 'image', 10, 400, nothing)

switch = "color/gray"
cv2.createTrackbar(switch, 'image', 0, 1, nothing)

while(True):
    img = cv2.imread('lena.jpg')
    pos =cv2.getTrackbarPos('cp', 'image')
    font =cv2.FONT_HERSHEY_SIMPLEX

    #put the text in the frame
    cv2.putText(img , str(pos), (50, 150),font, 4 , (0, 0, 255) )

    # press q to exit the frame
```

```
        if cv2.waitKey(1) & 0xFF == ord('q'):
            break

    p =cv2.getTrackbarPos(switch, "image")
    if p==0:
        pass
    else:
        img = cv2.cvtColor(img, cv2.COLOR_BGR2GRAY)

    # display the frame
    img =cv2.imshow('image', img)

cv2.destroyAllWindows()
```

In the preceding code, we first create a black image and a window to display the image. We then define a callback function for the trackbar (in this case, the function does not do anything), and create the trackbar using the **cv2.createTrackbar()** function.

Refer to the following figure for image trackbar operations in OpenCV:

Figure 3.18: Display the image trackbar

We then enter a loop where we continuously display the image and update its color based on the current position of the trackbar using the `cv2.getTrackbarPos()` function. Finally, we check for user input and exit the loop if the user presses the *q* key.

Overall, this code demonstrates how to use trackbars in OpenCV with Python. By creating and binding trackbars to various parameters, we can fine-tune the results of image processing operations in real-time.

Conclusion

In this chapter, we have discussed the basic image-processing techniques like cropping, rotating, resizing, wait key function and many more. Furthermore, we have discussed resizing and pausing the video frame, bitwise operations, and Trackbar control using the OpenCV library.

In the next chapter, we will discuss more image-processing techniques like smoothing, blurring, edge detection, matplot library, and image blending using OpenCV and Python.

Points to Remember

The display image will be closed after 5 seconds using cv2.waitkey(5000) or press the 'q' button to close the function while using cv2.waitkey(0).

References

Image processing techniques:

https://docs.opencv.org/4.x/d2/d96/tutorial_py_table_of_contents_imgproc.html

CHAPTER 4

Image Processing 2 using OpenCV

Introduction

This chapter will cover the other image processing techniques such as Matplotlib, smoothing, blurring, and edge detection using OpenCV. Image Gradients, pyramids, and blending techniques will be clearly explained using OpenCV and python programming language.

Structure

In this chapter, we will cover the following topics:

- Matplotlib with OpenCV
- Morphological Transformations using OpenCV
- Smoothing and Blurring Images using OpenCV
- Image Gradients using OpenCV
- Image Pyramids with OpenCV
- Image Blending using OpenCV
- Edge Detection using OpenCV

Matplotlib with OpenCV

Matplotlib is a useful Python library for creating visualizations and plotting data. It can also be used in conjunction with OpenCV for displaying images and visualizing data. Here are some common techniques for using Matplotlib with OpenCV:

- Displaying multiple images using Matplotlib:

    ```
    import cv2
    import matplotlib.pyplot as plt
    ```

```python
# Load two images
img1 = cv2.imread('out.jpg')
img2 = cv2.imread('apple.jpg')

# Convert the images to RGB color space
img1 = cv2.cvtColor(img1, cv2.COLOR_BGR2RGB)
img2 = cv2.cvtColor(img2, cv2.COLOR_BGR2RGB)

# Create a figure and two subplots
fig, (ax1, ax2) = plt.subplots(1, 2)

# Display the images on the subplots
ax1.imshow(img1)
ax1.set_title('Image 1')
ax2.imshow(img2)
ax2.set_title('Image 2')

# Show the figure
plt.show()
```

Refer to the following figure for displaying images using Matplotlib in OpenCV.

Figure 4.1: *Display the image using Matplotlib*

In this code, we first load two images using **cv2.imread()** and convert them to the RGB color space using **cv2.cvtColor()**. We then create a figure with two subplots using the **plt.subplots()** function. We display the two images on the subplots using **ax1.imshow()** and **ax2.imshow()** and set the titles of the subplots using **ax1.set_title()** and **ax2.set_title()**. Finally, we show the figure using **plt.show()**.

- Plotting a histogram of an image using Matplotlib:

    ```
    import cv2
    import matplotlib.pyplot as plt

    # Load an image
    img = cv2.imread('apple.jpg')

    # Convert the image to grayscale
    gray = cv2.cvtColor(img, cv2.COLOR_BGR2GRAY)

    # Calculate and plot the histogram of the grayscale image
    hist = cv2.calcHist([gray], [0], None, [256], [0, 256])
    plt.plot(hist)
    plt.xlim([0, 256])
    plt.show()
    ```

Refer to the following figure for plotting a histogram of an image in OpenCV:

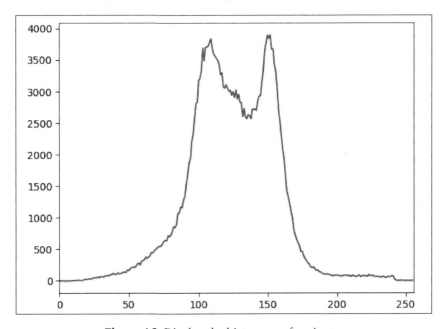

Figure 4.2: *Display the histogram of an image*

In this code, we first load an image using `cv2.imread()` and convert it to grayscale using `cv2.cvtColor()`. We then calculate the histogram of the grayscale image using `cv2.calcHist()`, and plot the histogram using `plt.plot()`. We set the *x*-axis limits using `plt.xlim()` and show the `plot using plt.show()`.

Overall, these examples demonstrate how to use Matplotlib with OpenCV techniques to display images and results and to visualize data such as histograms.

Morphological Transformations Using OpenCV

Morphological transformations are a set of image processing operations that process images based on their shapes. These operations are normally performed on binary images, such as those obtained from thresholding an image. OpenCV provides several functions for performing morphological transformations. Here are some of the most common ones:

- **Erosion:** Erosion is a morphological operation that shrinks the boundaries of foreground objects in a binary image. The basic idea is to slide a small kernel over the image and if all pixels under the kernel are white, the center pixel is set to white, otherwise, it is set to black. Here's an example of how to perform erosion using OpenCV:

```
import cv2
import numpy as np

# Load an image
img = cv2.imread('apple.jpg', 0)

# Define the kernel for erosion
kernel = np.ones((5,5), np.uint8)

# Apply erosion
erosion = cv2.erode(img, kernel, iterations=1)

# Display the results
cv2.imshow('Original Image', img)
cv2.imshow('Erosion', erosion)
```

```
cv2.waitKey(0)
cv2.destroyAllWindows()
```
Refer to the following figure for plotting an erosion of an image in OpenCV:

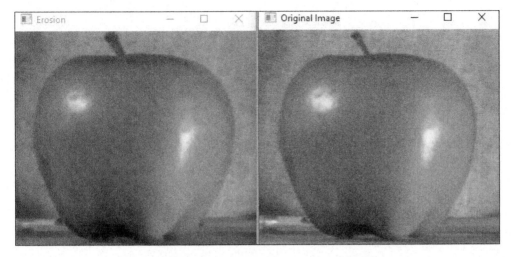

Figure 4.3: *Display the erosion of an image*

In this example, we load a binary image using OpenCV's `imread()` function and convert it to grayscale. We then define a 3x3 kernel using NumPy's `ones()` function and perform erosion on the image using OpenCV `erode()` function. Finally, we display the original image and the result of the erosion operation using OpenCV's `imshow()` function.

- **Dilation:** Dilation is a morphological operation that expands the boundaries of foreground objects in a binary image. The basic idea is to slide a small kernel over the image and if at least one pixel under the kernel is white, the center pixel is set to white, otherwise, it is set to black. Here's an example of how to perform dilation using OpenCV:

```
import cv2
import numpy as np

# Load an image
img = cv2.imread('apple.jpg', 0)

# Define the kernel for dilation
kernel = np.ones((5,5), np.uint8)
```

```python
# Apply dilation
dilation = cv2.dilate(img, kernel, iterations=1)

# Display the results
cv2.imshow('Original Image', img)
cv2.imshow('Dilation', dilation)
cv2.waitKey(0)
cv2.destroyAllWindows()
```

Refer to the following figure for plotting a dilation of an image in OpenCV.

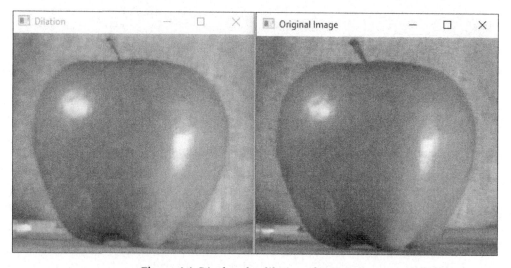

Figure 4.4: *Display the dilation of an image*

In this example, we load a binary image using OpenCV's **imread()** function and convert it to grayscale. We then define a 3×3 kernel using NumPy's **ones()** function, and perform dilation on the image using OpenCV's **dilate()** function. Finally, we display the original image and the result of the dilation operation using OpenCV's **imshow()** function

- **Opening**: Opening is a morphological operation that consists of an erosion followed by a dilation. It can be used to remove small objects in a binary image or to smooth the contours of an object. Here's an example of how to perform an opening using OpenCV:

```python
import cv2
import numpy as np

# Load an image
img = cv2.imread('apple.jpg', 0)

# Define the kernel for opening
```

Image Processing 2 using OpenCV

```
kernel = np.ones((5,5), np.uint8)

# Apply opening
opening = cv2.morphologyEx(img, cv2.MORPH_OPEN, kernel)

# Display the results
cv2.imshow('Original Image', img)
cv2.imshow('Opening', opening)
cv2.waitKey(0)
cv2.destroyAllWindows()
```

Refer to the following figure for plotting an opening of an image in OpenCV:

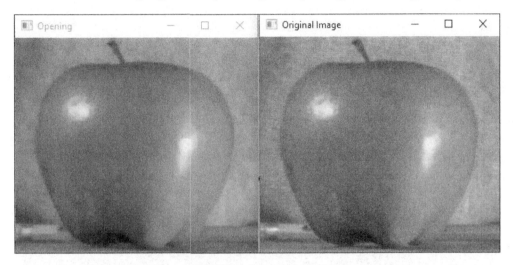

Figure 4.5: *Display the opening of an image*

In this example, we load a binary image using OpenCV's **imread()** function and convert it to grayscale. We then define a 3×3 kernel using NumPy's **ones()** function and perform opening on the image using OpenCV's **morphologyEx()** function with the **cv2.MORPH_OPEN** flag. Finally, we display the original image and the result of the opening operation using OpenCV's **imshow()** function.

- **Closing:** Closing is a morphological operation that consists of a dilation followed by an erosion. It can be used to fill small holes in a binary image or smooth an object's contours. Here's an example of how to perform closing using OpenCV:

```
import cv2
import numpy as np

# Load an image
img = cv2.imread('apple.jpg', 0)
```

```
# Define the kernel for closing
kernel = np.ones((5,5), np.uint8)

# Apply closing
closing = cv2.morphologyEx(img, cv2.MORPH_CLOSE, kernel)

# Display the results
cv2.imshow('Original Image', img)
cv2.imshow('Closing', closing)
cv2.waitKey(0)
cv2.destroyAllWindows()
```

Refer to the following figure for plotting a closing of an image in OpenCV:

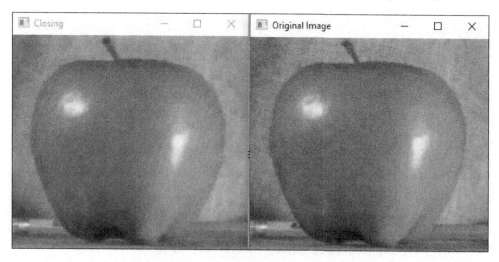

Figure 4.6: *Display the closing of an image*

In this example, we load a binary image using OpenCV's `imread()` function and convert it to grayscale. We then define a 3×3 kernel using NumPy's `ones()` function and perform closing on the image using OpenCV's `morphologyEx()` function with the `cv2.MORPH_CLOSE` flag. Finally, we display the original image and the result of the closing operation using OpenCV's `imshow()` function.

Smoothing and Blurring Images Using OpenCV

Smoothing and blurring are important techniques in image processing that can be used for various purposes such as noise reduction, edge detection, and feature extraction. In OpenCV, there are several smoothing and blurring filters available, each with its own unique characteristics and use cases.

Here's an overview of some of the most commonly used filters:

- **Gaussian Filter:** This filter is used to blur an image and reduce noise. It works by convolving the image with a Gaussian kernel, which emphasizes the central pixels and attenuates the surrounding pixels. It is implemented in OpenCV using the `cv2.GaussianBlur()` function:

  ```
  import cv2
  img = cv2.imread('image.jpg')
  blur = cv2.GaussianBlur(img, (5,5), 0)
  cv2.imshow('Blurred Image', blur)
  cv2.waitKey(0)
  cv2.destroyAllWindows()
  ```

Refer to the following figure for the gaussian filter of an image in OpenCV:

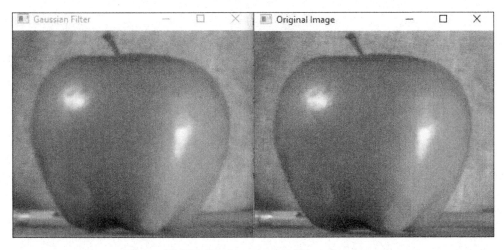

Figure 4.7: Display the gaussian filter of an image

- **Median Filter:** This filter is used to remove salt-and-pepper noise from an image. It works by replacing each pixel with the median value of its neighboring pixels. It is implemented in OpenCV using the `cv2.medianBlur()` function:

  ```
  import cv2
  img = cv2.imread('image.jpg')
  blur = cv2.medianBlur(img, 5)
  cv2.imshow('Blurred Image', blur)
  cv2.waitKey(0)
  cv2.destroyAllWindows()
  ```

Refer to the following figure for the median filter of an image in OpenCV:

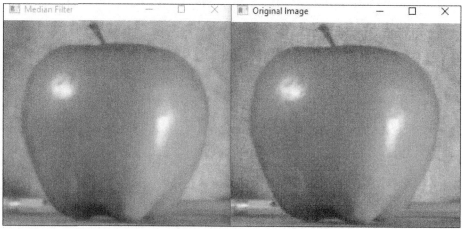

Figure 4.8: *Display the median filter of an image*

- **Bilateral Filter:** This filter is used to smooth an image while preserving its edges. It works by applying a Gaussian filter to the pixels based on their spatial distance and intensity difference. It is implemented in OpenCV using the **cv2.bilateralFilter()** function:

```
import cv2
img = cv2.imread('image.jpg')
blur = cv2.bilateralFilter(img, 9, 75, 75)
cv2.imshow('Blurred Image', blur)
cv2.waitKey(0)
cv2.destroyAllWindows()
```

Refer to the following figure for the bilateral filter of an image in OpenCV:

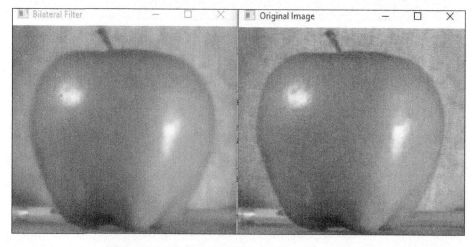

Figure 4.9: *Display the bilateral filter of an image*

- **Box Filter:** This filter is used to blur an image and reduce noise. It works by convolving the image with a rectangular kernel, which averages the pixels within the kernel. It is implemented in OpenCV using the **cv2.boxFilter()** function:

  ```
  import cv2
  img = cv2.imread('image.jpg')
  blur = cv2.boxFilter(img, -1, (5,5), normalize=True)
  cv2.imshow('Blurred Image', blur)
  cv2.waitKey(0)
  cv2.destroyAllWindows()
  ```

Refer to the following figure for the box filter of an image in OpenCV:

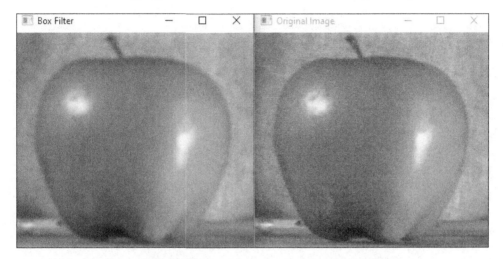

Figure 4.10: Display the box filter of an image

- **Mean Filter:** This filter is used to blur an image and reduce noise. It defines the size of the kernel that we want to use for the mean filter. In this case, we have set the kernel size to 5×5. We then define the kernel as a NumPy array with ones and divide it by the size of the kernel squared to normalize it.

  We apply the mean filter using the **cv2.filter2D()** function, which takes the input image, the depth of the output image (-1 means the same as the input), and the kernel as inputs and returns the filtered image:

  ```
  import cv2
  import numpy as np
  
  # Load the image
  img = cv2.imread('image.jpg')
  ```

```
# Define the kernel size
kernel_size = 5

# Define the kernel
kernel = np.ones((kernel_size, kernel_size), np.float32) / 
(kernel_size**2)

# Apply the mean filter
filtered_image = cv2.filter2D(img, -1, kernel)

# Display the original and filtered images
cv2.imshow('Original Image', img)
cv2.imshow('Filtered Image', filtered_image)
cv2.waitKey(0)
cv2.destroyAllWindows()
```
Refer to the following figure for plotting a mean filter of an image in OpenCV:

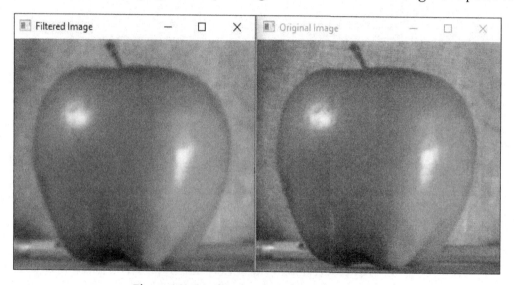

Figure 4.11: *Display the mean filter of an image*

Image Gradients Using OpenCV

Image gradients are used to measure the rate of change of pixel values in an image. They are useful for tasks such as edge detection, image segmentation, and feature extraction. In OpenCV, image gradients can be calculated using different filters such as the Sobel filter, Scharr filter, or Laplacian filter.

The Sobel and Scharr filters are used to calculate the first-order derivatives of an image, which represent the gradient in the x and y directions, respectively.

These filters work by convolving the image with a small kernel that approximates the derivative of the image.

The Laplacian filter, on the other hand, calculates the second-order derivative of an image, which represents the curvature of the image. This filter is useful for detecting edges and corners in an image.

Here's an example of how to calculate image gradients using the Sobel filter in OpenCV:

```
import cv2

# Load an image
img = cv2.imread('image.jpg')

# Convert the image to grayscale
gray = cv2.cvtColor(img, cv2.COLOR_BGR2GRAY)

# Calculate the horizontal and vertical Sobel gradients
grad_x = cv2.Sobel(gray, cv2.CV_64F, 1, 0, ksize=3)
grad_y = cv2.Sobel(gray, cv2.CV_64F, 0, 1, ksize=3)

# Calculate the absolute value of the gradients
abs_grad_x = cv2.convertScaleAbs(grad_x)
abs_grad_y = cv2.convertScaleAbs(grad_y)

# Combine the gradients using the magnitude and direction
grad_mag = cv2.addWeighted(abs_grad_x, 0.5, abs_grad_y, 0.5, 0)
grad_dir = cv2.phase(grad_x, grad_y, angleInDegrees=True)

# Display the results
cv2.imshow('Original Image', img)
cv2.imshow('Horizontal Gradient', abs_grad_x)
cv2.imshow('Vertical Gradient', abs_grad_y)
cv2.imshow('Combined Gradient (Magnitude)', grad_mag)
cv2.imshow('Gradient Direction', grad_dir)
cv2.waitKey(0)
cv2.destroyAllWindows()
```

Refer to the following figure for plotting an image gradient of an image in OpenCV:

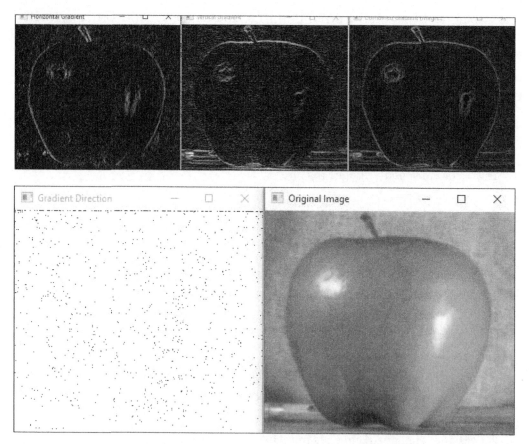

Figure 4.12: Display the image gradient of an image

In this example, we load an image using OpenCV's `imread()` function and convert it to grayscale using the `cv2.cvtColor()` function. We then calculate the horizontal and vertical Sobel gradients of the image using `cv2.Sobel()` function. We also calculate the absolute value of the gradients using the `cv2.convertScaleAbs()` function. We combine the gradients using the magnitude and direction using `cv2.addWeighted()` and `cv2.phase()` functions, respectively. Finally, we display all the results using the `cv2.imshow()` function.

Note that the size of the filter kernel used in the Sobel filter can be adjusted using the ksize parameter. Also, the gradient magnitude and direction can be calculated using other filters such as the Scharr filter or the Laplacian filter. You can experiment with different filters and parameters to find the values that work best for your application.

Image Pyramids with OpenCV

Image pyramids are a multi-scale representation of an image that can be used for tasks such as image blending, texture analysis, and object detection. In computer vision, image pyramids are a fundamental concept that allows the processing of an image at different scales. In OpenCV, there are two main types of image pyramids:

- **Gaussian pyramids:** It is formed by repeatedly smoothing the image using a Gaussian filter and then downsampling the image. Each level of the pyramid is half the size of the previous level. Gaussian pyramids can be created using the `cv2.pyrDown()` function which performs the downsampling operation, and `cv2.GaussianBlur()` function which performs the image smoothing operation.

- **Laplacian pyramids:** It is formed by taking the difference between each level of the Gaussian pyramid and the corresponding upsampled and smoothed version of the next level. Each level of the Laplacian pyramid represents the information that is lost when downsampling the previous level of the Gaussian pyramid. Laplacian pyramids can be created using the `cv2.pyrUp()` function which performs the upsampling operation, and the `cv2.subtract()` function which performs the difference operation.

Here's an example of how to create Gaussian and Laplacian pyramids in OpenCV:

```
import cv2

# Load an image
img = cv2.imread('apple.jpg')

# Create a Gaussian pyramid
gaussian = img.copy()
gaussian_pyramid = [gaussian]
for i in range(4):
    gaussian = cv2.pyrDown(gaussian)
    gaussian_pyramid.append(gaussian)

# Create a Laplacian pyramid
laplacian_pyramid = []
for i in range(3, 0, -1):
    gaussian_expanded = cv2.pyrUp(gaussian_pyramid[i])
    laplacian = cv2.subtract(gaussian_pyramid[i-1], gaussian_expanded)
    laplacian_pyramid.append(laplacian)
```

```
# Display the results
cv2.imshow('Original Image', img)
for i in range(4):
    cv2.imshow(f'Gaussian Pyramid Level {i}', gaussian_pyramid[i])
for i in range(3):
    cv2.imshow(f'Laplacian Pyramid Level {i}', laplacian_pyramid[i])
cv2.waitKey(0)
cv2.destroyAllWindows()
```

Refer to the following figure for plotting image pyramids of an image in OpenCV:

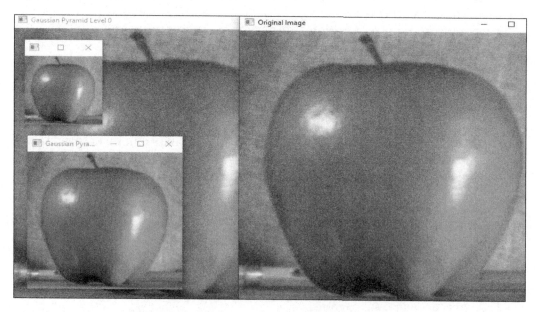

Figure 4.13: *Display the image pyramids of an image*

In this example, we load an image using OpenCV's **imread()** function. We then create a Gaussian pyramid by repeatedly applying the **cv2.pyrDown()** function to the image and storing each level in a list. We also create a Laplacian pyramid by taking the difference between each level of the Gaussian pyramid and the corresponding upsampled and smoothed version of the next level and storing each level in a list. Finally, we display the results using the **cv2.imshow()** function.

Note that the number of levels in the Gaussian and Laplacian pyramids can be adjusted depending on the desired scale of the image. Additionally, image pyramids can be useful in many image-processing tasks such as image blending, texture analysis, and object detection.

Image Blending Using OpenCV

Image blending is the process of combining two or more images into a single image by blending their pixel values. In computer vision, image blending can be used for tasks such as creating smooth transitions between images, creating panoramic images, and removing unwanted objects from images. OpenCV provides several methods for image blending, some of which are:

- **Additive Blending:** This method involves adding the pixel values of two images to produce the blended image. It is useful for adding two images with different exposure levels or brightness levels. The function **cv2.add()** can be used for additive blending.

Example code:

```
import cv2

# Load two images
img1 = cv2.imread('apple.jpg')
img2 = cv2.imread('dog.jpg')

# Resize the images to the same size
img1 = cv2.resize(img1, (320, 280))
img2 = cv2.resize(img2, (320, 280))

# Blend the images
blended_img = cv2.add(img1, img2)

# Display the results
cv2.imshow('Image 1', img1)
cv2.imshow('Image 2', img2)
cv2.imshow('Blended Image', blended_img)
cv2.waitKey(0)
cv2.destroyAllWindows()
```

Refer to the following figure for plotting an additive blending of an image in OpenCV:

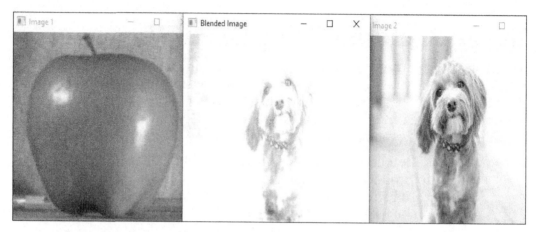

Figure 4.14: *Display the additive blending of an image*

- **Weighted Blending:** This method involves taking a weighted average of the pixel values of two images to produce the blended image. The weights can be adjusted to control the contribution of each image to the final output. The function `cv2.addWeighted()` can be used for weighted blending. Example code:

```
import cv2

# Load two images
img1 = cv2.imread('apple.jpg')
img2 = cv2.imread('dog.jpg')

# Resize the images to the same size
img1 = cv2.resize(img1, (320, 280))
img2 = cv2.resize(img2, (320, 280))

# Blend the images with a weight of 0.5
blended = cv2.addWeighted(img1, 0.5, img2, 0.5, 0)

# Display the results
cv2.imshow('Image 1', img1)
cv2.imshow('Image 2', img2)
cv2.imshow('Blended Image', blended)
```

Image Processing 2 using OpenCV 87

```
cv2.waitKey(0)
cv2.destroyAllWindows()
```
Refer to the following figure for the weighted blending of an image in OpenCV:

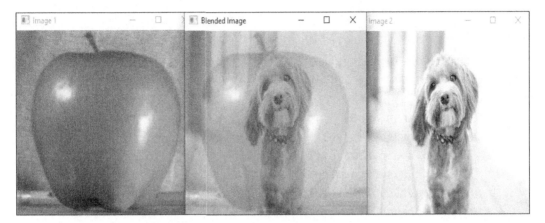

Figure 4.15: Display the weighted blending of an image

In this code, we have used the `cv2.addWeighted()` function to perform weighted blending. The alpha and beta parameters specify the weight of the first and second images, respectively. The gamma parameter is an optional scalar value added to the weighted sum.

- **Image Pyramids:** Image pyramids are a type of image representation that consists of a series of scaled-down images. Image blending can be performed by combining corresponding levels of two image pyramids. The function `cv2.pyrUp()` can be used to create an image pyramid, and `cv2.pyrDown()` can be used to downsample an image. Example code:

```
import cv2
import numpy as np

# Load the images
img1 = cv2.imread('image1.jpg')
img2 = cv2.imread('image2.jpg')

# Create Gaussian pyramids for each image
G1 = img1.copy()
G2 = img2.copy()
gp1 = [G1]
gp2 = [G2]
```

```python
for i in range(6):
    G1 = cv2.pyrDown(G1)
    G2 = cv2.pyrDown(G2)
    gp1.append(G1)
    gp2.append(G2)

# Create Laplacian pyramids for each image
lp1 = [gp1[5]]
lp2 = [gp2[5]]
for i in range(5, 0, -1):
    GE1 = cv2.pyrUp(gp1[i])
    GE2 = cv2.pyrUp(gp2[i])
    L1 = cv2.subtract(gp1[i-1], GE1)
    L2 = cv2.subtract(gp2[i-1], GE2)
    lp1.append(L1)
    lp2.append(L2)

# Merge the Laplacian pyramids
LS = []
for l1, l2 in zip(lp1, lp2):
    rows, cols, dpt = l1.shape
    ls = np.hstack((l1[:, 0:cols//2], l2[:, cols//2:]))
    LS.append(ls)

# Reconstruct the blended image
blended_img = LS[0]
for i in range(1, 6):
    blended_img = cv2.pyrUp(blended_img)
    blended_img = cv2.add(blended_img, LS[i])

# Display the blended image
cv2.imshow('Blended Image', blended_img)
cv2.waitKey(0)
cv2.destroyAllWindows()
```

Refer to the following figure for plotting image pyramids of an image in OpenCV:

Figure 4.16: *Display the image pyramids of an image*

We then create Laplacian pyramids for each image by subtracting each level of the Gaussian pyramid from its upsampled version at the next level. We append each level of the Laplacian pyramid to a list.

We then merge the Laplacian pyramids by horizontally concatenating the left and right halves of each level and appending the result to a list. Finally, we reconstruct the blended image by starting with the smallest level of the Laplacian pyramid, repeatedly upsampling it, and adding the corresponding level of the merged Laplacian pyramid until we reach the top of the pyramid.

We display the resulting blended image using `cv2.imshow()` and wait for a key press using `cv2.waitKey()` before closing the window using `cv2.destroyAllWindows()`.

Edge Detection Using OpenCV

Edge detection is the process of identifying the boundaries between objects in an image. In computer vision, edge detection is a fundamental step in many tasks such as object detection, image segmentation, and feature extraction.

In OpenCV, there are several methods available for edge detection, including the Canny edge detection algorithm, the Sobel operator, and the Laplacian of Gaussian (LoG) filter.

- **Sobel Operator:** The Sobel operator is a commonly used edge detection filter in OpenCV. It calculates the gradient of an image in the x and y directions and then combines the two gradients to produce an edge map. The Sobel operator can be applied using the `cv2.Sobel()` function.
- **Laplacian of Gaussian (LoG) Filter:** The LoG filter is a second-order derivative filter that is useful for detecting edges and corners in an image. It works by first smoothing the image using a Gaussian filter, and then calculating the Laplacian of the smoothed image. The LoG filter can be applied using the `cv2.GaussianBlur()` and `cv2.Laplacian()` functions.
- **Canny Edge Detection Algorithm:** The Canny algorithm is a widely used edge detection algorithm that is robust to noise and produces thin, well-defined edges. It works by first smoothing the image using a Gaussian filter, then calculating the gradient magnitude and direction using the Sobel operator, and finally applying non-maximum suppression and hysteresis thresholding to extract the edges. The Canny algorithm can be applied using the `cv2.Canny()` function.
- **Edge Detection Parameters:** The performance of edge detection algorithms can be affected by various parameters such as the size of the filter kernel, the threshold values, and the hysteresis thresholding parameters. These parameters can be adjusted to achieve the desired edge detection results.

Sobel Operator Using OpenCV

Here's an example of how to perform edge detection using the Sobel operator in OpenCV:

```
import cv2

# Load an image
img = cv2.imread('image.jpg')
```

```python
# Convert the image to grayscale
gray = cv2.cvtColor(img, cv2.COLOR_BGR2GRAY)

# Calculate the horizontal and vertical Sobel gradients
grad_x = cv2.Sobel(gray, cv2.CV_64F, 1, 0, ksize=3)
grad_y = cv2.Sobel(gray, cv2.CV_64F, 0, 1, ksize=3)

# Combine the gradients using the magnitude and direction
grad_mag = cv2.addWeighted(grad_x, 0.5, grad_y, 0.5, 0)

# Threshold the gradient magnitude to produce binary edge map
edges = cv2.threshold(grad_mag, 50, 255, cv2.THRESH_BINARY)[1]

# Display the results
cv2.imshow('Original Image', img)
cv2.imshow('Sobel Edges', edges)
cv2.waitKey(0)
cv2.destroyAllWindows()
```

Refer to the following figure for plotting the sobel edges of an image in OpenCV:

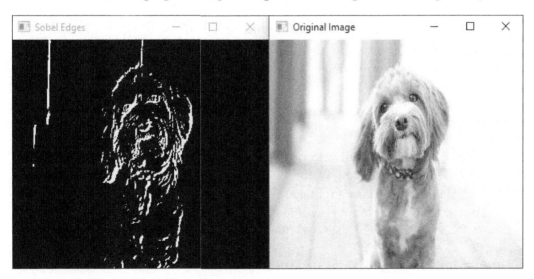

Figure 4.17: *Display the sobel edges of an image*

In this example, we load an image using OpenCV's **imread()** function and convert it to grayscale using the **cv2.cvtColor()** function. We then calculate the horizontal and vertical Sobel gradients of the image using **cv2.Sobel()** function. We combine the gradients using the magnitude and direction using the **cv2.addWeighted()** function. We threshold the gradient magnitude to produce a binary edge map using the `cv2.threshold()` function. Finally, we display the results using the `cv2.imshow()` function.

Note that the size of the filter kernel used in the Sobel operator can be adjusted using the `ksize` parameter. Also, the threshold values used in the thresholding step can be adjusted to produce different edge maps. You can experiment with different parameters and methods to find the values that work best for your application.

Laplacian of Gaussian (LoG) Filter Using OpenCV

Here is an example of OpenCV code for implementing the Laplacian of Gaussian (LoG) filter:

```
import cv2
import numpy as np

# Load image
img = cv2.imread('image.jpg', cv2.IMREAD_GRAYSCALE)

# Define kernel size and sigma value
kernel_size = 5
sigma = 1.4

# Apply LoG filter
filtered_img = cv2.GaussianBlur(img, (kernel_size, kernel_size), sigma)
filtered_img = cv2.Laplacian(filtered_img, cv2.CV_64F)

# Normalize the filtered image
filtered_img = cv2.normalize(filtered_img, None, alpha=0, beta=255, norm_type=cv2.NORM_MINMAX, dtype=cv2.CV_8U)

# Display the original and filtered images
cv2.imshow('Original Image', img)
cv2.imshow('Filtered Image', filtered_img)
cv2.waitKey(0)
cv2.destroyAllWindows()
```

Refer to the following figure for plotting a LOG filter of an image in OpenCV:

Figure 4.18: *Display the LOG filter of an image*

In this code, we first load the input image in grayscale format. Then, we define the kernel size and sigma value for the LoG filter. We apply the Gaussian blur and Laplacian filter using the `cv2.GaussianBlur()` and `cv2.Laplacian()` functions, respectively. Finally, we normalize the filtered image and display both the original and filtered images using the `cv2.imshow()` function.

Canny Edge Detection Using OpenCV

Here's an example of how to perform Canny edge detection in OpenCV using Python:

In this example, we load an image using OpenCV's `imread()` function and convert it to grayscale using the `cv2.cvtColor()` function. We then apply the Canny edge detection algorithm using `cv2.Canny()` function with threshold values of 100 and 200.

The Canny algorithm works by first removing noise from the image using a Gaussian filter, then calculating the gradient magnitude and direction of the image using the Sobel operator, and finally applying non-maximum suppression and hysteresis thresholding to extract the edges. Finally, we display the results using the `cv2.imshow()` function.

Note that the threshold values used in the Canny algorithm can be adjusted depending on the specific image and the desired effect. You can experiment with different threshold values to find the values that work best for your application. Additionally, it's a good practice to perform some pre-processing such as noise reduction and image smoothing before applying edge detection algorithms to get better results.

Here's another example of how to perform Canny edge detection on an image file using OpenCV and Python:

```
import cv2

# Load an image
img = cv2.imread('dog.jpg')
img = cv2.resize(img, (320, 280))

# Convert the image to grayscale
gray = cv2.cvtColor(img, cv2.COLOR_BGR2GRAY)

# Apply the Canny edge detection algorithm
edges = cv2.Canny(gray, 100, 200)

# Display the results
cv2.imshow('Original Image', img)
cv2.imshow('Canny Edges', edges)
cv2.waitKey(0)
cv2.destroyAllWindows()
```

Refer to the following figure for plotting a canny edge detection of an image in OpenCV:

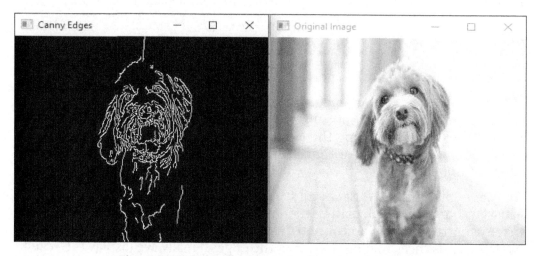

Figure 4.19: Display the canny edge detection of an image

Here's another example of how to perform Canny edge detection on a video file using OpenCV and Python:

```
import cv2
```

```python
# Load the video file
cap = cv2.VideoCapture(0)

# Loop through the video frames
while(cap.isOpened()):
    # Read a frame from the video
    ret, frame = cap.read()
    if not ret: break

    # Convert the frame to grayscale
    gray = cv2.cvtColor(frame, cv2.COLOR_BGR2GRAY)

    # Apply the Canny edge detection algorithm
    edges = cv2.Canny(gray, 100, 200)

    # Display the results
    cv2.imshow('Canny Edges', edges)

    # Exit the loop if the 'q' key is pressed
    if cv2.waitKey(25) & 0xFF == ord('q'):
        break

# Release the video capture object and close all windows
cap.release()
cv2.destroyAllWindows()
```

Refer to the following figure for plotting a canny edge detection of a video in OpenCV:

Figure 4.20: *Display the canny edge detection of a video*

In this example, we load a video file using OpenCV's `VideoCapture()` function. We then loop through the frames of the video using a while loop and the `read()` function. For each frame, we convert it to grayscale using the `cv2.cvtColor()` function and apply the Canny edge detection algorithm using `cv2.Canny()` function with threshold values of 100 and 200.

We display the results using the `cv2.imshow()` function. Finally, we exit the loop if the 'q' key is pressed, release the video capture object and close all windows using `cap.release()` and `cv2.destroyAllWindows()` functions. Note that the frame rate of the video can be adjusted using the `cv2.waitKey()` function.

The argument passed to this function is the delay in milliseconds between each frame. In this example, we use a delay of 25 milliseconds, which corresponds to a frame rate of 40 frames per second. You can adjust the delay to achieve the desired frame rate for your application.

Additionally, it's a good practice to perform some pre-processing such as noise reduction and image smoothing before applying edge detection algorithms to get better results.

Conclusion

In this chapter, we have discussed the second phase of image processing techniques like matplot library, morphological transformation, smoothing, and blurring in images using OpenCV. Furthermore, we have discussed image gradient, blending, and edge detection using OpenCV and Python.

In the next chapter, we will discuss contour and image thresholding techniques and Hough line theory using OpenCV and Python.

Points to Remember

Install the matplot library in Jupyter notebook using the following code:

```
! pip install matplotlib
```

References

Image processing techniques: https://docs.opencv.org/4.x/d2/d96/tutorial_py_table_of_contents_imgproc.html

CHAPTER 5

Thresholding and Contour Techniques Using OpenCV

Introduction

In this chapter, we will cover image thresholding, contour techniques, and the detection of simple geometric shapes using OpenCV. Additionally, image histograms, Hough Line Transform Theory, and camera calibration are explained in detail using OpenCV and the Python programming languages.

Structure

In this chapter, we will cover the following topics:
- Image thresholding using OpenCV
- Finding and drawing contours using OpenCV
- Detecting simple geometric shapes using OpenCV
- Understanding image histograms using OpenCV
- Hough line transform theory in OpenCV
- Circle detection using OpenCV Hough circle transform
- Camera calibration using OpenCV

Image Thresholding using OpenCV

There are several types of image thresholding techniques available in OpenCV. Here are some of the most commonly used ones:

Simple thresholding

This is the simplest form of thresholding, where each pixel in the image is compared with a fixed threshold value. If the pixel value is greater than the threshold, it is set to a maximum value. Otherwise, it is set to zero. This can be done using the `cv2.threshold()` function. Here is an example code for applying a simple thresholding technique using OpenCV in Python:

```
import cv2

# Load the image in grayscale mode
img = cv2.imread('image.jpg', cv2.IMREAD_GRAYSCALE)

# Apply simple thresholding
threshold_value = 127
max_value = 255
ret, thresh = cv2.threshold(img, threshold_value, max_value, cv2.THRESH_BINARY)

# Display the original and thresholded images
cv2.imshow('Original Image', img)
cv2.imshow('Thresholded Image', thresh)
cv2.waitKey(0)
cv2.destroyAllWindows()
```

Refer to the following figure for displaying simple thresholding using OpenCV:

Figure 5.1: *Display the simple thresholding*

Adaptive thresholding

In this technique, the threshold value is not fixed, but instead is calculated for each pixel based on the mean or Gaussian-weighted mean of its surrounding pixels. This is useful in cases where the lighting conditions are not consistent across the image. This can be done using the `cv2.adaptiveThreshold()` function. Here is an example code for applying the adaptive thresholding technique using OpenCV in Python:

```
import cv2

# Load the image in grayscale mode
img = cv2.imread('image.jpg', cv2.IMREAD_GRAYSCALE)

# Apply adaptive thresholding
max_value = 255
adaptive_method = cv2.ADAPTIVE_THRESH_GAUSSIAN_C
threshold_type = cv2.THRESH_BINARY_INV
block_size = 11
c = 2
thresh = cv2.adaptiveThreshold(img, max_value, adaptive_method, threshold_type, block_size, c)

# Display the original and thresholded images
cv2.imshow('Original Image', img)
cv2.imshow('Adaptive Thresholded Image', thresh)
cv2.waitKey(0)
cv2.destroyAllWindows()
```

In this code, we first load the input image using `cv2.imread()` with the `cv2.IMREAD_GRAYSCALE` flag to read the image in grayscale mode. We then apply adaptive thresholding using the `cv2.adaptiveThreshold()` function, specifying the maximum value as 255, and the adaptive thresholding method as `cv2.ADAPTIVE_THRESH_GAUSSIAN_C`, the thresholding type as `cv2.THRESH_BINARY_INV`, the block size is 11, and the constant value is 2.

Refer to the following figure for displaying adaptive thresholding using OpenCV:

Figure 5.2: Display the adaptive thresholding

The `cv2.ADAPTIVE_THRESH_GAUSSIAN_C` method calculates the threshold value for each pixel as the weighted sum of its surrounding pixels, with the weights being a Gaussian window. The `cv2.THRESH_BINARY_INV` flag is used to create a binary image with the thresholded pixels being black and the non-thresholded pixels being white.

Otsu's thresholding

This is a technique for automatically calculating the threshold value based on the image histogram. It assumes that there are two classes of pixels in the image - foreground and background - and finds the threshold that maximizes the variance between these two classes. This can be done using the `cv2.threshold()` function with the `cv2.THRESH_OTSU` flag. Here is an example code for applying Otsu's thresholding technique using OpenCV in Python:

```
import cv2

# read image in grayscale
img = cv2.imread('image.jpg', 0)

# apply Otsu's thresholding
```

```
ret, th = cv2.threshold(img, 0, 255, cv2.THRESH_BINARY + cv2.THRESH_
OTSU)

# display original and thresholded images
cv2.imshow('Original Image', img)
cv2.imshow('Thresholded Image', th)
cv2.waitKey(0)
cv2.destroyAllWindows()
```

In the preceding code, we first read an image in grayscale using the `cv2.imread()` function. Then, we apply Otsu's thresholding technique using the `cv2.threshold()` function with the `cv2.THRESH_BINARY + cv2.THRESH_OTSU` flag. This flag tells OpenCV to automatically determine the threshold value using Otsu's method.

Refer to the following figure for displaying Otsu's thresholding using OpenCV:

Figure 5.3: *Display the Otsu's thresholding*

Finally, we display the original and thresholded images using the `cv2.imshow()` function and wait for the user to press a key before closing the windows using the `cv2.waitKey()` and `cv2.destroyAllWindows()` functions.

Binary thresholding

This is similar to simple thresholding, but instead of setting the pixels above the threshold to a maximum value, they are set to a specific value (usually 1) to create a binary image. This can be done using the **cv2.threshold()** function with the **cv2.THRESH_BINARY** flag. Here's an example code for binary thresholding using OpenCV in Python:

```python
import cv2

# Load the image
img = cv2.imread('image.jpg', 0)

# Apply binary thresholding
thresh_val, thresh = cv2.threshold(img, 128, 255, cv2.THRESH_BINARY)

# Display the original and thresholded image
cv2.imshow('Original Image', img)
cv2.imshow('Thresholded Image', thresh)
cv2.waitKey(0)
cv2.destroyAllWindows()
```

In the preceding code, we first load an image using the **cv2.imread()** function. We then apply binary thresholding using the **cv2.threshold()** function. This function uses the input image, threshold value, max value, and thresholding type as arguments. In this case, we have used a threshold value of 128 and a max value of 255. The thresholding type is **cv2.THRESH_BINARY** indicates that pixel values greater than the threshold value will be set to the max value and those below the threshold value will be set to 0.

Refer to the following figure for displaying Binary thresholding using OpenCV:

Figure 5.4: Display the Binary thresholding

Finally, we display the original and thresholded images using the `cv2.imshow()` function and wait for a key press before closing the windows using the `cv2.destroyAllWindows()` function.

Inverted thresholding

This is similar to binary thresholding, but instead of setting the pixels above the threshold to a specific value, they are set to zero, and the pixels below the threshold are set to a specific value (usually 1). This can be done using the `cv2.threshold()` function with the `cv2.THRESH_BINARY_INV` flag.

Here's an example code for inverted thresholding using OpenCV in Python:

```
import cv2

# Load the image
img = cv2.imread('image.jpg', 0)

# Apply thresholding
thresh_val, thresh = cv2.threshold(img, 150, 255, cv2.THRESH_BINARY_INV)

# Show the original and thresholded images
cv2.imshow('Original Image', img)
cv2.imshow('Thresholded Image', thresh)

# Wait for key press and then close all windows
cv2.waitKey(0)
cv2.destroyAllWindows()
```

In this code, we load an image using the `cv2.imread()` function and then apply thresholding using the `cv2.threshold()` function. The second argument of the `cv2.threshold()` function is the threshold value, which is set to 150. The third and fourth arguments are the maximum value and the type of thresholding respectively. Here, we are using `cv2.THRESH_BINARY_INV` to apply inverted thresholding.

Refer to the following figure for displaying Inverted thresholding using OpenCV:

Figure 5.5: Display the Inverted thresholding using OpenCV

Finally, we display the original and thresholded images using the `cv2.imshow()` function and wait for a key press using the `cv2.waitKey()` function. When any key is pressed, we close all the windows using the `cv2.destroyAllWindows()` function.

Finding and Drawing Contours with OpenCV

Contours are the boundaries of the shapes in an image that represent the object's boundaries. In image processing, contours are used for object detection, shape analysis, and object recognition.

OpenCV provides a function called `findContours()` to find the contours in an image and `drawContours()` to draw the detected contours on the image. Here is the code snippet to find and draw contours using OpenCV:

```
import cv2
import numpy as np

# Load image
img = cv2.imread('image.jpg')

# Convert image to grayscale
gray = cv2.cvtColor(img, cv2.COLOR_BGR2GRAY)
```

```
# Apply threshold to the image
_, thresh = cv2.threshold(gray, 127, 255, cv2.THRESH_BINARY)

# Find contours in the image
contours, hierarchy = cv2.findContours(thresh, cv2.RETR_TREE, cv2.
CHAIN_APPROX_SIMPLE)

# Draw contours on the image
cv2.drawContours(img, contours, -1, (0, 255, 0), 2)

# Display the image with contours
cv2.imshow('Image with Contours', img)
cv2.waitKey(0)
cv2.destroyAllWindows()
```

In this code, we first load the input image and convert it to grayscale. Then, we apply thresholding to the image to create a binary image where the object is represented in white and the background is represented in black. We use the **cv2.findContours()** function to find all the contours in the binary image. The function returns a list of contours and the hierarchy of the contours. We then use the **cv2.drawContours()** function to draw the detected contours on the original image with a green color and thickness of 2.

Refer to the following figure for displaying draw contours using OpenCV:

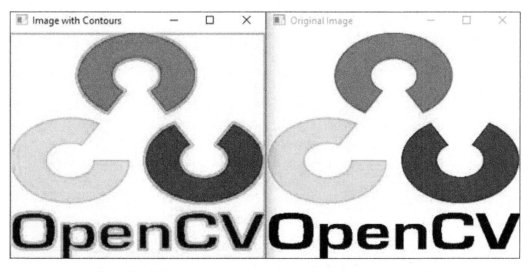

Figure 5.6: Display the draw contours in the image using OpenCV

Finally, we display the image with the detected contours using the **cv2.imshow()** function.

Here is an example code to find and draw contours in a video using OpenCV:

```python
import cv2
import numpy as np

# Load video
cap = cv2.VideoCapture('video.mp4')

while True:
    # Read frame from the video
    ret, frame = cap.read()

    if ret:
        # Convert frame to grayscale
        gray = cv2.cvtColor(frame, cv2.COLOR_BGR2GRAY)

        # Apply threshold to the frame
        _, thresh = cv2.threshold(gray, 127, 255, cv2.THRESH_BINARY)

        # Find contours in the frame
        contours, hierarchy = cv2.findContours(thresh, cv2.RETR_TREE, cv2.CHAIN_APPROX_SIMPLE)

        # Draw contours on the frame
        cv2.drawContours(frame, contours, -1, (0, 255, 0), 2)

        # Display the frame with contours
        cv2.imshow('Frame with Contours', frame)

        # Press 'q' to quit
        if cv2.waitKey(1) & 0xFF == ord('q'):
            break
    else:
        break

# Release video capture and destroy all windows
cap.release()
cv2.destroyAllWindows()
```

In this code, we first load the input video using `cv2.VideoCapture()` function. We then read the frames one by one in a loop using the `cap.read()` function.

For each frame, we convert it to grayscale, apply thresholding to create a binary image, find the contours in the binary image using the `cv2.findContours()` function, and draw the detected contours on the original frame using the `cv2.drawContours()` function.

Refer to the following figure for displaying draw contours using OpenCV:

Figure 5.7: Display the draw contours in the video using OpenCV

Finally, we display the frame with the detected contours using the `cv2.imshow()` function and wait for the user to press q to quit. Once the user presses q, we release the video capture using the `cap.release()` function and destroy all windows using the `cv2.destroyAllWindows()` function.

Detecting Simple Geometric Shapes Using OpenCV

The "Detect Simple Geometric Shapes" OpenCV code is a computer vision program that uses the OpenCV library to detect simple geometric shapes in an image. The code uses various OpenCV functions to perform image processing and shape detection.

The code first reads an image file using the `cv2.imread()` function and converts the image to grayscale using the `cv2.cvtColor()` function. The grayscale image is then thresholded using the `cv2.threshold()` function to create a binary image where the shapes are highlighted in white and the background is black.

Next, the code uses the `cv2.findContours()` function to find the contours (that is, the boundaries) of the shapes in the binary image. The contours are then filtered based on their area using the `cv2.contourArea()` function to remove small or noisy contours.

Once the contours have been filtered, the code loops through each contour and uses the `cv2.approxPolyDP()` function to approximate the shape of the contour as a polygon. The polygon is then classified based on the number of vertices it has, which determines the type of shape it represents. For example, a polygon with three vertices is classified as a triangle, a polygon with four vertices is classified as a rectangle or square, and so on.

Finally, the code draws the detected shapes on the original color image using the `cv2.drawContours()` function and displays the result using the `cv2.imshow()` function. Here is an example of an OpenCV code to detect simple geometric shapes such as circles, triangles, and squares in an image:

```
import cv2
import numpy as np

# Load the image and convert to grayscale
image = cv2.imread("shapes.jpg")
gray = cv2.cvtColor(image, cv2.COLOR_BGR2GRAY)

# Apply Canny edge detection to detect edges in the image
edges = cv2.Canny(gray, 50, 150, apertureSize=3)

# Find contours in the edge image
contours, hierarchy = cv2.findContours(edges, cv2.RETR_EXTERNAL, cv2.CHAIN_APPROX_SIMPLE)

# Loop through each contour and check if it matches a circle, triangle, or square
for cnt in contours:
    # Calculate the perimeter of the contour
    perimeter = cv2.arcLength(cnt, True)
```

```python
    # Approximate the shape of the contour
    approx = cv2.approxPolyDP(cnt, 0.04 * perimeter, True)

    # Calculate the number of vertices of the approximated shape
    num_vertices = len(approx)

    # If the shape has 3 vertices, it's a triangle
    if num_vertices == 3:
        cv2.drawContours(image, [approx], 0, (0, 255, 0), 2)
        cv2.putText(image, "Triangle", tuple(approx[0][0]), cv2.
        FONT_HERSHEY_SIMPLEX, 0.5, (0, 255, 0), 2)
    # If the shape has 4 vertices, it could be a square or a
    rectangle
    elif num_vertices == 4:
        # Calculate the aspect ratio of the shape
        x, y, w, h = cv2.boundingRect(cnt)
        aspect_ratio = float(w) / h

        # If the aspect ratio is close to 1, it's a square
        if 0.95 <= aspect_ratio <= 1.05:
            cv2.drawContours(image, [approx], 0, (0, 0, 255), 2)
            cv2.putText(image, "Square", tuple(approx[0][0]), cv2.
            FONT_HERSHEY_SIMPLEX, 0.5, (0, 0, 255), 2)
        # Otherwise, it's a rectangle
        else:
            cv2.drawContours(image, [approx], 0, (0, 255, 255), 2)
            cv2.putText(image, "Rectangle", tuple(approx[0][0]),
            cv2.FONT_HERSHEY_SIMPLEX, 0.5, (0, 255, 255), 2)
    # If the shape has more than 4 vertices, it's a circle
    else:
        cv2.drawContours(image, [approx], 0, (255, 0, 0), 2)
        cv2.putText(image, "Circle", tuple(approx[0][0]), cv2.FONT_
        HERSHEY_SIMPLEX, 0.5, (255, 0, 0), 2)

# Display the image with the detected shapes
cv2.imshow("Shapes", image)
cv2.waitKey(0)
cv2.destroyAllWindows()
```

Refer to the following figure for detecting simple geometric shapes using OpenCV:

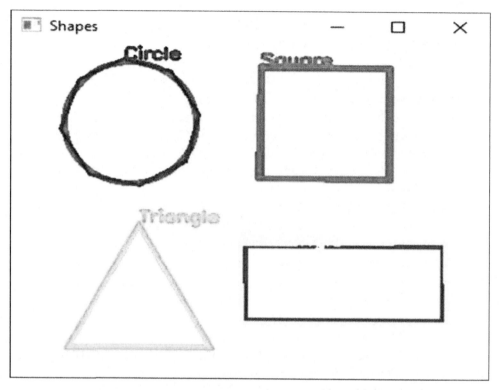

Figure 5.8: *Display simple Geometric shapes using OpenCV*

Overall, this code demonstrates how OpenCV can be used to perform shape detection in images and can be a useful starting point for more advanced computer vision applications.

Understanding Image Histograms Using OpenCV

An image histogram is a graphical representation of the distribution of pixel intensities in an image. Understanding image histograms in OpenCV can be useful for various image processing tasks, such as contrast enhancement, thresholding, and colour correction.

You can use image histograms in OpenCV to perform various image-processing tasks. For example, you can adjust the contrast of an image by stretching the histogram to fill the entire intensity range. You can also threshold an image by selecting a threshold value based on the histogram shape.

Overall, understanding image histograms in OpenCV can be a useful tool for image processing and analysis, as it provides insights into the distribution of pixel intensities in an image.

There are two types of image histograms in OpenCV.

1D Histograms: These histograms represent the distribution of pixel values in a single channel of the image. They are represented as a 1D array or a plot with pixel values on the x-axis and the frequency of their occurrence on the y-axis.

- **2D Histograms:** These histograms represent the joint distribution of pixel values in two channels of the image. They are represented as a 2D array or a heatmap with the pixel values of the two channels on the x- and y-axes and the frequency of their occurrence represented by the colour intensity.

Both 1D and 2D histograms can be used for various image processing tasks, such as contrast stretching, histogram equalization, thresholding, and colour correction.

In OpenCV, you can calculate both 1D and 2D histograms using the `cv2.calcHist()` function. The function takes several parameters, including the input image, the channel(s) of interest, the number of bins, and the range of pixel values. Once the histogram is calculated, you can visualize it using Matplotlib or OpenCV's built-in visualization functions.

Here is an example OpenCV code to understand image histograms:

```
import cv2
import numpy as np
from matplotlib import pyplot as plt

# Load an image in grayscale
image = cv2.imread("lena.jpg", cv2.IMREAD_GRAYSCALE)

# Calculate the histogram of the image
hist = cv2.calcHist([image], [0], None, [256], [0, 256])

# Plot the histogram using matplotlib
plt.plot(hist)
plt.xlim([0, 256])
plt.show()
```

```
# Display the image
cv2.imshow("Image", image)
cv2.waitKey(0)
cv2.destroyAllWindows()
```

In this code, we first load an image in grayscale. We then use the `calcHist()` function of OpenCV to calculate the histogram of the image. The `calcHist()` function takes the following arguments:

images: a list of input images

- **channels:** a list of indices specifying which channels to use for the histogram calculation. In this case, we only have one channel, so we set this to [0].
- **mask:** an optional mask used to compute a histogram for only a certain region of the image. We set this to None to compute the histogram for the entire image.
- **histSize:** the number of bins in the histogram. In this case, we use 256 bins.
- **ranges:** the range of values to be measured in the histogram. In this case, we use the full range of 0-255.

We then plot the histogram using matplotlib. Finally, we display the original image using OpenCV's imshow() function.

Refer to the following figure for displaying the image histogram using OpenCV:

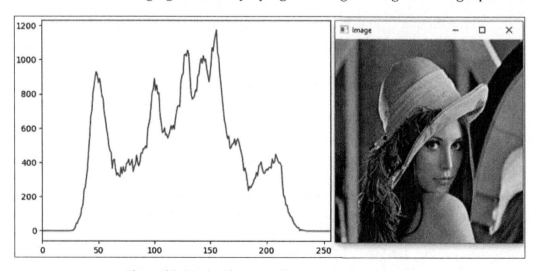

Figure 5.9: *Display the image histogram using OpenCV*

Note that this is just a basic example of how to calculate and plot image histograms using OpenCV and matplotlib. There are many other ways to manipulate and analyze image histograms, such as applying histogram equalization, histogram matching, or thresholding based on histogram values.

Template Matching Using OpenCV

Template matching is a technique used in computer vision to find a template (a small image) within a larger image. OpenCV provides functions that can be used to perform template matching in images.

The basic idea behind template matching is to slide a template image over a larger image and compare the pixel values in the template image with the corresponding pixels in the larger image. This comparison can be performed using different methods, such as the **sum of squared differences (SSD)**, correlation coefficient, or **normalized cross-correlation (NCC)**.

In OpenCV, the `cv2.matchTemplate()` function is used to perform template matching. This function takes the input image and the template image as input parameters and returns a response image that shows the similarity between the template and the input image at each pixel location.

Several types of template-matching methods can be used for finding a template image within a larger image. The choice of method depends on the specific application and the desired performance characteristics. Here are some of the most commonly used template-matching methods in OpenCV:

- **The sum of squared differences (`cv2.TM_SQDIFF`)**: This method calculates the sum of squared differences between the template and the input image at each pixel location. The minimum value in the resulting response image corresponds to the location of the best match.

- **The normalized sum of squared differences** (`cv2.TM_SQDIFF_NORMED`): This method is similar to the sum of squared differences method, but the resulting response image is normalized to have values between 0 and 1. The minimum value in the normalized response image corresponds to the location of the best match.

- **Cross-correlation (`cv2.TM_CCORR`)**: This method calculates the cross-correlation between the template and the input image at each pixel location. The maximum value in the resulting response image corresponds to the location of the best match.

- **Normalized cross-correlation (`cv2.TM_CCORR_NORMED`)**: This method is similar to the cross-correlation method, but the resulting response image is normalized to have values between 0 and 1. The maximum value in the normalized response image corresponds to the location of the best match.

- **Correlation coefficient (cv2.TM_CCOEFF):** This method calculates the correlation coefficient between the template and the input image at each pixel location. The maximum value in the resulting response image corresponds to the location of the best match.
- **Normalized correlation coefficient (cv2.TM_CCOEFF_NORMED):** This method is similar to the correlation coefficient method, but the resulting response image is normalized to have values between -1 and 1. The maximum value in the normalized response image corresponds to the location of the best match.

Each of these methods has its advantages and disadvantages, and the choice of method depends on the specific requirements of the application. Here are two examples of OpenCV codes for template matching

Basic code:

```python
import cv2
import numpy as np

# Load the main image and the template image
main_image = cv2.imread("dog.jpg")
template_image = cv2.imread("dog-head.jpg")

# Get the dimensions of the template image
template_height, template_width, _ = template_image.shape

# Apply template matching using the TM_CCOEFF_NORMED method
result = cv2.matchTemplate(main_image, template_image, cv2.TM_CCOEFF_NORMED)

# Set a threshold to filter out weak matches
threshold = 0.8
locations = np.where(result >= threshold)
locations = list(zip(*locations[::-1]))

# Draw rectangles around the matching regions
for loc in locations:
    top_left = loc
    bottom_right = (top_left[0] + template_width, top_left[1] + template_height)
    cv2.rectangle(main_image, top_left, bottom_right, (0, 0, 255), 1)

# Display the result
```

Thresholding and Contour Techniques Using OpenCV

```
cv2.imshow("Result", main_image)
cv2.waitKey(0)
cv2.destroyAllWindows()
```
Refer to the following figure for displaying Template matching using OpenCV:

Figure 5.10: *Display the Template matching using OpenCV*

Second code:

```
import cv2
import matplotlib.pyplot as plt

img = cv2.imread('dog.jpg',0)
img2 = img.copy()
template = cv2.imread('dog-head.jpg',0)
w, h = template.shape[::-1]

# All the 6 methods for comparison in a list
methods = ['cv2.TM_CCOEFF', 'cv2.TM_CCOEFF_NORMED', 'cv2.TM_CCORR',
           'cv2.TM_CCORR_NORMED', 'cv2.TM_SQDIFF', 'cv2.TM_SQDIFF_
```

NORMED']

```
for meth in methods:
    img = img2.copy()
    method = eval(meth)
    # Apply template Matching
    res = cv2.matchTemplate(img,template,method)
    min_val, max_val, min_loc, max_loc = cv2.minMaxLoc(res)
    # If the method is TM_SQDIFF or TM_SQDIFF_NORMED, take minimum
    if method in [cv2.TM_SQDIFF, cv2.TM_SQDIFF_NORMED]:
        top_left = min_loc
    else:
        top_left = max_loc
    bottom_right = (top_left[0] + w, top_left[1] + h)
    cv2.rectangle(img,top_left, bottom_right, 255, 5)
    plt.subplot(121),plt.imshow(res,cmap = 'gray')
    plt.title('Matching Result'), plt.xticks([]), plt.yticks([])
    plt.subplot(122),plt.imshow(img,cmap = 'gray')
    plt.title('Detected Point'), plt.xticks([]), plt.yticks([])
    plt.suptitle(meth)
    plt.show()
```

Refer to the following figure for displaying Template matching using OpenCV:

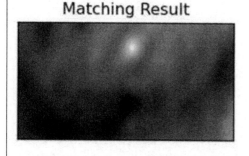

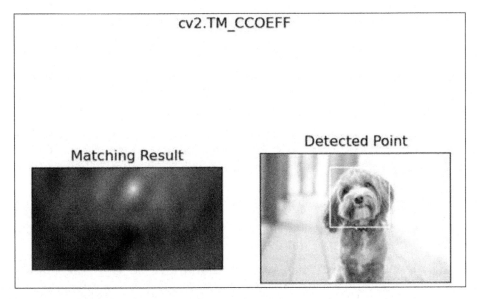

Figure 5.11: *Display the Template matching using OpenCV*

Once the response image is obtained, you can use the `cv2.minMaxLoc()` function to find the location(s) of the highest correlation value(s) in the response image. These locations correspond to the location(s) of the template in the input image.

Template matching can be useful in various computer vision applications, such as object detection, face recognition, and **optical character recognition (OCR)**. However, it has some limitations, such as sensitivity to changes in lighting, scale, and rotation, and it may not work well with complex or cluttered images.

Overall, template matching using OpenCV is a useful tool for finding a specific pattern or object in an image, but it should be used with caution and in conjunction with other computer vision techniques for more robust and accurate results.

Hough Line Transform Theory in OpenCV

The Hough Line Transform is a computer vision technique used to detect straight lines in an image. It is widely used in various applications such as lane detection in autonomous vehicles, edge detection, and shape analysis.

In OpenCV, the Hough Line Transform can be performed using the `cv2.HoughLines()` function. This function takes the input image, the rho and theta accuracies (in pixels and radians, respectively), and a threshold parameter as input. The function returns a list of lines detected in the image, represented as (rho, theta) pairs.

The Hough Line Transform works by converting each pixel in the input image to a set of lines in the parameter space (rho, theta). The rho parameter represents the distance from the origin to the line, and the theta parameter represents the angle between the line and the x-axis. Each pixel in the input image contributes to a set of lines in the parameter space that pass through that pixel.

The Hough Line Transform then looks for the most prominent lines in the parameter space by identifying the pixels that contribute to the largest number of lines. This is done by thresholding the parameter space at a certain value, which determines the minimum number of pixels required for a line to be detected.

Once the lines are detected using the `cv2.HoughLines()` function, they can be drawn on the input image using the `cv2.line()` function. The resulting image shows the detected lines overlaid on the original image.

The Hough Line Transform has several limitations, such as the inability to detect curved lines and the sensitivity to noise and image artifacts. However, it is a powerful tool for detecting straight lines in an image and can be used in various computer vision applications.

Overall, the Hough Line Transform in OpenCV provides a robust and efficient way to detect straight lines in an image, and it can be a useful tool for various computer vision tasks.

In OpenCV, there are two main types of Hough Line Transform methods: the Standard Hough Transform and the Probabilistic Hough Transform. Here is an overview of these two methods:

- **Standard Hough Transform**: The Standard Hough Transform is the original Hough Transform algorithm for detecting lines in an image. It works by creating a Hough Accumulator Array, which is a two-dimensional array that represents the parameter space (rho and theta) for detecting lines in the image.

  For each edge pixel in the image, the Standard Hough Transform computes the set of lines that pass through that pixel and increments the corresponding cells in the Hough Accumulator Array. The lines with the highest vote count in the Hough Accumulator Array are then selected as the detected lines in the image.

- **Probabilistic Hough Transform**: The Probabilistic Hough Transform is a modified version of the Standard Hough Transform that is more efficient and accurate for detecting lines in an image. It works by randomly selecting a subset of edge pixels in the image and computing the lines that pass through those pixels.

The algorithm then iteratively adds more edge pixels to the subset and updates the detected lines accordingly. This process continues until a certain number of lines have been detected or a specified accuracy level has been reached.

The Probabilistic Hough Transform is faster and more accurate than the Standard Hough Transform for detecting lines in an image, especially in complex or cluttered images. However, it requires more parameters to be specified than the Standard Hough Transform, such as the minimum and maximum line length and the maximum gap between segments.

Overall, both the Standard and Probabilistic Hough Transform methods are powerful tools for detecting lines in an image and can be used in various computer vision applications, depending on the specific requirements of the task.

Standard Hough line transform using OpenCV

The Hough Line Transform is a popular computer vision technique used to detect straight lines in an image. In OpenCV, you can use the `cv2.HoughLines()` function to perform the Hough Line Transform.

Here is an example code snippet that demonstrates how to use the `cv2.HoughLines()` function in OpenCV:

```
import cv2
import numpy as np

# Load image and convert to grayscale
img = cv2.imread('chess.png')
img = cv2.resize(img, (640, 480))
gray = cv2.cvtColor(img, cv2.COLOR_BGR2GRAY)

# Apply Canny edge detection
edges = cv2.Canny(gray, 50, 150, apertureSize=3)

# Apply Hough Line Transform
lines = cv2.HoughLines(edges, rho=1, theta=np.pi/180, threshold=100)

# Draw detected lines on original image
for line in lines:
    rho, theta = line[0]
    a = np.cos(theta)
    b = np.sin(theta)
    x0 = a * rho
    y0 = b * rho
```

```
        x1 = int(x0 + 1000 * (-b))
        y1 = int(y0 + 1000 * (a))
        x2 = int(x0 - 1000 * (-b))
        y2 = int(y0 - 1000 * (a))
        cv2.line(img, (x1, y1), (x2, y2), (0, 0, 255), 2)
# Display result
cv2.imshow('result', img)
cv2.waitKey(0)
cv2.destroyAllWindows()
```

In this code, we first load an image and convert it to grayscale. We then apply Canny edge detection to the grayscale image to obtain a binary edge map. We then call the `cv2.HoughLines()` function on the edge map, specifying the rho and theta accuracies and a threshold parameter. The function returns a list of lines detected in the image, represented as (rho, theta) pairs.

image: the input edge image

- **rho:** the distance resolution of the accumulator in pixels
- **theta:** the angular resolution of the accumulator in radians
- **threshold:** the minimum number of votes (intersections in Hough space) required to detect a line The function returns an array of lines in the form (rho, theta)

We then loop through each detected line and use the parameters to draw the line on the original image using the `cv2.line()` function. Finally, we display the result in a window using the `cv2.imshow()` function.

Refer to the following figure for displaying Standard Hough Line Transform using OpenCV:

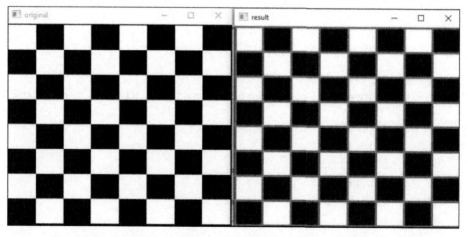

Figure 5.12: *Display the Standard Hough Line Transform using OpenCV*

Overall, the Hough Line Transform in OpenCV is a powerful tool for detecting straight lines in an image, and it can be used in various computer vision applications, such as lane detection, object recognition, and image segmentation.

Probabilistic Hough Transform Using OpenCV

The **Probabilistic Hough Transform (PHT)** is a modified version of the Hough Line Transform that is more efficient and accurate for detecting lines in an image. In OpenCV, you can use the `cv2.HoughLinesP()` function to perform the Probabilistic Hough Transform.

Here is an example code snippet that demonstrates how to use the `cv2.HoughLinesP()` function in OpenCV:

```
import cv2
import numpy as np

# Load image and convert to grayscale
img = cv2.imread('chess.png')
img = cv2.resize(img, (640, 480))
gray = cv2.cvtColor(img, cv2.COLOR_BGR2GRAY)

# Apply Canny edge detection
edges = cv2.Canny(gray, 50, 150, apertureSize=3)

# Apply Probabilistic Hough Line Transform
lines = cv2.HoughLinesP(edges, rho=1, theta=np.pi/180,
threshold=100, minLineLength=50, maxLineGap=10)

# Draw detected lines on original image
for line in lines:
    x1, y1, x2, y2 = line[0]
    cv2.line(img, (x1, y1), (x2, y2), (0, 0, 255), 2)

# Display result
cv2.imshow('result', img)
cv2.waitKey(0)
cv2.destroyAllWindows()
```

In this code, we first load an image and convert it to grayscale. We then apply Canny edge detection to the grayscale image to obtain a binary edge map.

We then call the `cv2.HoughLinesP()` function on the edge map, specifies the rho and theta accuracies, a threshold parameter, and the minimum line length and the maximum gap between line segments. The function returns a list of line segments detected in the image, represented as (x1, y1, x2, y2) tuples.

We then loop through each detected line segment and use the parameters to draw the line on the original image using the `cv2.line()` function. Finally, we display the result in a window using the `cv2.imshow()` function.

Refer to the following figure for displaying Probabilistic Hough Transform using OpenCV:

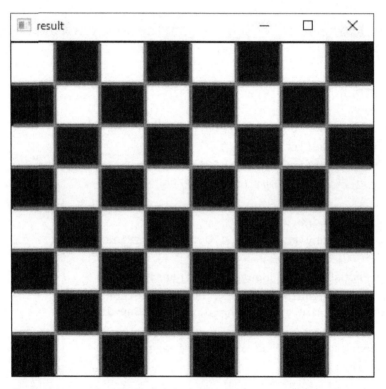

Figure 5.13: *Display the Probabilistic Hough Transform using OpenCV*

The Probabilistic Hough Transform is more efficient than the Standard Hough Transform because it randomly selects a subset of edge pixels in the image and computes the lines that pass through those pixels.

The algorithm then iteratively adds more edge pixels to the subset and updates the detected lines accordingly. This process continues until a certain number of lines have been detected or a specified accuracy level has been reached.

Overall, the Probabilistic Hough Transform in OpenCV is a powerful tool for detecting lines in an image, especially in complex or cluttered images. It can be used in various computer vision applications, such as object recognition, lane detection, and image segmentation.

Circle Detection Using OpenCV Hough Circle Transform

Circle detection is a common computer vision task that involves detecting circular shapes in an image. OpenCV provides a function called Hough Circle Transform that can be cused to detect circles in an image.

The Hough Circle Transform works by converting the image to grayscale, applying edge detection, and then searching for circular shapes on the edge map. The algorithm searches for circles of a specific radius range, and for each possible circle, it computes the center point and radius using the Hough Transform.

Here is an example code snippet that demonstrates how to perform circle detection using the Hough Circle Transform in OpenCV:

```
import cv2
import numpy as np

# Load image and convert to grayscale
img = cv2.imread('smarties.png')
output=img.copy()

# apply median blur
gray = cv2.cvtColor(img, cv2.COLOR_BGR2GRAY)
gray = cv2.medianBlur(gray, 5)
# Apply Hough Circle Transform
circles = cv2.HoughCircles(gray, cv2.HOUGH_GRADIENT, 1, 20,
                            param1=100, param2=30,
                            minRadius=1, maxRadius=30)

detected_circles = np.uint16(np.around(circles))
# Draw detected circles on original image
for (x, y, r) in detected_circles[0, :]:
    cv2.circle(output, (x,y) , r, (0,255,0), 3)
    cv2.circle(output, (x,y) , 2, (0,255,255), 3)
```

```
# Display result
cv2.imshow('output', output)
cv2.waitKey(0)
cv2.destroyAllWindows()
```

In this code, we first load an image and convert it to grayscale. We then apply Gaussian blur to the grayscale image to reduce noise and apply edge detection using the Canny algorithm.

We then call the `cv2.HoughCircles()` function on the edge map, specifying the Hough Gradient method, a distance parameter, a minimum distance between detected circles, and several threshold and radius parameters.

Refer to the following figure for displaying circle detection using OpenCV:

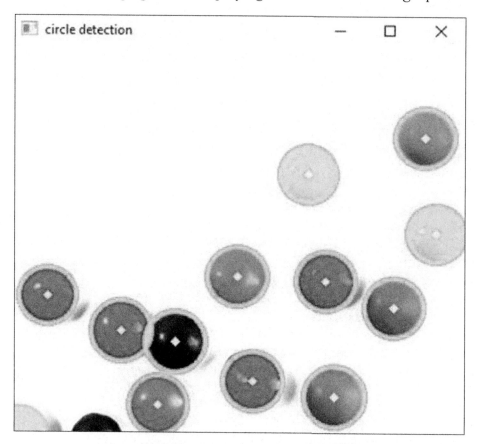

Figure 5.14: *Display the Circle detection using OpenCV*

The function returns a list of detected circles, represented as (x, y, r) tuples. We then loop through each detected circle and use the parameters to draw the circle on the original image using the `cv2.circle()` function. Finally, we display the result in a window using the `cv2.imshow()` function.

Overall, the Hough Circle Transform in OpenCV is a powerful tool for detecting circular shapes in an image, but it may require tuning the threshold parameters to obtain accurate and reliable results in a real-world setting.

Camera Calibration Using OpenCV

Camera calibration is the process of determining the intrinsic and extrinsic parameters of a camera. The intrinsic parameters include the focal length, image sensor size, and lens distortion, while the extrinsic parameters describe the position and orientation of the camera in 3D space. This process is essential for accurate measurements in computer vision applications such as object tracking, 3D reconstruction, and augmented reality.

In OpenCV, camera calibration is performed using a set of images of a known pattern, typically a chessboard or a grid of dots. The calibration process involves detecting the corners of the pattern in the images and using these correspondences to estimate the camera parameters. The calibration process involves finding the mapping between the 3D coordinates of the calibration pattern and their corresponding 2D image coordinates.

The calibration algorithm first estimates the intrinsic parameters of the camera, which can be used to correct lens distortion and determine the field of view. The extrinsic parameters are then estimated by solving a set of equations that relate the 3D coordinates of the pattern to their corresponding 2D image coordinates.

Once the camera parameters have been estimated, they can be used to undistorted images and perform other geometric transformations such as perspective correction and 3D reconstruction. The extrinsic parameters include the position and orientation of the camera relative to the calibration pattern. OpenCV uses several calibration methods, such as Zhang's method and Tsai's method, to estimate these parameters.

OpenCV provides a module called calib3d that includes functions for camera calibration. The basic steps for camera calibration using OpenCV are:

- Capture multiple images of a calibration pattern (for example, checkerboard) from different angles and positions
- Find the corners of the calibration pattern in each image using the **findChessboardCorners()** function
- Refine the corner positions using the **cornerSubPix()** function
- Compute the camera calibration parameters using the **calibrateCamera()** function

- Evaluate the calibration results using the `getOptimalNewCameraMatrix()` function

The output of camera calibration is the camera matrix, which is a 3x3 matrix that represents the intrinsic parameters of the camera. The camera matrix includes the focal length, principal point, and skew coefficient, as well as distortion coefficients that correct for lens distortion.

Here is an example code snippet that demonstrates how to perform camera calibration using OpenCV:

Datasets:

Figure 5.15: *Display the Datasets*

The code is as follows:

```
# import required modules
import numpy as np
import cv2
import glob

# Define the dimensions of the checkerboard pattern
CHECKERBOARD = (6, 9)

# Define the object points (3D coordinates of the checkerboard
corners)
objp = np.zeros((CHECKERBOARD[0] * CHECKERBOARD[1], 3), np.float32)
objp[:, :2] = np.mgrid[0:CHECKERBOARD[0],
0:CHECKERBOARD[1]].T.reshape(-1, 2)

# Create arrays to store the object points and image points from all
images
```

```python
objpoints = []
imgpoints = []

# Get a list of all calibration images
images = glob.glob('checkerboard*.jpg')

# Loop through each image and detect the checkerboard corners
for fname in images:
    img = cv2.imread(fname)
    gray = cv2.cvtColor(img, cv2.COLOR_BGR2GRAY)
    ret, corners = cv2.findChessboardCorners(gray, CHECKERBOARD, None)

    # If corners are detected, add object points and image points to
    their respective lists
    if ret == True:
        objpoints.append(objp)
        imgpoints.append(corners)

        # Draw and display the corners
        img = cv2.drawChessboardCorners(img, CHECKERBOARD, corners, ret)
        cv2.imshow('img', img)
        cv2.waitKey(0)

cv2.destroyAllWindows()
# Calibrate the camera using the object points and image points
ret, mtx, dist, rvecs, tvecs = cv2.calibrateCamera(objpoints, imgpoints, gray.shape[::-1], None, None)

# Displaying required output
print("Camera matrix:")
print(mtx)

print("\n Distortion coefficient:")
print(dist)

print("\n Rotation Vectors:")
print(rvecs)

print("\n Translation Vectors:")
print(tvecs)
```

Refer to the following figure for displaying camera calibration using OpenCV:

Figure 5.16: Display the Camera calibration using OpenCV

```
Camera matrix:
[[32.2300153    0.           85.54750147]
 [ 0.          32.67873363  94.78169015]
 [ 0.           0.           1.         ]]

Distortion coefficient:
[[-2.57178768e-04 -6.99011689e-05 -3.18355381e-03  1.08244458e-03
   6.21509925e-06]]

Rotation Vectors:
(array([[-0.076667  ],
       [ 0.046132  ],
       [ 1.50724635]]), array([[-0.12776343],
       [-0.01755455],
       [ 3.07728866]]), array([[-0.02683613],
       [ 0.07007699],
       [-0.0741852 ]]))

Translation Vectors:
(array([[ 4.54475152],
       [-3.73046037],
       [ 2.18631095]]), array([[2.23031191],
       [4.03142583],
       [2.20441646]]), array([[-3.25423753],
       [-3.41660746],
       [ 2.21579478]]))
```

Figure 5.17: Display the Camera calibration matrix values

Overall, camera calibration is an important step in many computer vision applications, such as object detection and tracking, augmented reality, and 3D scanning. This projection allows for the measurement of distances, angles, and other properties of objects in the scene.

Conclusion

In this chapter, we have discussed the detailed techniques of image thresholding and drawing contours using OpenCV. Furthermore, we discussed the image histogram, Hough Line Transform Theory, circle detection, and camera calibration are explained using OpenCV and Python programming language.

In the next chapter, we will discuss detecting corners and road lane detection techniques using OpenCV and Python.

Points to Remember

Install the matplot library in Jupyter Notebook using the following code:

```
! pip install matplotlib
```

References

Image thresholding techniques:

https://docs.opencv.org/4.x/d2/d96/tutorial_py_table_of_contents_imgproc.html

CHAPTER 6

Detect Corners and Road Lane Using OpenCV

Introduction

This chapter will cover road lane detection, corner detection, and their types using OpenCV. Additionally, we will cover feature matching techniques, and background subtraction, and their types will be explained using OpenCV and Python programming language.

Structure

In this chapter, we will cover the following topics:

- Road lane line detection with OpenCV
- Detecting corners in OpenCV
- Types of detecting corners in OpenCV
- Feature matching with FLANN
- Background subtraction methods in OpenCV
- Types of background subtraction methods in OpenCV

Road Lane Line Detection Using OpenCV

Road lane line detection is a common computer vision task that involves detecting the lane lines on a road from an image or video stream. OpenCV provides several functions that can be used for road lane line detection, such as edge detection, line detection, and image processing techniques.

Here is a general overview of the road lane line detection pipeline using OpenCV: Preprocessing: The input image or video frame is preprocessed to enhance the lane lines and remove noise.

This can involve techniques such as color space conversion, contrast adjustment, and noise reduction:

Edge Detection: The preprocessed image is then subjected to an edge detection algorithm, such as Canny edge detection, to detect the edges of the road and lane lines.

- **Region of Interest Selection:** A region of interest (ROI) is selected in the image or video frame, which contains the lane lines. The ROI is typically a trapezoidal shape that covers the area of the road directly in front of the vehicle.

- **Hough Line Transform:** The Hough Line Transform is then applied to the ROI to detect the straight lines that represent the lane lines. This can be done using either the Standard Hough Transform or the Probabilistic Hough Transform, as discussed earlier.

- **Line Filtering and Averaging:** The detected lines are then filtered and averaged to obtain a single line that represents the lane line. This can involve techniques such as outlier removal, line smoothing, and line interpolation.

- **Lane Tracking:** Once the lane lines have been detected in the first frame, subsequent frames can use the detected lines to track the position and orientation of the lane lines in real-time. This can involve techniques such as Kalman filtering and optical flow.

Overall, road lane line detection using OpenCV is a complex task that involves multiple image processing techniques and computer vision algorithms. However, with the right combination of techniques, it is possible to accurately detect and track lane lines in real-time, which is a crucial component of many autonomous driving and driver assistance systems.

Road Lane Detection using OpenCV is a computer vision project that involves detecting and tracking the lane markings on the road using the OpenCV library in Python. This project can be useful in autonomous driving, driver assistance systems, and other related applications.

Here is an example code snippet that demonstrates how to perform road lane line detection using OpenCV:

```
import cv2
import numpy as np
```

```python
# Load image and convert to grayscale
img = cv2.imread('road.png')
img = cv2.resize(img, (640, 480))
gray = cv2.cvtColor(img, cv2.COLOR_BGR2GRAY)

# Apply Canny edge detection
edges = cv2.Canny(gray, 50, 150, apertureSize=3)

# Define region of interest
roi_vertices = np.array([[(0, img.shape[0]), (img.shape[1] // 2,
img.shape[0] // 2), (img.shape[1], img.shape[0])]], dtype=np.int32)
mask = np.zeros_like(edges)
cv2.fillPoly(mask, roi_vertices, 255)
masked_edges = cv2.bitwise_and(edges, mask)

# Apply Hough Line Transform
lines = cv2.HoughLinesP(masked_edges, rho=1, theta=np.pi/180,
threshold=50, minLineLength=100, maxLineGap=50)

# Draw detected lines on original image
for line in lines:
    x1, y1, x2, y2 = line[0]
    cv2.line(img, (x1, y1), (x2, y2), (0, 0, 255), 2)

# Display result
cv2.imshow('result', img)
cv2.waitKey(0)
cv2.destroyAllWindows()
```

In this code, we first load an image and convert it to grayscale. We then apply Canny edge detection to the grayscale image to obtain a binary edge map. We then define a ROI that covers the area of the road directly in front of the vehicle. The ROI is defined using a trapezoidal shape and is used to mask the edge map to ignore edges outside the ROI.

Refer to the following figure for displaying road lane line detection using OpenCV:

Figure 6.1: Road lane line detection using OpenCV

We then call the `cv2.HoughLinesP()` function on the masked edge map, specifying the rho and theta accuracies, a threshold parameter, and the minimum line length and the maximum gap between line segments. The function returns a list of line segments detected in the ROI, represented as (x1, y1, x2, y2) tuples.

We then loop through each detected line segment and use the parameters to draw the line on the original image using the `cv2.line()` function. Finally, we display the result in a window using the `cv2.imshow()` function.

Here is an example code snippet that demonstrates how to perform road lane line detection on a video stream using OpenCV:

Download the video file by using the following link and running the code.

https://www.kaggle.com/datasets/dpamgautam/video-file-for-lane-detection-project

```python
import cv2
import numpy as np

# Define region of interest
def roi_mask(img, vertices):
    mask = np.zeros_like(img)
    cv2.fillPoly(mask, vertices, 255)
    masked_img = cv2.bitwise_and(img, mask)
    return masked_img

# Apply Hough Line Transform
def hough_lines(img, rho, theta, threshold, min_line_len, max_line_gap):
    lines = cv2.HoughLinesP(img, rho, theta, threshold,
        np.array([]), minLineLength=min_line_len, maxLineGap=max_line_gap)
    return lines

# Draw detected lines on original image
def draw_lines(img, lines, color=[255, 0, 0], thickness=5):
    for line in lines:
        for x1, y1, x2, y2 in line:
            cv2.line(img, (x1, y1), (x2, y2), color, thickness)

# Road Lane Line Detection on video stream
cap = cv2.VideoCapture('road.mp4')
while True:
    ret, frame = cap.read()
    if ret:
        try:
            # Convert to grayscale
            gray = cv2.cvtColor(frame, cv2.COLOR_BGR2GRAY)

            # Apply Gaussian blur
            blur = cv2.GaussianBlur(gray, (5, 5), 0)

            # Apply Canny edge detection
            edges = cv2.Canny(blur, 50, 150)


            # Define region of interest
            roi_vertices = np.array([[(0, frame.shape[0]), (frame.
            shape[1] // 2, frame.shape[0] // 2 + 50), (frame.
```

```
                shape[1], frame.shape[0])]], dtype=np.int32)
                roi = roi_mask(edges, roi_vertices)

                # Apply Hough Line Transform
                lines = hough_lines(roi, rho=2, theta=np.pi/180,
                 threshold=50, min_line_len=100, max_line_gap=50)

                # Draw detected lines on original image
                line_img = np.zeros((frame.shape[0], frame.shape[1], 3),
                dtype=np.uint8)
                draw_lines(line_img, lines)

                # Overlay detected lane lines on original image
                result = cv2.addWeighted(frame, 0.8, line_img, 1, 0)

                # Display result
                cv2.imshow('result', result)

                # Exit on 'q' key press
                if cv2.waitKey(25) & 0xFF == ord('q'):
                    break

            except: pass
        else:
            break

    # Release resources
    cap.release()
    cv2.destroyAllWindows()
```

In this code, we first define three helper functions: `roi_mask()` to define the region of interest, `hough_lines()` to apply the Hough Line Transform, and `draw_lines()` to draw the detected lines on the original image. We then open the input video stream and loop through each frame. For each frame, we perform the following processing steps:

Convert the frame to grayscale.

1. Apply Gaussian blur to the grayscale image to reduce noise.
2. Apply Canny edge detection to obtain a binary edge map.
3. Define the region of interest using a trapezoidal shape and mask the edge map to ignore edges outside the ROI.
4. Apply the Hough Line Transform to detect the lane lines in the ROI.
5. Draw the detected lines on a blank image.

6. Overlay the detected lane lines on the original image using the `cv2.addWeighted()` function. Display the result in a window.

The processing steps are repeated for each frame of the input video stream until the end of the video or until the *q* key is pressed to exit the program.

Refer to the following figure for displaying road lane line detection using OpenCV:

Figure 6.2: Road lane line detection in video using OpenCV

Overall, this code provides a basic implementation of road lane line detection using OpenCV, but further processing and filtering may be needed to obtain accurate and reliable results in a real-world setting.

Detecting Corners in OpenCV

Corner detection is a fundamental computer vision task that involves detecting points in an image where there is a change in intensity or color. Corners are important features in an image because they can be used for tasks such as image registration, object recognition, and tracking.

OpenCV provides several methods for corner detection, each with its own strengths and weaknesses.

Here are some of the commonly used methods for corner detection in OpenCV:

- **Harris Corner Detection:** Harris Corner Detection is a popular method for detecting corners in an image. It works by computing the corner response function for each pixel in the image using the second-order derivatives of the image intensity. The algorithm then thresholds the corner response map to obtain binary corner points.

- **Shi-Tomasi Corner Detection:** Shi-Tomasi Corner Detection is a modification of the Harris Corner Detection method that is more robust to noise and produces a more uniform distribution of detected corners. It works by computing the minimum eigenvalue of a 2×2 gradient matrix at each pixel in the image. The algorithm then selects the most prominent corners based on a threshold and a maximum number of corners.

- **FAST Corner Detection:** FAST (Features from Accelerated Segment Test) Corner Detection is a fast and efficient method for detecting corners in an image. It works by testing a circular patch of pixels around each pixel in the image and determining whether the patch contains a corner. The algorithm then selects the most prominent corners based on a threshold and a maximum number of corners.

- **Blob Detection:** Blob Detection is a method for detecting circular or elliptical regions of uniform intensity in an image. It works by applying a Laplacian of Gaussian filter to the image and then thresholding the result to obtain binary blobs. The algorithm can be tuned to detect blobs of different sizes and shapes.

- **Scale-Invariant Feature Transform (SIFT):** SIFT is a method for detecting and describing local features in an image. It works by identifying key points in an image that are invariant to scale, rotation, and affine distortion. The algorithm then computes a descriptor for each key point based on the image gradient orientation and magnitude.

- **Speeded-Up Robust Feature (SURF):** SURF is a method for detecting and describing local features in an image that is similar to SIFT but is more efficient and robust to noise. It works by identifying key points based on the Hessian matrix of the image and then computing a descriptor based on the image gradient orientation and magnitude.

Each of these methods has its own advantages and disadvantages, and the choice of method will depend on the specific application and image characteristics.

Types of Detect Corners in OpenCV

Harris Corner Detector

Harris Corner Detector is an algorithm used to detect corners in an image. It was introduced by Chris Harris and Mike Stephens in 1988, and it is widely used in computer vision and image processing applications. In OpenCV, you can use the `cv2.cornerHarris()` function to apply the Harris Corner Detector to an image.

Here's an example code that demonstrates how to detect corners with the Harris Corner Detector in OpenCV:

```
import cv2
import numpy as np

# Load image
img = cv2.imread('blox.jpg')

# Convert image to grayscale
gray = cv2.cvtColor(img, cv2.COLOR_BGR2GRAY)

# Apply Harris Corner Detector
dst = cv2.cornerHarris(gray, 2, 3, 0.04)

# Threshold for an optimal value
thresh = 0.01 * dst.max()

# Create a black image to display the corners
corner_img = np.zeros_like(img)

# Draw detected corners on the black image
for row_index in range(dst.shape[0]):
    for column_index in range(dst.shape[1]):
        if dst[row_index ,column_index] > thresh:
            cv2.circle(img, (column_index,row_index), 3, (0,255,0), 1)
```

```
# Display the original image and the detected corners
cv2.imshow('Image', img)
# cv2.imshow('Corners', corner_img)
cv2.waitKey(0)
cv2.destroyAllWindows()
```

In this example, we first load an image and convert it to grayscale. Then we apply the `cv2.cornerHarris()` function to the grayscale image, with parameters `blockSize=2`, `ksize=3`, and `k=0.04`. These parameters determine the size of the neighborhood considered for each pixel, the size of the Sobel operator used to calculate the gradients, and the sensitivity of the corner detector, respectively. The result of the Harris Corner Detector is a grayscale image with high values at the corners and low values elsewhere.

Refer to the following figure for displaying Harris Corner Detector using OpenCV:

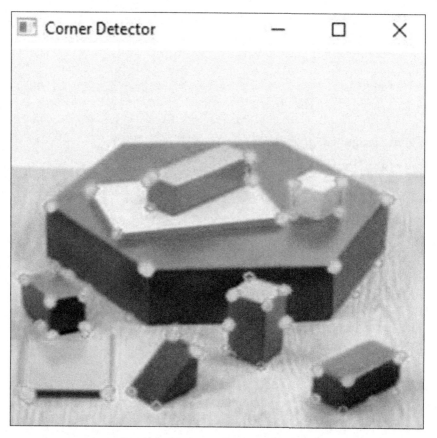

Figure 6.3: *Harris Corner Detector using OpenCV*

We then set a threshold value (thresh) based on the maximum value of the Harris Corner Detector output and create a black image (`corner_img`) to display the detected corners. We iterate through each pixel in the Harris Corner Detector output, and if the value is greater than the threshold, we draw a green circle at that position on the black image.

Finally, we display the original image and the detected corners using the `cv2.imshow()` function and wait for a key press to close the windows.

Shi Tomasi Corner Detector

Shi-Tomasi Corner Detector is an algorithm used to detect corners in an image. It is similar to the Harris Corner Detector, but it uses a different measure of corner quality that is more accurate and efficient. In OpenCV, you can use the `cv2.goodFeaturesToTrack()` function to apply the Shi-Tomasi Corner Detector to an image.

Here's an example code that demonstrates how to detect corners with the Shi-Tomasi Corner Detector in OpenCV:

```
import cv2
import numpy as np

# Load image
img = cv2.imread('blox.jpg')

# Convert image to grayscale
gray = cv2.cvtColor(img, cv2.COLOR_BGR2GRAY)

# Set parameters for Shi-Tomasi Corner Detector
max_corners = 100
quality_level = 0.3
min_distance = 7
block_size = 7

# Apply Shi-Tomasi Corner Detector
corners = cv2.goodFeaturesToTrack(gray, max_corners, quality_level, min_distance, blockSize=block_size)

# Draw detected corners on the original image
corners = np.int0(corners)
for i in corners:
    x, y = i.ravel()
    cv2.circle(img, (x, y), 5, (0, 255, 0), -1)
```

```
# Display the original image with detected corners
cv2.imshow('Image', img)
cv2.waitKey(0)
cv2.destroyAllWindows()
```

In this example, we first load an image and convert it to grayscale. Then we set the parameters for the Shi-Tomasi Corner Detector, including the maximum number of corners to be detected (`max_corners`), the minimum quality level of corners (`quality_level`), the minimum distance between corners (`min_distance`), and the size of the window used to calculate the minimum eigenvalue (`block_size`).

Refer to the following figure for displaying Shi-Tomasi Corner Detector using OpenCV:

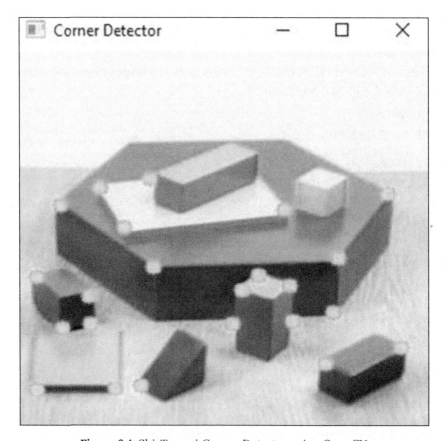

Figure 6.4: *Shi-Tomasi Corner Detector using OpenCV*

We then apply the `cv2.goodFeaturesToTrack()` function to the grayscale image, with the specified parameters, to obtain the detected corners. The result is an array of corner points, where each point is a 2D coordinate.

Finally, we iterate through each corner point and draw a green circle at that position on the original image using the `cv2.circle()` function. We then display the original image with the detected corners using the `cv2.imshow()` function and wait for a key press to close the window.

FAST corner detection

Features from Accelerated Segment Test (FAST) is a corner detection algorithm that is both accurate and fast. In OpenCV, you can use the `cv2.FastFeatureDetector()` function to apply the FAST corner detection algorithm to an image.

Here's an example code that demonstrates how to detect corners with the FAST algorithm in OpenCV:

```
import cv2

# Load image
img = cv2.imread('blox.jpg')

# Convert image to grayscale
gray = cv2.cvtColor(img, cv2.COLOR_BGR2GRAY)

# Set parameters for FAST corner detection
fast = cv2.FastFeatureDetector_create(threshold=25)

# Detect corners using FAST algorithm
kp = fast.detect(gray, None)

# Draw detected corners on the original image
img2 = cv2.drawKeypoints(img, kp, None, color=(0, 255, 0))

# Display the original image with detected corners
cv2.imshow('Image', img2)
cv2.waitKey(0)
cv2.destroyAllWindows()
```

In this example, we first load an image and convert it to grayscale. Then, we set the threshold value for FAST corner detection using the `cv2.FastFeatureDetector_create()` function.

We then apply the `cv2.FastFeatureDetector()` function to the grayscale image, with the specified threshold value, to obtain the detected corners. The result is an array of `cv2.KeyPoint` objects, where each object represents a corner point and contains its 2D coordinate and other information such as the response and size.

Refer to the following figure for displaying FAST Corner Detector using OpenCV:

Figure 6.5: *FAST corner detector using OpenCV*

Finally, we use the `cv2.drawKeypoints()` function to draw green circles at the detected corner points on the original image and display the image using the `cv2.imshow()` function.

Blob Detection

Blob detection is a technique used for detecting regions in an image that have similar properties, such as color or texture. In OpenCV, you can use the `cv2.SimpleBlobDetector()` function to apply the blob detection algorithm to an image.

Here's an example code that demonstrates how to detect corners with the blob detection algorithm in OpenCV:

```python
import cv2

# Load image
img = cv2.imread('blox.jpg')

# Convert image to grayscale
gray = cv2.cvtColor(img, cv2.COLOR_BGR2GRAY)

# Set parameters for blob detection
params = cv2.SimpleBlobDetector_Params()

# Filter by color and size
params.filterByColor = True
params.blobColor = 255
params.filterByArea = True
params.minArea = 100

# Create a blob detector object
detector = cv2.SimpleBlobDetector_create(params)

# Detect blobs using the blob detector
keypoints = detector.detect(gray)

# Draw detected blobs on the original image
img_with_keypoints = cv2.drawKeypoints(img, keypoints, np.array([]), (0,0,255), cv2.DRAW_MATCHES_FLAGS_DRAW_RICH_KEYPOINTS)

# Display the original image with detected blobs
cv2.imshow('Image', img_with_keypoints)
cv2.waitKey(0)
cv2.destroyAllWindows()
```

In this example, we first load an image and convert it to grayscale. Then, we set the parameters for blob detection using **cv2.SimpleBlobDetector_Params()** function. In this case, we filter blobs by color and size.

Refer to the following figure for displaying Blob detection using OpenCV:

Figure 6.6: *Blob detection using OpenCV*

We then create a blob detector object using the `cv2.SimpleBlobDetector_create()` function with the specified parameters. Next, we apply the blob detection algorithm to the grayscale image using the `detector.detect()` function. The result is an array of `cv2.KeyPoint` objects, where each object represents a blob and contains its 2D coordinate and other information such as the size and response.

Finally, we use the `cv2.drawKeypoints()` function to draw red circles at the detected blob points on the original image and display the image using the `cv2.imshow()` function.

Scale-invariant feature transform

Scale-invariant feature transform (SIFT) is a widely used algorithm for detecting key points in an image. In OpenCV, you can use the `cv2.xfeatures2d.SIFT_create()` function to apply the SIFT algorithm to an image.

Here's an example code that demonstrates how to detect corners with the SIFT algorithm in OpenCV:

```
import cv2

# Load image
img = cv2.imread('blox.jpg')

# Convert image to grayscale
gray = cv2.cvtColor(img, cv2.COLOR_BGR2GRAY)

# Create a SIFT detector object
sift = cv2.SIFT_create()

# Detect keypoints using the SIFT detector
keypoints = sift.detect(gray, None)

# Draw detected keypoints on the original image
img_with_keypoints = cv2.drawKeypoints(img, keypoints, None)

#Display the original image with detected keypoints
cv2.imshow('Image', img_with_keypoints)
cv2.waitKey(0)
cv2.destroyAllWindows()
```

In this example, we first load an image and convert it to grayscale. Then, we create a SIFT detector object using the `cv2.SIFT_create()` function. We then apply the SIFT algorithm to the grayscale image using the `sift.detect()` function.

Refer to the following figure for displaying SIFT detection using OpenCV:

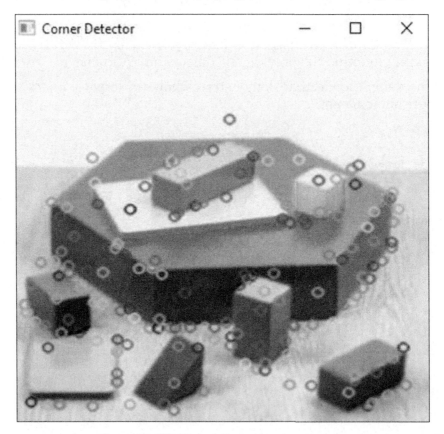

Figure 6.7: *SIFT Corner Detector using OpenCV*

The result is an array of `cv2.KeyPoint` objects, where each object represents a key point and contains its 2D coordinate and other information such as the scale and orientation.

Finally, we use the `cv2.drawKeypoints()` function to draw circles at the detected keypoint points on the original image and display the image using the `cv2.imshow()` function.

Feature Matching with FLANN

Feature matching is a common computer vision technique to identify corresponding features in two or more images. The goal is to find a set of feature points in one image that corresponds to a set of feature points in another image. This can be useful for a variety of applications, such as image stitching, object recognition, and 3D reconstruction.

FLANN (Fast Library for Approximate Nearest Neighbors) is an algorithm for feature matching in OpenCV. It is a fast and efficient algorithm for finding approximate nearest neighbors in high-dimensional spaces. FLANN works by building a hierarchical index structure that allows for a fast and efficient search of the feature space.

To use FLANN for feature matching in OpenCV, you typically follow these steps:

1. Detects feature points in each image using a feature detection algorithm such as SIFT, SURF, or ORB.
2. Compute descriptors for each feature point using a descriptor extraction algorithm such as SIFT, SURF, or ORB.
3. Create a FLANN index for the descriptor vectors in one image using the `flann.Index()` function in OpenCV. This index is used to find the nearest neighbors of each descriptor vector in the other image.
4. For each descriptor vector in the other image, use the FLANN index to find its nearest neighbor(s) in the first image.
5. Apply a matching threshold to the nearest neighbor distances to filter out false matches.
6. Use the matched feature points to perform further analysis or processing, such as image-stitching or object recognition.

FLANN can be a powerful tool for feature matching in OpenCV, as it provides fast and efficient approximate nearest neighbor search. However, it is important to choose the appropriate feature detection and descriptor extraction algorithms for your specific application and to fine-tune the matching parameters to achieve the best results:

```python
import cv2
import numpy as np

# Load images
img1 = cv2.imread('dog.jpg', cv2.IMREAD_GRAYSCALE)
img2 = cv2.imread('dog-head.jpg', cv2.IMREAD_GRAYSCALE)

# Initiate SIFT detector
sift = cv2.SIFT_create()

# Find keypoints and descriptors for both images
kp1, des1 = sift.detectAndCompute(img1, None)
kp2, des2 = sift.detectAndCompute(img2, None)
```

```python
# FLANN parameters
FLANN_INDEX_KDTREE = 1
index_params = dict(algorithm=FLANN_INDEX_KDTREE, trees=5)
search_params = dict(checks=50)

# Create FLANN matcher
flann = cv2.FlannBasedMatcher(index_params, search_params)

# Match descriptors
matches = flann.knnMatch(des1, des2, k=2)

# Ratio test as per Lowe's paper
good_matches = []
for m, n in matches:

"""

m: This variable represents the first best match between a feature
descriptor in des1 and the feature descriptors in des2.
n: This variable represents the second-best match between a feature
descriptor in des1 and the feature descriptors in des2

"""

    if m.distance < 0.7 * n.distance:
        good_matches.append(m)

# Draw matches
img3 = cv2.drawMatches(img1, kp1, img2, kp2, good_matches, None,
flags=cv2.DrawMatchesFlags_NOT_DRAW_SINGLE_POINTS)

# Display image
cv2.imshow('Matches', img3)
cv2.waitKey(0)
cv2.destroyAllWindows()
```

Refer to the following figure for displaying Feature matching using OpenCV:

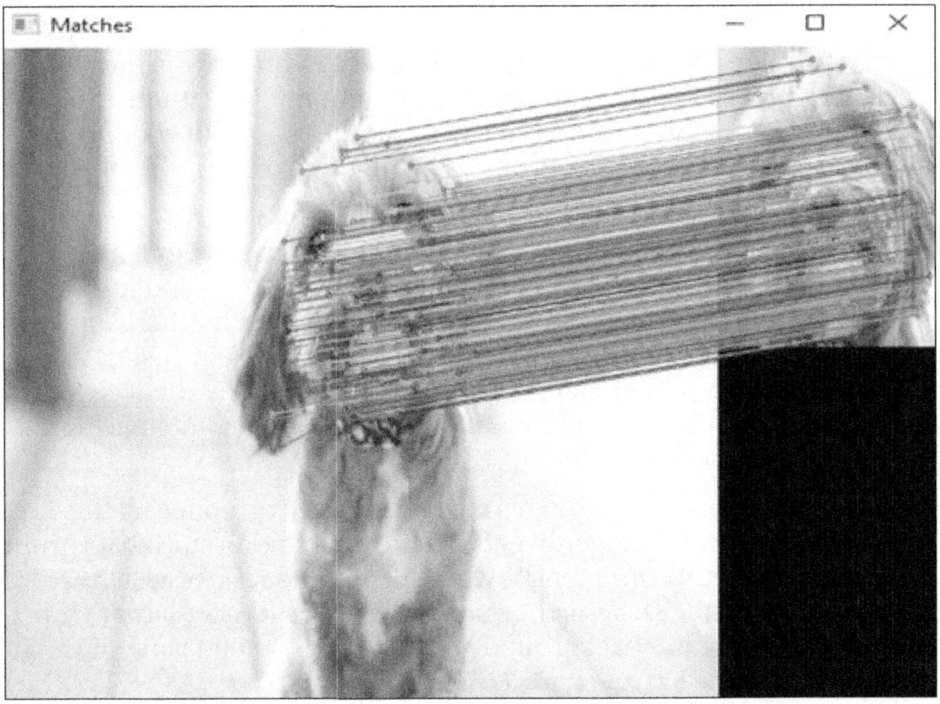

Figure 6.8: *Feature Matching with FLANN using OpenCV*

In this code, we load two images and use the SIFT feature detector to extract key points and descriptors for both images. We then create a FLANN-based matcher and use it to match the descriptors between the two images. We apply the ratio test to select good matches, and finally, draw the matches on a new image and display it.

Background Subtraction Methods in OpenCV

Background subtraction is a commonly used technique in computer vision that involves separating the foreground objects in an image or video from the static background. This technique is used in many applications such as object tracking, motion detection, and surveillance.

OpenCV provides several methods for performing background subtraction, including `BackgroundSubtractorMOG2`, `BackgroundSubtractorKNN`, and `BackgroundSubtractorCNT`. These methods differ in their underlying algorithms and their ability to handle dynamic or static backgrounds.

- **BackgroundSubtractorMOG2:** This method is based on a Gaussian mixture model and is capable of handling dynamic backgrounds and lighting changes. To use this method in OpenCV, we first create a `BackgroundSubtractorMOG2` object using the `cv2.createBackgroundSubtractorMOG2()` function. We then apply the background subtraction to each frame of the input video using the `bg_sub.apply(frame)` function. This function returns a binary mask indicating the foreground pixels.

- **BackgroundSubtractorKNN:** This method is based on a k-nearest neighbors algorithm and is also capable of handling dynamic backgrounds and lighting changes. To use this method in OpenCV, we first create a `BackgroundSubtractorKNN` object using the `cv2.createBackgroundSubtractorKNN()` function. We then apply the background subtraction to each frame of the input video using the `bg_sub.apply(frame)` function.

- **BackgroundSubtractorCNT:** This method is based on counting the number of pixels that have changed over time and is suitable for static backgrounds. To use this method in OpenCV, we first create a `BackgroundSubtractorCNT` object using the `cv2.bgsegm.createBackgroundSubtractorCNT()` function. We then apply the background subtraction to each frame of the input video using the `bg_sub.apply(frame)` function.

After applying the background subtraction, we usually need to perform some post-processing on the binary mask to remove noise and improve the accuracy of the foreground detection. This can be achieved using morphological operations such as erosion and dilation, which are available in OpenCV.

In summary, background subtraction is a powerful technique for separating foreground objects from the background in an image or video, and OpenCV provides several methods for performing this task. The choice of method will depend on the specific application and the characteristics of the image or video.

Types of Background Subtraction Methods in OpenCV

BackgroundSubtractorMOG2

Here is an example code snippet that demonstrates how to use the BackgroundSubtractorMOG2 method in OpenCV:

```
import cv2
```

```python
# Create background subtraction object
bg_sub = cv2.createBackgroundSubtractorMOG2()

# Open video file or stream
cap = cv2.VideoCapture('output.mp4')

while True:
    # Read frame
    ret, frame = cap.read()

    if ret:
        # Apply background subtraction
        fg_mask = bg_sub.apply(frame)

        # Apply morphological operations to clean up mask
        kernel = cv2.getStructuringElement(cv2.MORPH_ELLIPSE, (3, 3))
        fg_mask = cv2.morphologyEx(fg_mask, cv2.MORPH_OPEN, kernel)

        # Display result
        cv2.imshow('Foreground Mask', fg_mask)
        cv2.imshow('Original Frame', frame)

        # Exit on ESC key
        if cv2.waitKey(25) & 0xFF == ord('q'):
            break
    else: break

# Release resources
cap.release()
cv2.destroyAllWindows()
```

In this code, we first create a **BackgroundSubtractorMOG2** object using the **cv2.createBackgroundSubtractorMOG2()** function.

We then open a video file or stream using the **cv2.VideoCapture()** function. In the main loop, we read a frame from the video using the **cap.read()** function. We then apply the background subtraction to the frame using the **bg_sub.apply()** function, which returns a binary foreground mask. We then apply morphological operations to clean up the mask using the **cv2.morphologyEx()** function.

Refer to the following figure for displaying Background subtraction using OpenCV:

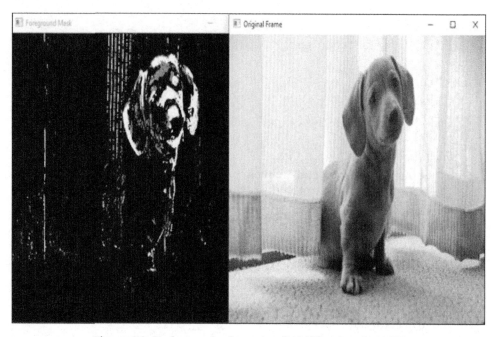

Figure 6.9: *Background subtraction (MOG2) using OpenCV*

Finally, we display the original frame and the foreground mask using the `cv2.imshow()` function. We exit the loop when the ESC key is pressed and release the resources using the `cap.release()` and `cv2.destroyAllWindows()` functions.

BackgroundSubtractorKNN

Here is an example code snippet that demonstrates how to use the `BackgroundSubtractorKNN` method in OpenCV:

```
import cv2

# Create a video capture object
cap = cv2.VideoCapture('output.mp4')

# Create a BackgroundSubtractorKNN object
bg_subtractor = cv2.createBackgroundSubtractorKNN()

while True:
    # Read a frame from the video
    ret, frame = cap.read()
```

```
        if not ret:
            break

        # Apply the background subtraction
        fg_mask = bg_subtractor.apply(frame)

        # Display the original frame and the foreground mask
        cv2.imshow('Original Frame', frame)
        cv2.imshow('Foreground Mask', fg_mask)

        # Check for user input to exit
        if cv2.waitKey(25) & 0xFF == ord('q'):
            break

    # Release the video capture object and destroy all windows
    cap.release()
    cv2.destroyAllWindows()
```

The **BackgroundSubtractorKNN** method is similar to the **BackgroundSubtractorMOG2** method, but it uses a different algorithm to model the background. The usage of the **BackgroundSubtractorKNN** method is the same as the **BackgroundSubtractorMOG2** method, but with the **createBackgroundSubtractorKNN()** function instead of the **createBackgroundSubtractorMOG2()** function.

Refer to the following figure for displaying Background subtraction using OpenCV:

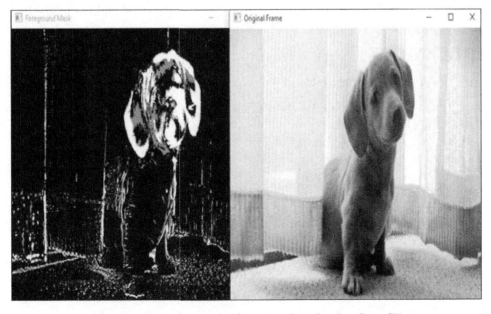

***Figure 6.10**: Background subtraction (KNN) using OpenCV*

Note that you can also set the parameters of the `BackgroundSubtractorKNN` object, such as the number of history frames to use for background modelling, the learning rate, and the number of Gaussian mixtures.

For example, you can create a `BackgroundSubtractorKNN` object with the following code:

```
bg_subtractor = cv2.createBackgroundSubtractorKNN(history=1000, dist2Threshold=100, detectShadows=True)
```

In this case, we set the number of history frames to 1000, the distance threshold to 100, and the shadow detection to `True`. You can experiment with different parameter values to get better results for your specific application.

Conclusion

In this chapter, we have discussed the detailed techniques of road lane detection, corner detection, and their types using OpenCV. Furthermore, we discussed the feature matching techniques, and background subtraction, and their types are explained using OpenCV and Python programming language.

In the next chapter, we will discuss object and motion detection techniques using OpenCV and Python.

Points to Remember

Press the q button to close or exit the image or video processing using OpenCV.

References

Corner detection techniques:

https://docs.opencv.org/3.4/db/d27/tutorial_py_table_of_contents_feature2d.html

CHAPTER 7

Object And Motion Detection Using Opencv

Introduction

In this chapter, we will cover the HSV color space and its role in object detection and tracking using OpenCV. Additionally, we will discuss motion detection, mean shift, camshaft methods in the object tracking method and basic augmented reality using OpenCV and Python programming language.

Structure

In this chapter, we will cover the following topics:

- HSV color space
- Object detection using HSV color space
- Object tracking using HSV color space
- Motion detection and tracking using OpenCV
- Mean Shift object tracking using OpenCV
- Camshift object tracking method using OpenCV
- Augmented reality (AR) in OpenCV

HSV Color Space

The HSV color space is a color model that stands for Hue, Saturation, and Value. It is also sometimes referred to as HSB (Hue, Saturation, Brightness). In the HSV color model, the color is defined by three parameters:

- **Hue:** The hue is the color itself, represented as a value between 0 to 360 degrees. It is also sometimes represented as a value between 0 to 1. The hue value determines the actual color of the pixel, such as red, blue, green, and so on.

- **Saturation:** The saturation parameter represents how intense the color is, or how much of the hue is present. It is represented as a value between 0 to 1, where 0 represents a completely unsaturated color (grayscale), and 1 represents a fully saturated color.
- **Value:** The value parameter represents the brightness or intensity of the color. It is also represented as a value between 0 to 1, where 0 represents black, and 1 represents the brightest possible color.

Refer to the following figure for HSV color in OpenCV.

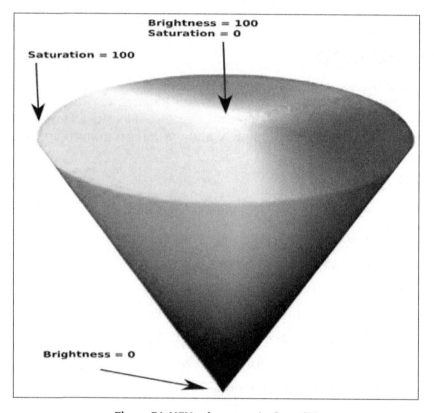

Figure 7.1: HSV color space in OpenCV

The HSV color space is particularly useful in computer vision and image processing applications because it is more intuitive and easier to work with than other color models like RGB. For example, it is easier to isolate a particular color in an image using the HSV color space than using the RGB color space.

In OpenCV, the HSV color space can be used for various image processing tasks such as color filtering, object tracking, and image segmentation. The `cv2.cvtColor()` function can be used to convert an image from one color space to another, including converting an image from RGB to HSV.

Object Detection Using HSV Color Space

Object detection using HSV (Hue, Saturation, Value) is a popular method in computer vision for detecting objects based on their color. The HSV color space separates color information into three components: hue, saturation, and value.

In this method, we first convert an image to the HSV color space and then use thresholding to isolate a specific range of colors that correspond to the object we want to detect. Here's an example of how to perform object detection using HSV in OpenCV:

```
import cv2
import numpy as np

# Define the callback function for the trackbar
def nothing(x):
    pass

# Create a named window for the trackbars
cv2.namedWindow('Trackbars')

# Create trackbars for Hue, Saturation, and Value
cv2.createTrackbar('Hue_Low', 'Trackbars', 0, 179, nothing)
cv2.createTrackbar('Hue_High', 'Trackbars', 179, 179, nothing)
cv2.createTrackbar('Saturation_Low', 'Trackbars', 0, 255, nothing)
cv2.createTrackbar('Saturation_High', 'Trackbars', 255, 255, nothing)
cv2.createTrackbar('Value_Low', 'Trackbars', 0, 255, nothing)
cv2.createTrackbar('Value_High', 'Trackbars', 255, 255, nothing)

# Load an image
img = cv2.imread('smarties.png')

# Convert the image to HSV color space
hsv = cv2.cvtColor(img, cv2.COLOR_BGR2HSV)

while True:
    # Get the current trackbar positions
    h_low = cv2.getTrackbarPos('Hue_Low', 'Trackbars')
    h_high = cv2.getTrackbarPos('Hue_High', 'Trackbars')
    s_low = cv2.getTrackbarPos('Saturation_Low', 'Trackbars')
    s_high = cv2.getTrackbarPos('Saturation_High', 'Trackbars')
    v_low = cv2.getTrackbarPos('Value_Low', 'Trackbars')
    v_high = cv2.getTrackbarPos('Value_High', 'Trackbars')
```

```
# Define the lower and upper bounds of the color to detect
lower_bound = np.array([h_low, s_low, v_low])
upper_bound = np.array([h_high, s_high, v_high])

# Create a mask using the lower and upper bounds
mask = cv2.inRange(hsv, lower_bound, upper_bound)

# Apply the mask to the original image
result = cv2.bitwise_and(img, img, mask=mask)

# Show the original image and the result
cv2.imshow('Original', img)
cv2.imshow('Result', result)

# Wait for the user to press 'q' to quit
if cv2.waitKey(1) & 0xFF == ord('q'):
    break

# Clean up
cv2.destroyAllWindows()
```

In this example, we load an image using OpenCV's **imread()** function. We then convert the image to the HSV color space using OpenCV's **cvtColor()** function. We define the range of colors we want to isolate by creating lower and upper color arrays. We then use the **cv2.inRange()** function to create a mask based on the color range. Finally, we apply the mask to the original image using the **cv2.bitwise_and()** function and display the original image, mask, and result using OpenCV's **imshow()** function.

Refer to the following figure for object detection using HSV in OpenCV:

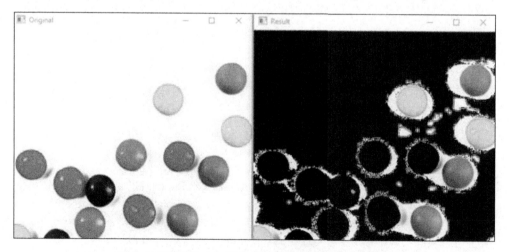

Figure 7.2: Object detection using images with HSV

Refer to the following figure for Trackbar using HSV in OpenCV:

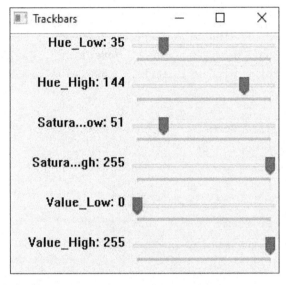

Figure 7.3: *Trackbar using HSV in OpenCV*

Note that the values in the lower and upper color arrays may need to be adjusted depending on the image's specific object and lighting conditions. You can experiment with different color ranges to find the values that work best for your application.

Object Tracking Using HSV Color Space

Object tracking using HSV (Hue, Saturation, Value) is a popular method in computer vision for tracking objects based on their color. Here's an example of how to perform object tracking using HSV in OpenCV:

```
import cv2
import numpy as np

def nothing(x):
    pass

# Load the video file
cap = cv2.VideoCapture('dog.mp4')

# Create a window and trackbars to adjust the color thresholds
cv2.namedWindow('Object Detection')
```

```python
cv2.createTrackbar('Low H', 'Object Detection', 0, 179, nothing)
cv2.createTrackbar('High H', 'Object Detection', 179, 179, nothing)
cv2.createTrackbar('Low S', 'Object Detection', 0, 255, nothing)
cv2.createTrackbar('High S', 'Object Detection', 255, 255, nothing)
cv2.createTrackbar('Low V', 'Object Detection', 0, 255, nothing)
cv2.createTrackbar('High V', 'Object Detection', 255, 255, nothing)

while True:
    # Read the video frame
    ret, frame = cap.read()
    if not ret:
        break

    # Convert the frame to HSV color space
    hsv = cv2.cvtColor(frame, cv2.COLOR_BGR2HSV)

    # Get the color thresholds from the trackbars
    low_h = cv2.getTrackbarPos('Low H', 'Object Detection')
    high_h = cv2.getTrackbarPos('High H', 'Object Detection')
    low_s = cv2.getTrackbarPos('Low S', 'Object Detection')
    high_s = cv2.getTrackbarPos('High S', 'Object Detection')
    low_v = cv2.getTrackbarPos('Low V', 'Object Detection')
    high_v = cv2.getTrackbarPos('High V', 'Object Detection')

    # Define the color thresholds
    lower_color = np.array([low_h, low_s, low_v])
    upper_color = np.array([high_h, high_s, high_v])

    # Threshold the HSV image to get only the object in the color
    range
    mask = cv2.inRange(hsv, lower_color, upper_color)

    # Apply morphological operations to remove noise
    kernel = np.ones((5,5), np.uint8)
    mask = cv2.erode(mask, kernel)
    mask = cv2.dilate(mask, kernel)

    # Find contours of the object in the mask
    contours, _ = cv2.findContours(mask, cv2.RETR_TREE, cv2.CHAIN_
    APPROX_SIMPLE)
```

```
    # Draw the contours on the original frame
    for contour in contours:
        area = cv2.contourArea(contour)
        if area > 100:
            cv2.drawContours(frame, contour, -1, (0, 255, 0), 3)

    # Display the frames
    cv2.imshow('Object Detection', frame)
    cv2.imshow('Mask', mask)

    # Press 'q' to exit the program
    if cv2.waitKey(1) == ord('q'):
        break
# Release the video capture and destroy all windows
cap.release()
cv2.destroyAllWindows()
```

Note that the values in the lower and upper color arrays may need to be adjusted depending on the image's specific object and lighting conditions. You can experiment with different color ranges to find the values that work best for your application.

Refer to the following figure for object tracking using HSV in OpenCV:

Figure 7.4: *Object tracking using images with HSV*

Refer to the following figure for Trackbar using HSV in OpenCV:

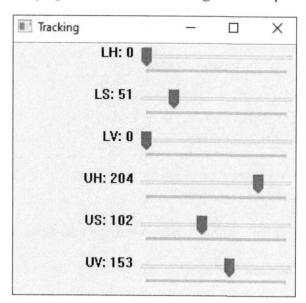

Figure 7.5: Trackbar using HSV in OpenCV

Motion Detection and Tracking Using OpenCV

Motion detection and tracking are important computer vision techniques used in various applications, such as surveillance, object tracking, and activity recognition. In general, motion detection is the process of detecting changes in the position of objects in a video sequence over time.

This can be done by comparing consecutive frames of a video and analyzing the differences between them. Motion tracking, on the other hand, involves estimating the trajectory of moving objects in a video and predicting their future positions. OpenCV provides several methods for motion detection and tracking, including background subtraction, optical flow, and template matching. Here is a brief overview of these methods:

Background Subtraction: This method involves creating a background model of a scene by averaging multiple frames of a video. Then, the current frame is compared with the background model to detect moving objects. Any pixel that is significantly different from the corresponding background pixel is considered a foreground pixel. OpenCV provides several algorithms for background subtraction, including MOG, MOG2, and GMG.

- **Optical Flow:** This method involves analyzing the movement of pixels between consecutive frames of a video. It works by estimating the motion vector of each pixel in the current frame relative to the previous frame. The motion vectors can be used to track the movement of objects in the video. OpenCV provides several algorithms for optical flow, including Lucas-Kanade and Farneback methods.
- **Template Matching:** This method involves detecting objects in a video by searching for a template image in each frame. The template image is a small image that represents the object to be detected. The search is performed by sliding the template over the image and comparing the template with each sub-image. When the template matches a sub-image, the location of the sub-image corresponds to the location of the object in the video.
- **Kalman filter:** The Kalman filter is a mathematical algorithm that can be used to estimate the state of a system based on noisy measurements. By combining CAMShift with a Kalman filter, it is possible to improve the accuracy of the tracking and to handle occlusions or other challenges that may arise.

Motion detection and tracking are important techniques for analyzing video data and extracting useful information from it. By using OpenCV's built-in algorithms, it is possible to implement these techniques in a relatively straightforward manner.

Mean Shift Object Tracking Using OpenCV

Mean Shift is a computer vision algorithm used for object tracking in videos. It is based on finding the mode of the **probability density function (PDF)** of the color distribution of the object being tracked. In other words, it tries to find the pixel value that is most representative of the object being tracked and then iteratively shifts a window around that pixel to track the object as it moves.

In OpenCV, Mean Shift object tracking is implemented using the `cv2.meanShift()` function. The function takes two arguments: the input image and the initial window location. The function returns two values: the updated window location and the convergence criteria. Here's an example code snippet that demonstrates how to use the Mean Shift algorithm for object tracking in OpenCV:

```
import cv2
```

```python
# Load the input video file
cap = cv2.VideoCapture('dog.mp4')

# Read the first frame from the input video
ret, frame = cap.read()

# Define the initial window location
x, y, w, h = 300, 200, 100, 100
track_window = (x, y, w, h)

# Extract the region of interest (ROI) from the first frame
roi = frame[y:y+h, x:x+w]

# Convert the ROI to the HSV color space
hsv_roi = cv2.cvtColor(roi, cv2.COLOR_BGR2HSV)

# Compute the histogram of the HSV color distribution in the ROI
roi_hist = cv2.calcHist([hsv_roi], [0], None, [180], [0, 180])

# Normalize the histogram
cv2.normalize(roi_hist, roi_hist, 0, 255, cv2.NORM_MINMAX)

# Define the termination criteria for the Mean Shift algorithm
term_crit = (cv2.TERM_CRITERIA_EPS | cv2.TERM_CRITERIA_COUNT, 10, 1)

# Loop through the frames in the input video
while True:
    # Read a frame from the input video
    ret, frame = cap.read()

    # Stop the loop if the end of the video is reached
    if not ret:
        break

    # Convert the frame to the HSV color space
    hsv = cv2.cvtColor(frame, cv2.COLOR_BGR2HSV)

    # Calculate the back projection of the histogram onto the frame
    dst = cv2.calcBackProject([hsv], [0], roi_hist, [0, 180], 1)

    # Apply the Mean Shift algorithm to the back projection
    ret, track_window = cv2.meanShift(dst, track_window, term_crit)
```

```
    # Draw a rectangle around the tracked object
    x, y, w, h = track_window
    cv2.rectangle(frame, (x, y), (x+w, y+h), (0, 255, 0), 2)

    # Display the output video frame with the rectangle
    cv2.imshow('Mean Shift Object Tracking', frame)

    # Exit on ESC key
    if cv2.waitKey(1) == 27:
        break

# Release resources
cap.release()
cv2.destroyAllWindows()
```

In this code, we first load the input video file using `cv2.VideoCapture()` function. We read the first frame from the input video using the `cap.read()` function and define the initial window location using the x, y, w, and h variables.

Refer to the following figure for Mean Shift object tracking using OpenCV:

Figure 7.6: *Mean Shift object tracking using videos*

We extract the region of interest (ROI) from the first frame using the window location and convert it to the HSV color space using the `cv2.cvtColor()` function. We then compute the histogram of the HSV color distribution in the ROI using the `cv2.calcHist()` function and normalize it using the `cv2.normalize()` function.

We define the termination criteria for the Mean Shift algorithm using the `cv2.TERM_CRITERIA_EPS` and `cv2.TERM_CRITERIA_COUNT` constants. We then loop through the frames in the input video and apply Mean Shift object tracking to each frame.

We convert each frame to the HSV color space using the `cv2.cvtColor()` function and calculate the back projection of the histogram onto the frame using the `cv2.calcBackProject()` function. We apply the Mean Shift algorithm to the back projection using the `cv2.meanShift()` function and draw a rectangle around the tracked object using the `cv2.rectangle()` function.

Finally, we display the output video frame with the rectangle using the `cv2.imshow()` function and exit the loop when the ESC key is pressed. We release the resources using the `cap.release()` and `cv2.destroyAllWindows()` functions.

Overall, Mean Shift object tracking is a powerful technique for tracking objects in videos using color histograms. By combining this technique with other computer vision algorithms, it is possible to build sophisticated applications for surveillance, robotics, and autonomous vehicles.

Camshift Object Tracking Method Using OpenCV

CAMShift (Continuously Adaptive Mean Shift) is a computer vision algorithm used for object tracking in videos. It is an extension of the Mean Shift algorithm that adapts to changes in the size and orientation of the object being tracked. CAMShift works by iteratively shifting a window around the mode of the probability density function (PDF) of the color distribution of the object being tracked, and then updating the size and orientation of the window based on the shape of the object.

In OpenCV, CAMShift object tracking is implemented using the `cv2.CamShift()` function. The function takes two arguments: the input image and the initial window location. The function returns two values: the updated window location and the convergence criteria. Here's an example code snippet that demonstrates how to use the CAMShift algorithm for object tracking in OpenCV:

```
import cv2
import numpy as np
```

```python
# Load the input video file
cap = cv2.VideoCapture('dog.mp4')

# Read the first frame from the input video
ret, frame = cap.read()

# Define the initial window location
x, y, w, h = 300, 200, 100, 100
track_window = (x, y, w, h)

# Extract the region of interest (ROI) from the first frame
roi = frame[y:y+h, x:x+w]

# Convert the ROI to the HSV color space
hsv_roi = cv2.cvtColor(roi, cv2.COLOR_BGR2HSV)

# Compute the histogram of the HSV color distribution in the ROI
roi_hist = cv2.calcHist([hsv_roi], [0], None, [180], [0, 180])

# Normalize the histogram
cv2.normalize(roi_hist, roi_hist, 0, 255, cv2.NORM_MINMAX)

# Define the termination criteria for the CAMShift algorithm
term_crit = (cv2.TERM_CRITERIA_EPS | cv2.TERM_CRITERIA_COUNT, 10, 1)

# Loop through the frames in the input video
while True:
    # Read a frame from the input video
    ret, frame = cap.read()

    # Stop the loop if the end of the video is reached
    if not ret:
        break

    # Convert the frame to the HSV color space
    hsv = cv2.cvtColor(frame, cv2.COLOR_BGR2HSV)

    # Calculate the back projection of the histogram onto the frame
    dst = cv2.calcBackProject([hsv], [0], roi_hist, [0, 180], 1)

    # Apply the CAMShift algorithm to the back projection
    ret, track_window = cv2.CamShift(dst, track_window, term_crit)
```

```
        # Draw an ellipse around the tracked object
        pts = cv2.boxPoints(ret)
        pts = np.int0(pts)
        cv2.polylines(frame, [pts], True, (0, 255, 0), 2)

        # Display the output video frame with the ellipse
        cv2.imshow('CAMShift Object Tracking', frame)

        # Exit on ESC key
        if cv2.waitKey(1) == 27:
            break

    # Release resources
    cap.release()
    cv2.destroyAllWindows()
```
In this code, we first load the input video file using `cv2.VideoCapture()` function. We read the first frame from the input video using the `cap.read()` function and define the initial window location using the x, y, w, and h variables.

Refer to the following figure for Camshift object tracking using OpenCV:

Figure 7.7: *Camshift object tracking using OpenCV*

We extract the region of interest (ROI) from the first frame using the window location and convert it to the HSV color space using the `cv2.cvtColor()` function. We then compute the histogram of the HSV color distribution in the ROI using the `cv2.calcHist()` function and normalize it using the `cv2.normalize()` function.

We define the termination criteria for the CAMShift algorithm using the `cv2.TERM_CRITERIA_EPS` and `cv2.TERM_CRITERIA_COUNT` constants. We then loop through the frames in the input video and apply CAMShift object tracking to each frame.

We convert each frame to the HSV color space using the `cv2.cvtColor()` function and calculate the back projection of the histogram onto the frame using the `cv2.calcBackProject()` function. We apply the CAMShift algorithm to the back projection using the `cv2.CamShift()` function and draw an ellipse around the tracked object using the `cv2.polylines()` function.

Finally, we display the output video frame with the ellipse using the `cv2.imshow()` function and exit the loop when the ESC key is pressed. We release the resources using the `cap.release()` and `cv2.destroyAllWindows()` functions.

Overall, CAMShift object tracking is a powerful technique for tracking objects in videos that can adapt to changes in the size and orientation of the object. By combining this technique with other computer vision algorithms, it is possible to build sophisticated applications for surveillance, robotics, and autonomous vehicles.

Augmented Reality in OpenCV

Augmented reality (AR) is a technology that allows users to superimpose computer-generated content into the real world. It is typically used in applications that enhance the user's perception of reality by adding virtual objects, information, or graphics to their view of the physical world. AR applications can be found in various fields, such as entertainment, education, marketing, and gaming.

OpenCV provides a set of tools and algorithms for image and video processing, object detection, and recognition, and 3D reconstruction. OpenCV is widely used in computer vision research and industrial applications, such as robotics, surveillance, and medical imaging.

The combination of AR and OpenCV can lead to exciting applications that allow users to interact with the real world and digital content in a more intuitive and immersive way.

Here are some of the key steps involved in developing an AR application using OpenCV:

Camera calibration: In order to accurately overlay digital content onto the real world, the camera used to capture the real-world scene needs to be calibrated. This involves determining the intrinsic and extrinsic parameters of the camera, such as focal length, principal point, and lens distortion.

- Feature detection and tracking: In order to overlay virtual objects in the real world, the AR application needs to be able to detect and track features in the camera image, such as corners or edges. OpenCV provides various algorithms for feature detection and tracking, such as the Harris corner detector and the Kanade-Lucas-Tomasi (KLT) tracker.
- **Pose estimation:** Once the features are detected and tracked, the AR application needs to estimate the pose of the camera relative to the real-world scene. This involves determining the position and orientation of the camera with respect to a known reference frame, such as a calibration pattern or a set of tracked features.
- **Rendering:** Once the pose of the camera is estimated, the AR application can render virtual objects onto the camera image using computer graphics techniques, such as texture mapping, lighting, and shading.
- **User interaction:** Finally, the AR application can allow the user to interact with virtual objects, such as manipulating them or triggering events based on their position or orientation.

Here's an example code snippet that demonstrates how to use detecting markers with images using augmented reality (AR) in OpenCV.

> **NOTE:** Download ArUco Markers images for the following exercise.

```
import cv2
import numpy as np

# Load the dictionary and create the detector parameters
dictionary = cv2.aruco.getPredefinedDictionary(cv2.aruco.DICT_6X6_250)
parameters = cv2.aruco.DetectorParameters()
detector = cv2.aruco.ArucoDetector(dictionary, parameters)
```

```python
# Load the image
img = cv2.imread("aruco_marker.png")

# Convert the frame to grayscale
gray = cv2.cvtColor(img, cv2.COLOR_BGR2GRAY)

# Detect the markers in the frame
corners, ids, rejectedImgPoints = detector.detectMarkers(gray)

# Draw the detected markers and their IDs on the frame
if len(corners) > 0:
    ids = ids.flatten()
    for i, corner in enumerate(corners):
        cv2.aruco.drawDetectedMarkers(img, corners, ids)

# Show the frame
img = cv2.resize(img, (1600, 1200))
cv2.imshow('frame', img)

#close the function
cv2.waitKey(0)
# lose all windows
cv2.destroyAllWindows()
```

Refer to the following figure for Augmented reality in OpenCV using images:

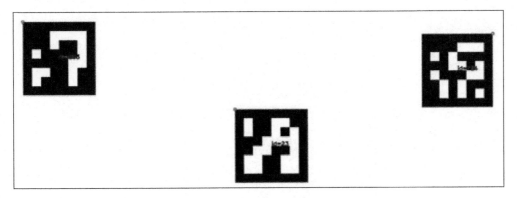

Figure 7.8: *Detecting markers using an image in OpenCV*

Here's an example code snippet that demonstrates how to use detecting markers with videos using augmented reality (AR) in OpenCV:

```
import cv2
import numpy as np
# Load the dictionary and create the detector parameters
dictionary = cv2.aruco.getPredefinedDictionary(cv2.aruco.DICT_6X6_250)
parameters = cv2.aruco.DetectorParameters()
detector = cv2.aruco.ArucoDetector(dictionary, parameters)

# Start the camera capture
cap = cv2.VideoCapture(0)

while True:
    # Read the current frame
    ret, frame = cap.read()
    if not ret:
        break

    # Convert the frame to grayscale
    gray = cv2.cvtColor(frame, cv2.COLOR_BGR2GRAY)

    # Detect the markers in the frame
    corners, ids, rejectedImgPoints = detector.detectMarkers(gray)

    # Draw the detected markers and their IDs on the frame
    if len(corners) > 0:
        ids = ids.flatten()
        for i, corner in enumerate(corners):
            cv2.aruco.drawDetectedMarkers(frame, corners, ids)

    # Show the frame
    cv2.imshow('frame', frame)
    if cv2.waitKey(1) == ord('q'):
        break
```

Object And Motion Detection Using Opencv

```
# Release the camera and close all windows
cap.release()
cv2.destroyAllWindows()
```

Refer to the following figure for Augmented reality in OpenCV using video:

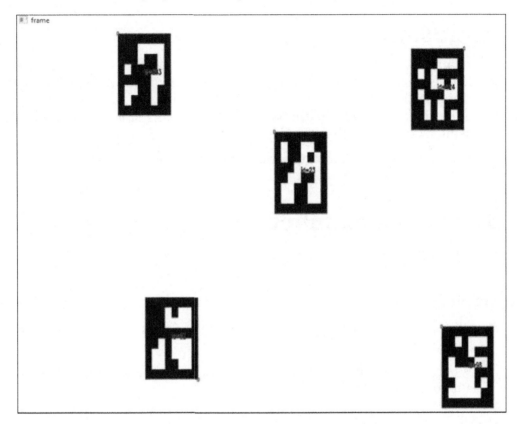

Figure 7.9: Detecting markers using a video in OpenCV

Before we can perform AR, we need to calibrate the camera to correct for any distortion or other factors that might affect the accuracy of object detection and tracking. This involves taking multiple images of a known calibration pattern, such as a checkerboard, from different viewpoints and using them to compute the intrinsic and extrinsic camera parameters.

Here's an example code snippet that demonstrates how to use camera calibration in OpenCV. (Refer the *Chapter 5: Thresholding and Contour Techniques using OpenCV* and *Figure 5.15*).

Overall, creating an augmented reality application using OpenCV requires expertise in computer vision, graphics programming, and image processing.

It involves a complex pipeline of image acquisition, feature detection and matching, object tracking, and virtual object rendering. While the specific implementation details may vary depending on the application, the underlying principles and techniques are similar.

Conclusion

In this chapter, we have discussed the HSV color space and its parameters. HSV role in object detection and tracking using OpenCV. Additionally, we will discuss motion detection and its types which is a mean shift, and camshaft methods in object tracking methods and a basic explanation of augmented reality using OpenCV and Python programming language.

In the next chapter, we will discuss Image Segmentation and Detecting faces and their features using OpenCV.

Points to Remember

Explore the Trackbar values in the object detection code.

Questions

1. What is HSV color space and its parameters usage in OpenCV applications?
2. What are Augmented Reality (AR) and real-time usage in OpenCV applications?

References

HSV color techniques:

https://docs.opencv.org/4.x/df/d9d/tutorial_py_colorspaces.html

Detection of ArUco Markers:

https://docs.opencv.org/4.x/d5/dae/tutorial_aruco_detection.html

CHAPTER 8

Image Segmentation and Detecting Faces Using OpenCV

Introduction

In this chapter, we will cover image segmentation techniques, QR code recognition and optical character recognition using OpenCV. We will also discuss the detailed introduction to Haar Cascade Classifiers and their use in face and eye detection using OpenCV and Python programming language.

Structure

In this chapter, we will cover the following topics:

- Image segmentation using OpenCV
- Introduction to Haar Cascade Classifiers
- Face detection using Haar Cascade Classifiers
- Eye detection Haar Feature-based Cascade Classifiers
- Smile detection Haar Feature-based Cascade Classifiers
- QR code detection using OpenCV
- Optical character recognition using OpenCV

Image Segmentation Using OpenCV

Image segmentation is a process of dividing an image into multiple segments, with each segment representing a different object or region within the image. One popular algorithm for image segmentation is the Watershed algorithm, which is based on mathematical morphology and is commonly used in computer vision and image processing.

The Watershed algorithm works by treating the image as a topographic map, where the pixel intensities represent elevations. The algorithm starts by identifying the local minima or markers in the image, areas where the intensity is lower than that of its surrounding pixels. The markers are then used to create a gradient image, which assigns higher values to pixels farther away from the markers.

Next, the gradient image is segmented into regions using the Watershed algorithm, which treats the image as a landscape with valleys and ridges. The algorithm starts flooding the landscape from the markers, and the valleys between the ridges are used as boundaries between the segments.

Here are the basic steps for implementing the Watershed algorithm for image segmentation:

Convert the image to grayscale and apply any necessary pre-processing, such as noise reduction or contrast enhancement.

- Identify the local minima or markers in the image using a thresholding or edge detection algorithm.
- Create a gradient image based on the markers, using techniques such as morphological gradients or distance transforms.
- Apply the Watershed algorithm to the gradient image to segment the image into regions. Post-process the segmentation results to remove noise, fill gaps, or merge small regions.

The Watershed algorithm can be a powerful tool for image segmentation, as it can handle complex and irregular shapes, and can segment images with multiple objects or regions.

However, it can also be sensitive to noise and requires careful parameter tuning to achieve good segmentation results. Additionally, it can be computationally intensive and may not be suitable for real-time applications or large datasets:

```
import cv2
import numpy as np

# Load the image
img = cv2.imread('image.jpg')

# Convert the image to grayscale
gray = cv2.cvtColor(img, cv2.COLOR_BGR2GRAY)
```

```python
# Threshold the image to obtain a binary image
ret, thresh = cv2.threshold(gray, 0, 255, cv2.THRESH_BINARY_INV+cv2.THRESH_OTSU)

# Morphological opening to remove noise
kernel = np.ones((3,3),np.uint8)
opening = cv2.morphologyEx(thresh,cv2.MORPH_OPEN,kernel, iterations = 2)

# Background area using dilate
sure_bg = cv2.dilate(opening,kernel,iterations=3)

# Finding sure foreground area
dist_transform = cv2.distanceTransform(opening,cv2.DIST_L2,5)
ret, sure_fg = cv2.threshold(dist_transform,0.7*dist_transform.max(),255,0)

# Finding unknown region
sure_fg = np.uint8(sure_fg)
unknown = cv2.subtract(sure_bg,sure_fg)

# Marker labelling
_, markers = cv2.connectedComponents(sure_fg)

# Adding one to all labels so that sure background is not 0, but 1
markers = markers+1

# Marking the region of unknown with zero
markers[unknown==255] = 0

# Applying watershed algorithm
markers = cv2.watershed(img,markers)
img[markers == -1] = [255,0,0]

# Display the result
cv2.imshow('Segmented Image', img)
cv2.waitKey(0)
cv2.destroyAllWindows()
```

Refer to the following figure for Image Segmentation in OpenCV:

Figure 8.1: *Image Segmentation in OpenCV*

Introduction to Haar Cascade Classifiers

Haar Cascade classifiers are machine learning-based algorithms that are commonly used for object detection in images and videos. They were introduced by Viola and Jones in 2001 and have been widely adopted in computer vision applications.

One of the most popular applications of Haar Cascade classifiers is face detection. The algorithm works by training a classifier on a large dataset of positive and negative images. Positive images contain faces, while negative images do not. The classifier learns to identify the features that are common in positive images, such as the contrast between the eyes and the nose, and the curvature of the mouth.

Once the classifier is trained, it can be used to detect faces in new images or video frames. The detection process involves scanning the image or video frame with a sliding window of different sizes and aspect ratios. At each position of the sliding window, the classifier is used to determine whether the window contains a face or not. If a face is detected, the position and size of the window are recorded.

Haar Cascade classifiers can also be trained to detect other objects, such as eyes, mouths, and smiles. In these cases, the positive images contain examples of the desired object, while the negative images do not. The classifier learns to identify the features that are specific to the object, such as the shape and texture of the eye or the curvature of the mouth. The Haar Cascade classifiers are often used in combination with other computer vision techniques, such as image segmentation and feature extraction, to improve the accuracy and robustness of object detection. They are widely used in applications such as face recognition, security systems, and driver assistance systems.

In summary, Haar Cascade classifiers are powerful tools for object detection in images and videos and can be trained to detect a wide range of objects, including faces, eyes, mouths, and smiles. The algorithm is based on machine learning and involves training a classifier on a large dataset of positive and negative images.

The trained classifier can then be used to detect objects in new images or video frames by scanning the image or video frame with a sliding window and using the classifier to determine whether the window contains the desired object or not.

Face Detection Using Haar Cascade Classifiers

Haar Cascade classifiers are a powerful tool for face detection in images, and OpenCV provides a simple interface for using these classifiers in Python.

Here's an example code snippet that demonstrates how to perform face detection using Haar Cascade classifiers in OpenCV:

> **NOTE: Keep the haarcascade.xml and input image file in the same folder where the code file exists.**

```
import cv2

# Load the Haar Cascade classifier for face detection
face_cascade = cv2.CascadeClassifier('haarcascade_frontalface_default.xml')

# Load the input image
img = cv2.imread('smile.jpg')
```

```
# Convert the image to grayscale for face detection
gray = cv2.cvtColor(img, cv2.COLOR_BGR2GRAY)

# Detect faces in the grayscale image using the Haar Cascade classifier
faces = face_cascade.detectMultiScale(gray, scaleFactor=1.1,
minNeighbors=5)

# Draw rectangles around the detected faces
for (x, y, w, h) in faces:
    cv2.rectangle(img, (x, y), (x+w, y+h), (0, 255, 0), 2)

# Display the output image with detected faces
cv2.imshow('Face Detection', img)

# Wait for a key press and then exit
cv2.waitKey(0)
cv2.destroyAllWindows()
```

In this code, we first load the Haar Cascade classifier for face detection using the `cv2.CascadeClassifier()` function. We then load the input image using the `cv2.imread()` function. We then convert the image to grayscale using the `cv2.cvtColor()` function, which is required for face detection.

Refer to the following figure for face detection in images using OpenCV:

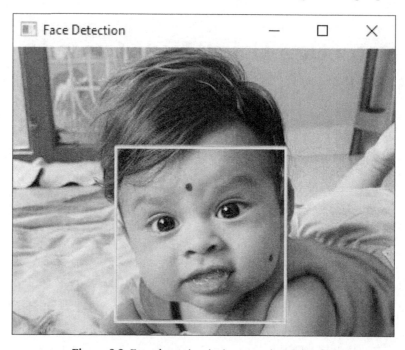

Figure 8.2: Face detection in image using OpenCV

Image Segmentation and Detecting Faces Using OpenCV

We use the `cv2.CascadeClassifier.detectMultiScale()` function to detect faces in the grayscale image. This function returns a list of rectangles that represent the detected faces. We draw these rectangles on the output image using the `cv2.rectangle()` function.

Finally, we display the output image with detected faces using the `cv2.imshow()` function and wait for a key press before exiting.

Here's an example code snippet that demonstrates how to perform face detection using Haar Cascade classifiers in OpenCV for an input video:

```
import cv2

# Load the Haar Cascade classifier for face detection
face_cascade = cv2.CascadeClassifier('haarcascade_frontalface_default.xml')

# Create a video capture object
cap = cv2.VideoCapture(0)

while True:
    # Read a frame from the video
    ret, frame = cap.read()

    if not ret:
        break

    # Convert the frame to grayscale
    gray = cv2.cvtColor(frame, cv2.COLOR_BGR2GRAY)

    # Detect faces in the grayscale image using the Haar Cascade
    classifier
    faces = face_cascade.detectMultiScale(gray, scaleFactor=1.1, minNeighbors=5, minSize=(30, 30))
    """
    scaleFactor: This parameter compensates for the fact that faces can appear at different sizes in an image.
    It specifies how much the image size is reduced at each image scale.
    A smaller value will increase the detection time but can lead to better detection, while a larger value will decrease the detection time but may miss smaller smiles.
    The default value is 1.3, but in this case, it has been set to 2.1.

    minNeighbors: This parameter controls the sensitivity of the detector.
    It specifies how many neighbors a candidate smile rectangle should have to be retained.
```

Higher values will result in fewer detections but with higher confidence, and lower values will result in more detections but with lower confidence.

The default value is 3, but in this case, it has been set to 12
"""

```
# Draw rectangles around the detected faces
for (x, y, w, h) in faces:
    cv2.rectangle(frame, (x, y), (x + w, y + h), (0, 255, 0), 2)

# Display the resulting frame
cv2.imshow('Face Detection', frame)

# Check for user input to exit
if cv2.waitKey(25) & 0xFF == ord('q'): break
```

```
# Release the video capture object and destroy all windows
cap.release()
cv2.destroyAllWindows()
```

In this code, we first load the Haar Cascade classifier for face detection using the **cv2.CascadeClassifier()** function. We then load the input image using the **cv2.imread()** function. We then convert the image to grayscale using the **cv2.cvtColor()** function, which is required for face detection.

Refer to the following figure for face detection in the video using OpenCV:

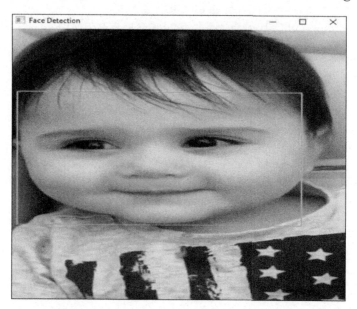

Figure 8.3: *Face detection in video using OpenCV*

We use the **cv2.CascadeClassifier.detectMultiScale()** function to detect faces in the grayscale image. This function returns a list of rectangles that represent the detected faces. We draw these rectangles on the output image using the `cv2.rectangle()` function.

Finally, we display the output image with detected faces using the `cv2.imshow()` function and wait for a key press before exiting.

Eye Detection Haar Feature-based Cascade Classifiers

Haar Cascade classifiers are a powerful tool for eye detection in images, and OpenCV provides a simple interface for using these classifiers in Python.

Here's an example code snippet that demonstrates how to perform eye detection using Haar Cascade classifiers in OpenCV for an input image:

```
import cv2

# Load the Haar Cascade classifier for eye detection
eye_cascade = cv2.CascadeClassifier('haarcascade_eye.xml')

# Load the input image
img = cv2.imread('input.jpg')

# Convert the image to grayscale for eye detection
gray = cv2.cvtColor(img, cv2.COLOR_BGR2GRAY)

# Detect eyes in the grayscale image using the Haar Cascade classifier
eyes = eye_cascade.detectMultiScale(gray, scaleFactor=1.1, minNeighbors=5)

# Draw rectangles around the detected eyes
for (x, y, w, h) in eyes:
    cv2.rectangle(img, (x, y), (x+w, y+h), (0, 0, 255), 2)

# Display the output image with detected eyes
cv2.imshow('Eye Detection', img)

# Wait for a key press and then exit
cv2.waitKey(0)
cv2.destroyAllWindows()
```

In this code, we first load the Haar Cascade classifier for eye detection using the `cv2.CascadeClassifier()` function. We then load the input image using the `cv2.imread()` function. We then convert the image to grayscale using the `cv2.cvtColor()` function, which is required for eye detection. We use the `cv2.CascadeClassifier.detectMultiScale()` function to detect eyes in the grayscale image. This function returns a list of rectangles that represent the detected eyes.

Refer to the following figure for eye detection in images using OpenCV:

Figure 8.4: *Eye detection in image using OpenCV*

We draw these rectangles on the output image using the `cv2.rectangle()` function. Finally, we display the output image with detected eyes using the `cv2.imshow()` function and wait for a key press before exiting.

Here's an example code snippet that demonstrates how to perform eye detection using Haar Cascade classifiers in OpenCV for an input video:

```python
import cv2

# Load the Haar Cascade classifier for eye detection
eye_cascade = cv2.CascadeClassifier('haarcascade_eye.xml')

# Load the input video file
cap = cv2.VideoCapture('input.mp4')

# Loop through the frames in the input video
while True:
    # Read a frame from the input video
    ret, frame = cap.read()

    # Stop the loop if the end of the video is reached
    if not ret:
        break

    # Convert the frame to grayscale for eye detection
    gray = cv2.cvtColor(frame, cv2.COLOR_BGR2GRAY)

    # Detect eyes in the grayscale image using the Haar Cascade
    classifier
    eyes = eye_cascade.detectMultiScale(gray, scaleFactor=1.1,
    minNeighbors=5)

    # Draw rectangles around the detected eyes
    for (x, y, w, h) in eyes:
        cv2.rectangle(frame, (x, y), (x+w, y+h), (0, 0, 255), 2)

    # Display the output video frame with detected eyes
    cv2.imshow('Eye Detection', frame)

    # Exit on ESC key
    if cv2.waitKey(25) & 0xFF == ord('q'):
        break

# Release resources
cap.release()
cv2.destroyAllWindows()
```

In this code, we first load the Haar Cascade classifier for eye detection using the `cv2.CascadeClassifier()` function. We then load the input video file using the `cv2.VideoCapture()` function. In the main loop, we read a frame from the input video using the `cap.read()` function. We then convert the frame to grayscale using the `cv2.cvtColor()` function, which is required for eye detection.

Refer to the following figure for eye detection in video using OpenCV:

Figure 8.5: *Eye detection in video using OpenCV*

We then use the `cv2.CascadeClassifier.detectMultiScale()` function to detect eyes in the grayscale image. This function returns a list of rectangles that represent the detected eyes. We draw these rectangles on the output video frame using the `cv2.rectangle()` function.

Finally, we display the output video frame with detected eyes using the `cv2.imshow()` function and exit the loop when the ESC key is pressed. We release the resources using the `cap.release()` and `cv2.destroyAllWindows()` functions.

Smile Detection Haar Feature-based Cascade Classifiers

Haar Cascade classifiers are a powerful tool for smile detection in images, and OpenCV provides a simple interface for using these classifiers in Python.

Here's an example code snippet that demonstrates how to perform smile detection using Haar Cascade classifiers in OpenCV for an input image:

```
import cv2

# Load the Haar Cascade classifier for smile detection
smile_cascade = cv2.CascadeClassifier('haarcascade_smile.xml')

# Load the input image
img = cv2.imread('smile.jpg')

# Convert the image to grayscale for smile detection
gray = cv2.cvtColor(img, cv2.COLOR_BGR2GRAY)

# Detect smiles in the grayscale image using the Haar Cascade
classifier
smiles = smile_cascade.detectMultiScale(gray, scaleFactor=2.1,
minNeighbors=12)

# Draw rectangles around the detected smiles
for (x, y, w, h) in smiles:
    cv2.rectangle(img, (x, y), (x+w, y+h), (0, 255, 0), 2)

# Display the output image with detected smiles
cv2.imshow('Smile Detection', img)

# Wait for a key press and then exit
cv2.waitKey(0)
cv2.destroyAllWindows()
```

In this code, we first load the Haar Cascade classifier for smile detection using the **cv2.CascadeClassifier()** function. We then load the input image using the **cv2.imread()** function. We then convert the image to grayscale using the **cv2.cvtColor()** function, which is required for smile detection.

 # scaleFactor: This parameter compensates for the fact that faces can appear at different #sizes in an image. It specifies how much the image size is reduced at each image scale. # The default value is 1.3, but in this case, it has been set to 2.1.

 # minNeighbors: This parameter controls the sensitivity of the detector. It specifies how # many neighbors a candidate smile rectangle should have to be retained. The default #value is 3, but in this case, it has been set to 12.

Refer to the following figure for smile detection in images using OpenCV:

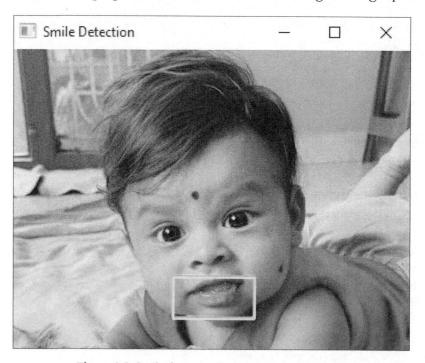

Figure 8.6: Smile detection in image using OpenCV

We use the `cv2.CascadeClassifier.detectMultiScale()` function to detect smiles in the grayscale image. This function returns a list of rectangles that represent the detected smiles. We draw these rectangles on the output image using the `cv2.rectangle()` function.

Finally, we display the output image with detected smiles using the `cv2.imshow()` function and wait for a key press before exiting.

Here's an example code snippet that demonstrates how to perform smile detection using Haar Cascade classifiers in OpenCV for an input video:

```
import cv2

# Load the pre-trained Haar Cascade classifier for face and smile detection
```

```python
face_cascade = cv2.CascadeClassifier('haarcascade_frontalface_default.xml')
smile_cascade = cv2.CascadeClassifier('haarcascade_smile.xml')

# Open the video capture device (0 is usually the built-in camera)
cap = cv2.VideoCapture("baby.mp4")

while True:
    # Read a frame from the video capture device
    ret, frame = cap.read()

    # Stop the loop if the end of the video is reached
    if not ret:
        break

    # Convert the frame to grayscale for face and smile detection
    gray = cv2.cvtColor(frame, cv2.COLOR_BGR2GRAY)

    # Detect faces in the grayscale image
    faces = face_cascade.detectMultiScale(gray, scaleFactor=1.1, minNeighbors=8, minSize=(30, 30))

    # For each detected face, detect smiles
    for (x, y, w, h) in faces:
        # Draw a rectangle around the face
        cv2.rectangle(frame, (x, y), (x + w, y + h), (255, 0, 0), 2)

        # Region of Interest (ROI) for the detected face
        roi_gray = gray[y:y + h, x:x + w]
        roi_color = frame[y:y + h, x:x + w]

        # Detect smiles in the ROI
        smiles = smile_cascade.detectMultiScale(roi_gray, scaleFactor=1.7, minNeighbors=15, minSize=(25, 25))

        # For each detected smile, draw a rectangle
        for (sx, sy, sw, sh) in smiles:
            cv2.rectangle(roi_color, (sx, sy), (sx + sw, sy + sh), (0, 0, 255), 2)

    frame = cv2.resize(frame, (512, 512))
```

```
    # Display the resulting image with detected faces and smiles
    cv2.imshow('Smile Detection', frame)

    # Break the loop when 'q' is pressed
    if cv2.waitKey(1) & 0xFF == ord('q'):
        break

# Release the video capture device and close all windows
cap.release()
cv2.destroyAllWindows()
```

In this code, we first load the Haar Cascade classifier for smile detection using the `cv2.CascadeClassifier()` function. We then load the input video file using the `cv2.VideoCapture()` function. In the main loop, we read a frame from the input video using the `cap.read()` function. We then convert the frame to grayscale using the `cv2.cvtColor()` function, which is required for smile detection.

Refer to the following figure for eye detection in video using OpenCV:

Figure 8.7: *Smile detection in video using OpenCV*

We then use the `cv2.CascadeClassifier.detectMultiScale()` function to detect smiles in the grayscale image. This function returns a list of rectangles that represent the detected smiles. We draw these rectangles on the output video frame using the `cv2.rectangle()` function.

Finally, we display the output video frame with detected smiles using the `cv2.imshow()` function and exit the loop when the Q key is pressed. We release the resources using the `cap.release()` and `cv2.destroyAllWindows()` functions.

QR Code Detection Using OpenCV

It involves a series of image processing and computer vision techniques to locate and decode QR codes in a digital image. Here's a high-level overview of the main steps involved:

- **Image acquisition:** The first step is to acquire an image containing the QR code. This can be done using a digital camera or by loading an existing image file.
- **Preprocessing:** The next step is to preprocess the image to enhance the QR code and reduce noise. This may involve operations such as image thresholding, blurring, and edge detection.
- **QR code detection:** Once the image has been preprocessed, the next step is to detect the QR code within the image. This typically involves looking for patterns in the image that match the known structure of QR codes. One common approach is to use a Hough transform to detect the alignment patterns in the corners of the QR code.
- **QR code decoding**: Once the QR code has been detected, the final step is to decode the information encoded in the QR code. This involves reading the patterns of black and white squares in the QR code and interpreting them according to the QR code specification.

OpenCV provides several functions and classes that can be used for QR code detection and decoding, including the `cv2.QRCodeDetector` class. This class provides methods for detecting and decoding QR codes in an image, as well as for drawing bounding boxes around the detected QR codes.

To use the `cv2.QRCodeDetector` class, you first need to create an instance of the class using the constructor. You can then use the detect and decode method to detect and decode QR codes in an image. This method takes an image as input and returns the decoded data, as well as the bounding boxes around the detected QR codes. You can then use the `cv2.rectangle` function to draw the bounding boxes on the image.

Here's an example code snippet that demonstrates how to perform QR code detection using OpenCV for an input image:

```python
import cv2

# QR detector
qcd = cv2.QRCodeDetector()

# read the image

frame = cv2.imread('QR.png')

ret_qr, decoded_info, points, _ = qcd.detectAndDecodeMulti(frame)
if ret_qr:
    for s, p in zip(decoded_info, points):
        """
        s = decoded_info: This is a list of decoded QR codes and their corresponding information.
        p = points: This is a list of lists, where each sublist contains four (x, y) coordinates that represent the corners of a detected QR code in the image.
        """
        if s:
            print(s)
            color = (0, 255, 0)
        else:
            color = (0, 0, 255)

        # Put the date and time on the frame
        font = cv2.FONT_HERSHEY_SIMPLEX
        cv2.putText(frame, s, (2, 15), font, .5, (0, 255, 0), 1, cv2.LINE_AA)
        frame = cv2.polylines(frame, [p.astype(int)], True, color, 8)
cv2.imshow("QR code", frame)

#close the function
cv2.waitKey(0)
cv2.destroyAllWindows()
```

Refer to the following figure for QR code detection in images using OpenCV:

Figure 8.8: QR code detection in image using OpenCV

Here's an example code snippet that demonstrates how to perform QR code detection using OpenCV for an input video:

```
import cv2

delay = 1
window_name = 'OpenCV QR Code'

qcd = cv2.QRCodeDetector()
cap = cv2.VideoCapture(0)

while True:
    ret, frame = cap.read()

    if ret:
        ret_qr, decoded_info, points, _ = qcd.
        detectAndDecodeMulti(frame)
```

```
        if ret_qr:
            for s, p in zip(decoded_info, points):
                if s:
                    print(s)
                    color = (0, 255, 0)
                else:
                    color = (0, 0, 255)
                frame = cv2.polylines(frame, [p.astype(int)], True,
                    color, 8)
            cv2.imshow(window_name, frame)
    else: break
    # Exit on the Q key
    if cv2.waitKey(delay) & 0xFF == ord('q'):
        break

# Release the capture and destroy all windows
cap.release()
cv2.destroyAllWindows()
```

Refer to the following figure for QR code detection in video using OpenCV:

Figure 8.9: QR code detection in video using OpenCV

Overall, QR code detection using OpenCV is a complex process that involves several steps of image processing and computer vision. However, with the right tools and techniques, it is possible to accurately detect and decode QR codes in a variety of applications.

Optical Character Recognition Using OpenCV

OCR (Optical Character Recognition) is a technology that allows computers to recognize and extract text from images, such as scanned documents or photographs. OCR technology is widely used in various applications, such as digitizing printed books, recognizing license plates, and extracting data from forms.

OpenCV (Open Source Computer Vision) is a popular open-source library for computer vision and image processing. OpenCV provides a wide range of functions and tools for image processing, including image filtering, segmentation, feature detection, and object recognition.

In the context of OCR, OpenCV can be used to preprocess images and extract text regions, which can then be passed to an OCR engine or algorithm for recognition. Some of the key steps in an OCR pipeline using OpenCV may include:

Image preprocessing: This may involve techniques such as image binarization, noise reduction, and edge detection to enhance the text regions and remove unwanted elements from the image.

- **Text region detection:** This involves identifying the regions of the image that contain text. This can be done using techniques such as connected component analysis, contour detection, or machine learning-based approaches.
- **Text segmentation:** This involves separating the text regions into individual characters or words. This can involve techniques such as blob analysis or morphological operations.
- **Recognizing the characters:** This involves passing the segmented characters or words to an OCR engine or algorithm, which can recognize the text and convert it into machine-readable form.

OpenCV provides a wide range of tools and functions that can be used for each of these steps, as well as for post-processing and analysis of the recognized text. Overall, OpenCV is a powerful tool for OCR, as it provides a flexible and customizable framework for preprocessing and analyzing images, which can improve the accuracy and efficiency of OCR algorithms.

Here's some basic code using images for OCR (Optical Character Recognition).

> **NOTE: You'll need to install pytesseract and the Tesseract OCR engine for this code to work.**

```
import cv2
import pytesseract
pytesseract.pytesseract.tesseract_cmd = r'C:/Program Files/
Tesseract-OCR/tesseract.exe'

# read image using OpenCV
img = cv2.imread('invoice.jpg')
img = cv2.cvtColor(img, cv2.COLOR_BGR2RGB)

# perform OCR using pytesseract
print(pytesseract.image_to_string(img))

# Detecting Characters
hImg, wImg,_ = img.shape
boxes = pytesseract.image_to_boxes(img)
for b in boxes.splitlines():
    b = b.split(' ')
    x, y, w, h = int(b[1]), int(b[2]), int(b[3]), int(b[4])
    cv2.rectangle(img, (x,hImg- y), (w,hImg- h), (50, 50, 255), 2)
    #cv2.putText(img,b[0],(x,hImg- y+25),cv2.FONT_HERSHEY_
    SIMPLEX,1,(50,50,255),2)

img = cv2.resize(img, (640, 480))
cv2.imshow('img', img)
cv2.waitKey(0)
cv2.destroyAllWindows()
```

Explanation:

- Import the necessary libraries, OpenCV and tesseract.
- Read the image using OpenCV's **imread()** function.
- Convert the image from BGR to RGB using OpenCV's cvtColor function.
- Use **pytesseract's image_to_string** function to perform OCR on the dilated image. The language used here is eng (English).

- Print the extracted text.
- Fetch the box values from Pytesseract and draw the box over the image using the box coordinates.

Refer to the following figure for OCR detection in images using OpenCV:

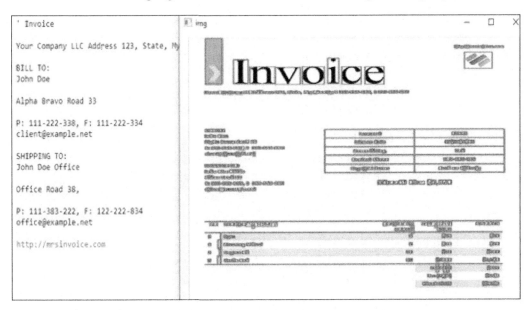

Figure 8.10: *OCR detection in image using OpenCV*

Here's some basic code using videos for OCR:

```
import cv2
import pytesseract

pytesseract.pytesseract.tesseract_cmd = r'C:/Program Files/Tesseract-OCR/tesseract.exe'

## load the video
cap = cv2.VideoCapture('text_vid.webm')
cap.set(3,640)
cap.set(4,480)

# capture the Screen value
def captureScreen(bbox=(300,300,1500,1000)):
    capScr = np.array(ImageGrab.grab(bbox))
    capScr = cv2.cvtColor(capScr, cv2.COLOR_RGB2BGR)
    return capScr
```

```python
while True:
    timer = cv2.getTickCount()
    ret,img = cap.read()

    if not ret: break

    #DETECTING CHARACTERES
    hImg, wImg,_ = img.shape
    boxes = pytesseract.image_to_boxes(img)

    # Detecting Characters
    for b in boxes.splitlines():

        b = b.split(' ')
        #Draw the rectangle the over the text in video
        x, y, w, h = int(b[1]), int(b[2]), int(b[3]), int(b[4])
        cv2.rectangle(img, (x,hImg- y), (w,hImg- h), (50, 50, 255),
2)

        #Draw the text the over the video
        cv2.putText(img,b[0],(x,hImg- y+25),cv2.FONT_HERSHEY_
        SIMPLEX,1,(50,50,255),2)

    fps = cv2.getTickFrequency() / (cv2.getTickCount() - timer);
    cv2.putText(img, str(int(fps)), (75, 40), cv2.FONT_HERSHEY_
    SIMPLEX, 0.7, (20,230,20), 2);

    # resize and display the frame
    img = cv2.resize(img, (640, 540))
    cv2.imshow("Text Detection",img)

    # press 'q' key stops the process
    if cv2.waitKey(1) & 0xFF == ord('q'):
        break

cap.release()
cv2.destroyAllWindows()
```

Explanation:

- Import the necessary libraries, OpenCV and **pytesseract**.
- Read the video using OpenCV's **VideoCapture()** function.
- Convert the image to BGB to RGB using OpenCV's **cvtColor** function.

- Use pytesseract's `image_to_string` function to perform OCR on the dilated image. The language used here is eng (English).
- Print the extracted text.
- Fetch the box values from `pytesseract` and draw the box over the video using the box coordinates.

Refer to the following figure for OCR detection in video using OpenCV:

Figure 8.11: *OCR detection in video using OpenCV*

Conclusion

In this chapter, we have discussed image segmentation techniques, QR code recognition using image and video as input, and optical character recognition using OpenCV. We will also discuss the detailed introduction to Haar Cascade Classifiers and their use in face and eye detection using image and video as input with OpenCV and Python programming language.

In the next chapter, we will discuss a basic introduction to Deep Learning and its algorithms along with their real-time project explanation using OpenCV.

Points to Remember

Install pytesseract to run the optical character recognition code.

```
! pip install pytesseract
```

Download the haarcascades.xml file from Haar Cascade GitHub.

https://github.com/opencv/opencv/tree/master/data/haarcascades

References

OCR with Tesseract

https://nanonets.com/blog/ocr-with-tesseract/

CHAPTER 9

Introduction to Deep Learning with OpenCV

Introduction

In this chapter, we will cover the introduction to machine learning, deep learning concepts and their architectures. We will also discuss deep learning projects using TensorFlow, OpenCV and Python programming languages.

Structure

In this chapter, we will cover the following topics:

- Introduction to machine learning
- Introduction to deep learning
- Artificial neural networks
- Introduction to deep learning in OpenCV
- Integration of OpenCV with robotics
- Iris dataset in TensorFlow
- Fashion-MNIST in TensorFlow
- Digit recognition in TensorFlow with OpenCV
- Dog vs. cat classification in TensorFlow with OpenCV

Introduction to Machine Learning

Machine learning is a subfield of artificial intelligence (AI) that focuses on designing algorithms that enable computers to learn from and make predictions or decisions based on data. Machine learning techniques are widely used in computer vision applications, including image classification, object detection, and tracking.

In this introduction to machine learning with OpenCV, we'll cover the basic theory behind some of these algorithms and demonstrate how to use them in practice.

Machine learning is the study of algorithms that can learn from and make predictions on data. In computer vision, machine learning is often used to recognize patterns in images, classify objects, and segment images into regions.

One popular approach to machine learning is called supervised learning, which involves training a model on a labeled dataset to predict the correct label for new, unseen data. OpenCV provides several algorithms for supervised learning, including **k-nearest neighbors (k-NN)**, **support vector machines (SVMs)**, and decision trees.

Another common approach to machine learning is unsupervised learning, where the goal is to find patterns in the data without any prior knowledge of the labels. One example of unsupervised learning is clustering, where the algorithm groups similar data points together. OpenCV provides several clustering algorithms, such as k-means and hierarchical clustering.

Types of machine learning

Machine learning can be broadly categorized into three types:

Supervised learning: Supervised learning is the most common type of machine learning. In this type, the algorithm is trained on a labeled dataset, where the correct outputs are already known. The model learns to map the input data to the correct output labels so that when it is presented with new, unseen data, it can predict the corresponding output labels.

- **Unsupervised learning:** Unsupervised learning is used when there is no labeled dataset available. In this type of machine learning, the algorithm tries to find patterns and relationships in the input data, without any prior knowledge of the correct output labels. The model identifies clusters of data points that are similar to each other and groups them.

- **Reinforcement learning:** Reinforcement learning is a type of machine learning where the algorithm learns through trial and error. In this type, the algorithm is trained to make decisions based on the feedback it receives from its environment. The model receives a reward for making a correct decision and a penalty for making an incorrect decision. The objective of the model is to learn to make the best decisions possible and to maximize the rewards received.

Refer to the following figure for types of machine learning:

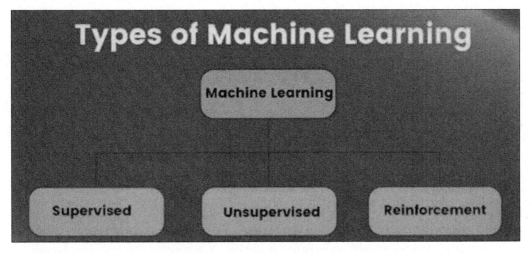

Figure 9.1: *Types of machine learning*

Here are some subtopics we'll cover in this introduction:

Preprocessing data for machine learning: Before training a machine learning model, it's often necessary to pre-process the data to make it more suitable for learning. We'll cover techniques such as normalization, feature scaling, and feature extraction.

- **k-Nearest Neighbors (k-NN) classification:** k-NN is a simple yet powerful algorithm for classification that can be used for image recognition. We'll cover how to train a k-NN classifier and use it for object recognition.
- **Support vector machines (SVMs) classification:** SVMs are powerful algorithms for classification that can be used for image recognition, object detection, and more. We'll cover how to train an SVM classifier and use it for object recognition.
- **Decision trees:** Decision trees are a simple yet powerful algorithm for classification that can be used for image recognition. We'll cover how to train a decision tree classifier and use it for object recognition.
- **Principal component analysis (PCA):** PCA is a technique for dimensionality reduction that can be used to pre-process data for machine learning. We'll cover how to use PCA to reduce the dimensionality of image features.
- **Clustering:** Clustering is an unsupervised learning technique that can be used to find patterns in data without any prior knowledge of the

labels. We'll cover how to use k-means and hierarchical clustering for image segmentation.

- **Neural networks:** Neural networks are powerful machine learning algorithms that can be used for image recognition, object detection, and more. We'll cover the basic theory behind neural networks and how to use them for image recognition.

Overall, this introduction to machine learning with OpenCV will provide a foundation for understanding how to use machine learning algorithms for computer vision applications.

Introduction to Deep Learning

Introduction to deep Learning is a course or study program that aims to provide an overview of deep learning and its applications. Deep learning is a subset of machine learning that uses artificial neural networks with multiple layers to learn from data and make predictions or decisions. It is a subfield of machine learning that uses neural networks to perform complex tasks such as image and speech recognition, natural language processing, and decision-making. It is a type of **artificial intelligence (AI)** that is based on the structure and function of the human brain. The goal of deep learning is to enable machines to learn and make decisions on their own without being explicitly programmed to do so.

The success of deep learning is primarily attributed to the development of **artificial neural networks (ANNs)** that simulate the way the human brain works. ANNs consist of multiple layers of interconnected nodes that process input data and produce output based on learned patterns. These networks can be trained using a variety of algorithms such as backpropagation, which adjusts the weights of connections between nodes to minimize the error between the predicted and actual outputs.

OpenCV is an open-source library for computer vision and machine learning that provides a variety of tools and algorithms for deep learning. It supports popular deep learning frameworks such as TensorFlow and Keras and provides tools for image and video processing, object detection, and more. With OpenCV, developers can build and train their deep-learning models or use pre-trained models to solve complex problems.

Throughout the course, learners are provided with hands-on exercises and projects that allow them to apply the concepts learned in each section. By the end of the course, learners should have a basic understanding of deep learning and its applications, as well as the skills to implement and train deep neural networks for their projects.

Artificial Neural Networks

Artificial neural networks (ANNs) is a computational approach inspired by the structure and function of the human brain. ANNs consist of interconnected nodes or neurons that process information in parallel and learn from examples through a training process.

The structure of an ANN can be visualized as a graph, with nodes representing neurons and edges representing the connections between them. Typically, ANNs consist of three types of layers: input, hidden, and output. The input layer receives the raw data, while the output layer produces the final output of the network. The hidden layers are responsible for processing the input and generating the output.

Each neuron in an ANN receives input from other neurons and applies a mathematical function to produce an output. The output of a neuron is then fed as input to other neurons in the network. The function that a neuron applies is typically a weighted sum of the inputs, followed by a nonlinear activation function that introduces nonlinearity into the network.

The weights in an ANN determine the strength of the connections between neurons and are learned through a training process that involves minimizing a loss function. The loss function measures the difference between the predicted output of the network and the true output, and the training process updates the weights to minimize this difference.

Types of neural networks

In this explanation, we will cover the most common types of ANNs and how they work:

Feedforward neural networks: Feedforward neural networks are the simplest type of ANNs. They consist of three layers: the input layer, one or more hidden layers, and finally the output layer. Each neuron in the input layer is connected to every neuron in the first hidden layer, and each neuron in the hidden layers is connected to every neuron in the next layer. The output of the final layer represents the prediction or classification made by the network.

Refer to the following figure for feedforward neural networks:

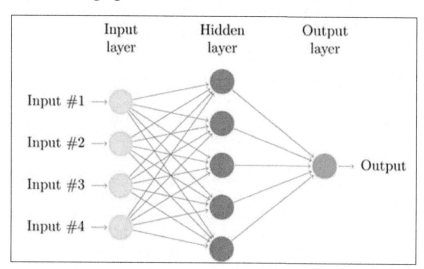

Figure 9.2: *Feedforward neural networks*

Convolutional neural networks (CNNs): CNNs are specifically designed for processing two-dimensional data, such as images. They consist of multiple layers of filters that learn to detect specific features in an image, such as edges, corners, and textures. The output of each filter is then passed through a non-linear activation function, such as the **Rectified Linear Unit (ReLU)**, before being fed into the next layer. The final layer of a CNN is typically a fully connected layer that performs the actual classification.

Refer to the following figure for convolutional neural networks:

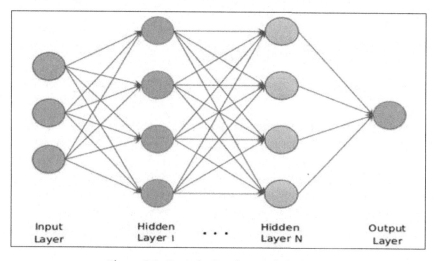

Figure 9.3: *Convolutional neural networks*

Recurrent neural networks (RNNs): RNNs are designed for processing sequential data, such as speech or text. They consist of a hidden state that is passed from one-time step to the next, allowing the network to remember information from previous time steps. The most common type of RNN is the **Long Short-Term Memory (LSTM)** network, which can selectively forget or remember information from previous time steps.

Refer to the following figure for recurrent neural networks:

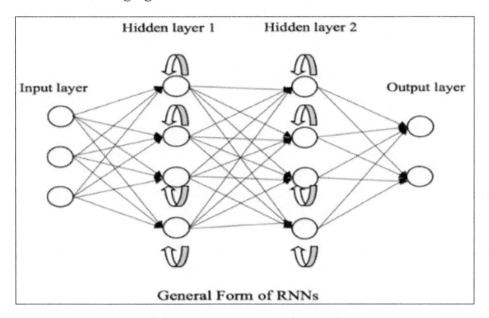

Figure 9.4: Recurrent neural networks

Autoencoders: Autoencoders are a type of neural network that is used for unsupervised learning, meaning that they learn to extract features from data without the need for labeled examples. They consist of two layers which are the encoder and decoder, and their function is an encoder network that compresses the input data into a lower dimensional and a decoder network that reconstructs the original data from the compressed. Autoencoders are often used for tasks such as data compression and anomaly detection.

Refer to the following figure for Autoencoders:

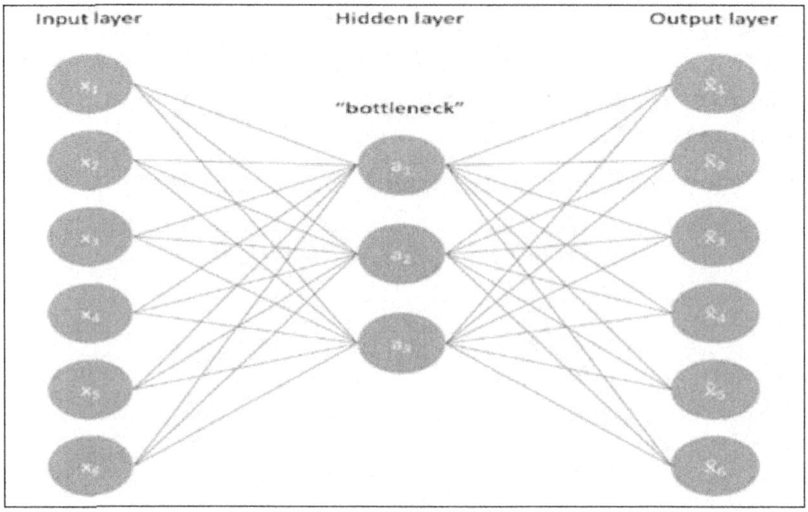

Figure 9.5: Autoencoders architecture

Generative adversarial networks (GANs): GANs are a type of neural network that is used for generative modeling, meaning that they learn to generate new data that is similar to a given dataset. GANs consist of two networks: a generator network that generates new data, and a discriminator network that tries to distinguish between the generated data and real data. The two networks are trained in an adversarial manner, with the generator trying to generate data that fools the discriminator, and the discriminator trying to correctly identify the generated data.

Refer to the following figure for generative adversarial networks:

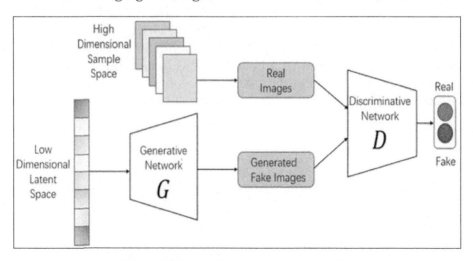

Figure 9.6: Generative adversarial networks

In summary, artificial neural networks are a powerful tool for solving a wide range of machine-learning tasks.

Neural network architecture

Neural network architecture refers to the arrangement of neurons and layers that make up the network. The architecture of a neural network can have a significant impact on its performance and ability to learn complex patterns in data. There are several types of neural network architectures, including:

Single-layer perceptron: The single-layer perceptron is the simplest type of neural network, consisting of a single layer of neurons that are connected to the input and output layers. It is used for linearly separable problems, such as binary classification.

- **Multi-layer perceptron (MLP):** The MLP is a type of feedforward neural network that consists of multiple layers of neurons, including an input layer, one or more hidden layers, and an output layer. The neurons in each layer are fully connected to the neurons in the previous and next layers, and each neuron applies an activation function to its input.

- **Convolutional neural network (CNN):** The CNN is a type of neural network that is designed to work with image data. It consists of multiple convolutional layers, which apply a set of filters to the input image, and pooling layers, which reduce the spatial dimensions of the output of the convolutional layers. The output of the last pooling layer is passed through one or more fully connected layers to produce the final output.

- **Recurrent neural network (RNN):** The RNN is a type of neural network that is designed to work with sequential data, such as text or speech. It uses feedback loops to pass information from one time step to the next, allowing it to capture temporal dependencies in the data. The output of each time step is passed through one or more fully connected layers to produce the final output.

Overall, the architecture of a neural network depends on the nature of the data and the task at hand. The choice of architecture can have a significant impact on the performance of the network, and different architectures are appropriate for different types of problems.

Activation functions

Activation functions are mathematical functions applied to the output of each neuron in a neural network. They introduce non-linearity into the network, which allows it to learn complex patterns and relationships in the data.

There are several types of activation functions used in neural networks, including:

- **Sigmoid:** The sigmoid function is a commonly used activation function that maps the output of a neuron to a value between 0 and 1. It is used in binary classification problems where the output should be either 0 or 1.
- **Hyperbolic tangent (tanh):** The hyperbolic tangent function is similar to the sigmoid function but maps the output to a value between -1 and 1. It is commonly used in feedforward neural networks for multiclass classification problems.
- **Rectified linear unit (ReLU):** The ReLU function is a non-linear activation function that maps the output of a neuron to the maximum of 0 and the input value. It is commonly used in deep neural networks and has been shown to improve their performance by reducing the problem of vanishing gradients.
- **Leaky ReLU:** The Leaky ReLU function is a variant of the ReLU function that allows small negative values to pass through the neuron. It is used to address the problem of "dead" neurons, which can occur when the ReLU function outputs 0 for all inputs.
- **Exponential linear unit (ELU):** The ELU function is a variant of the ReLU function that allows negative values to pass through the neuron. It is used to address the problem of "dead" neurons and has been shown to improve the performance of deep neural networks.
- **Softmax:** The softmax function is used in the output layer of neural networks for multiclass classification problems. It maps the output of each neuron to a probability distribution over the different classes.

Refer to the following figure for types of Activation functions:

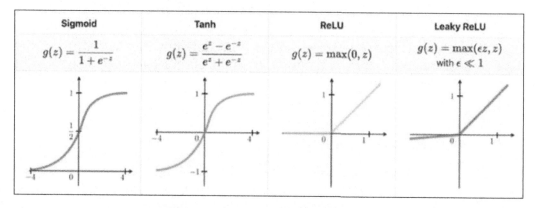

Figure 9.7: *Types of activation functions*

Overall, the choice of activation function can have a significant impact on the performance of a neural network, and different activation functions are appropriate for different types of problems.

Neural networks optimization techniques

Neural network optimization techniques are used to train the neural network and adjust the weights of the connections between neurons in order to minimize the error between the network's predictions and the actual output. Several optimization techniques can be used with neural networks, including:

- **Stochastic gradient descent (SGD):** SGD is a widely used optimization technique that updates the weights after each training example is processed. It uses the gradient of the loss function with respect to the weights to update the weights in the direction of the steepest descent.
- **Mini-batch gradient descent:** Mini-batch gradient descent is a variant of SGD that updates the weights after processing a small batch of training examples instead of a single example. This can lead to faster convergence and more stable training.
- **Momentum:** Momentum is a technique that adds a fraction of the previous weight update to the current weight update. This helps to accelerate convergence and smooth out the oscillations in the weight updates.
- **Adaptive learning rate methods:** Adaptive learning rate methods, such as AdaGrad, RMSProp, and Adam, adjust the learning rate of the optimization algorithm based on the history of the weight updates. This helps to prevent the learning rate from becoming too small or too large and can lead to faster convergence.
- **Regularization:** Regularization techniques, such as L1 and L2 regularization, add a penalty term to the loss function to prevent overfitting. This penalty term encourages the weights to be small, which helps to reduce the complexity of the model and prevents it from memorizing the training data.
- **Dropout:** Dropout is a technique that randomly drops out some neurons during training to prevent overfitting. This forces the network to learn more robust features and reduces the dependence of the network on any single neuron.

Overall, the choice of optimization technique can have a significant impact on the performance of a neural network, and different optimization techniques are appropriate for different types of problems.

Steps for training neural networks

Training deep neural networks refers to the process of adjusting the weights and biases of the network so that the output matches the target output as closely as possible. Deep neural networks are neural networks with multiple layers, and they require special techniques to be trained effectively. The training process involves the following steps:

Data preparation: The first step is to prepare the data by cleaning, preprocessing, and splitting it into training, validation, and test sets. The training set is used to train the network, the validation set is used to tune the hyperparameters of the network, and the test set is used to evaluate the performance of the network on unseen data.

1. **Initialization:** The weights and biases of the network are initialized randomly using a suitable initialization technique. The initial values can have a significant impact on the performance of the network, and it is important to choose an appropriate initialization technique.

2. **Forward propagation:** The input data is fed forward through the network, and the output of each layer is calculated using the weights and biases.

3. **Loss calculation:** The difference between the predicted output and the target output is calculated using a suitable loss function. The loss function measures how well the network is performing on the training data.

4. **Back propagation:** The error is backpropagated through the network, and the gradients of the loss function with respect to the weights and biases of each layer are calculated. This is done using the chain rule of calculus.

5. **Weight update:** The weights and biases of the network are updated using an optimization algorithm, such as stochastic gradient descent (SGD), to minimize the loss function. The optimization algorithm adjusts the weights and biases in the direction of the negative gradient of the loss function.

6. **Hyperparameter tuning:** The hyperparameters of the network, such as the learning rate, batch size, and regularization strength, are tuned using the validation set. This is done to find the values of the hyperparameters that result in the best performance on the validation set.

7. **Evaluation:** The performance of the network is evaluated on the test set using suitable metrics such as accuracy, precision, recall, and F1 score.

This step is important to ensure that the network is able to generalize well to unseen data.

The training process is repeated for multiple epochs until the network converges to a stable solution. Training deep neural networks can be computationally expensive and time-consuming, and it requires careful tuning of the hyperparameters to achieve the best performance.

Deep learning frameworks

Keras, TensorFlow, and PyTorch are three of the most popular open-source libraries for building and training deep learning models:

Keras: Keras is a high-level neural network API written in Python. It is designed to enable fast experimentation with deep neural networks, with a focus on user-friendliness, modularity, and extensibility. Keras supports both convolutional neural networks (CNNs) and recurrent neural networks (RNNs) and can be run on top of either TensorFlow or Theano.

Keras provides a simple and intuitive interface for building and training neural networks. It allows you to easily construct models by stacking layers, and it provides a range of pre-built layers, including convolutional layers, pooling layers, and recurrent layers. Keras also supports a range of loss functions, optimizers, and metrics, which makes it easy to configure and train your models.

TensorFlow: TensorFlow is an open-source deep learning framework developed by Google. It is one of the most popular deep-learning libraries and is widely used in research and industry. TensorFlow is highly scalable and can run on a range of devices, including CPUs, GPUs, and TPUs.

TensorFlow provides a flexible and efficient way to build and train deep learning models. It includes a range of pre-built layers, loss functions, and optimizers, as well as support for custom layers and models. TensorFlow also includes a range of high-level APIs, including Keras, which makes it easy to get started with deep learning.

PyTorch: PyTorch is an open-source deep learning framework developed by Facebook. It is designed to be easy to use and highly efficient, with a focus on dynamic computation graphs. PyTorch is particularly well-suited for building and training deep learning models for research purposes.

PyTorch provides a range of pre-built modules, including convolutional layers, pooling layers, and recurrent layers, as well as support for custom modules. PyTorch also includes a range of loss functions and optimizers, as well as support for custom loss functions and optimizers. PyTorch's dynamic computation graph makes it easy to build and debug models, as well as to incorporate new ideas and techniques.

Keras, TensorFlow, and PyTorch are three of the most popular deep-learning libraries. They each have their strengths and weaknesses, and the choice of which one to use depends on your specific needs and requirements. However, all three libraries provide a powerful and flexible way to build and train deep learning models, and they are all well-supported by the community.

Deep learning applications

Deep learning is a subfield of machine learning that has revolutionized the field of artificial intelligence in recent years. Its ability to learn from large amounts of data and automatically discover complex patterns and relationships has led to a wide range of applications in various fields. Some of the most common applications of deep learning are:

Computer vision: Deep learning has had a significant impact on computer vision, with applications such as object detection, image classification, and facial recognition. CNNs are commonly used in computer vision tasks, and they have achieved state-of-the-art performance on benchmark datasets.

- **Natural language processing (NLP):** Deep learning has also had a significant impact on NLP, with applications such as sentiment analysis, language translation, and chatbots. RNNs and transformer models are commonly used in NLP tasks, and they have achieved state-of-the-art performance on benchmark datasets.
- **Speech recognition:** Deep learning has been used to improve the accuracy of speech recognition systems, with applications such as speech-to-text transcription, speaker identification, and voice assistant systems.
- **Healthcare:** Deep learning has the potential to revolutionize the healthcare industry, with applications such as disease diagnosis, drug discovery, and personalized medicine. Deep learning models can analyze medical images, electronic health records, and genomic data to discover new insights and improve patient outcomes.
- **Autonomous vehicles:** Deep learning has been used to develop autonomous vehicles, with applications such as object detection, lane detection, and pedestrian detection. Deep learning models can analyze sensor data from cameras, lidar, and radar to help vehicles navigate safely and avoid collisions.

- **Robotics:** Deep learning has been used in robotics applications such as object recognition, motion planning, and control. Deep learning models can analyze sensor data from cameras and other sensors to help robots interact with their environment and perform complex tasks.

Overall, deep learning has a wide range of applications in various fields, and its potential for solving complex problems and improving outcomes is continuing to grow as the field advances.

Introduction to Deep Learning in OpenCV

Introduction to deep learning with OpenCV is a course that aims to introduce learners to the basics of deep learning and its application in computer vision using the OpenCV library. The course is designed for individuals who have a basic understanding of Python programming and are interested in learning about deep learning.

Throughout the course, learners are provided with hands-on exercises and projects that allow them to apply the concepts learned in each section. By the end of the course, learners should have a basic understanding of deep learning and its application in computer vision using OpenCV.

Neural networks in the image and video analytics

Neural networks are a type of machine learning algorithm that is widely used in image and video analytics. In image and video analytics, neural networks are used to recognize patterns and features in images and videos and to make predictions or decisions based on that information.

CNNs are a type of neural network that is commonly used in image and video analytics. CNNs are designed to work with image data and are able to learn the important features of an image by filtering and processing it through multiple layers of neurons. This makes them useful for tasks such as image classification, object detection, and segmentation.

In image classification, a CNN is trained to recognize different classes of images, such as animals or vehicles. The network is fed a large dataset of labeled images and is trained to identify the features that are most important for distinguishing between the different classes.

In image and video analytics, neural networks are used to extract meaningful features from raw visual data. This is typically done using a technique called CNNs, which are designed to process two-dimensional data such as images and videos. CNNs work by applying a set of filters to the input image, which detects various features such as edges, corners, and textures. The output of each filter is then passed through a non-linear activation function, which helps to identify patterns and relationships between the features.

Once the features have been extracted from the visual data, they can be used for a variety of tasks such as object detection, classification, and segmentation. For example, in object detection, a neural network can be trained to recognize the presence of specific objects in an image or video by detecting the features that are commonly associated with those objects. Similarly, in image segmentation, a neural network can be used to identify the boundaries between different objects in an image by detecting the features that distinguish them.

Object detection is another task that is commonly performed using neural networks in image and video analytics. In object detection, a CNN is used to identify the location and size of objects within an image or video. This is typically done by training the network to recognize a set of object classes and then using it to detect those objects within an image or video.

Neural networks are also used in video analytics to perform tasks such as action recognition and video segmentation. In action recognition, a CNN is trained to recognize different actions or activities within a video, such as walking, running, or jumping. In video segmentation, a CNN is used to separate the different objects or regions within a video and assign them to different classes or categories.

Overall, neural networks are a powerful tool for image and video analytics and have been used to achieve state-of-the-art results on a wide range of tasks in these fields.

Image classification with deep neural networks

Image classification with deep neural networks is a task in machine learning that involves training a model to correctly classify images into different categories. This task is achieved using a type of neural network called a convolutional neural network, which is specifically designed to work with image data.

CNNs consist of multiple layers that are responsible for learning and extracting features from the input images. The first layer is typically a convolutional layer, which applies a set of filters to the input image to extract spatial features. This is followed by a pooling layer, which reduces the spatial dimensions of the output of the convolutional layer.

After several convolutional and pooling layers, the output is flattened and passed through one or more fully connected layers, which perform classification on the features extracted by the convolutional layers. The final layer typically uses a softmax activation function to output the probability distribution of the input image belonging to each of the predefined categories.

The training of a CNN involves a process known as backpropagation, which involves calculating the gradient of the loss function with respect to the parameters of the network and using this gradient to update the parameters via stochastic gradient descent.

The loss function used for image classification is typically cross-entropy loss, which compares the predicted probability distribution of the model with the true labels and penalizes the model for incorrect predictions.

Refer to the following figure for image classification using neural networks:

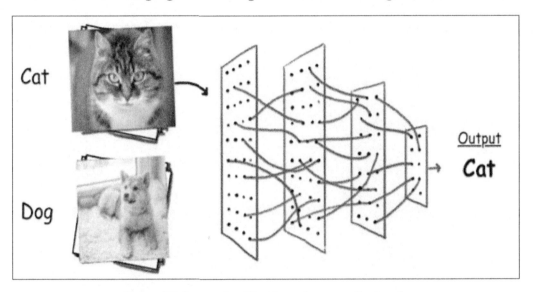

Figure 9.8: *Image classification using neural networks*

Once the CNN is trained, it can be used to classify new images into predefined categories. The performance of the CNN is evaluated on a test set of images, which were not used during training. The metrics used to evaluate the performance of the CNN include accuracy, precision, recall, and F1 score.

Object detection with neural networks

Object detection with neural networks is a task in machine learning that involves identifying the location and category of objects within an image. This task is achieved using a type of neural network called an object detection network, which is typically composed of two main components: a **region proposal network (RPN)** and a classification network.

The RPN is responsible for generating proposals for object locations within the image. It does this by sliding a small window (or "anchor") across the input image and predicting the probability of an object being present at each anchor location. It also predicts the coordinates of a bounding box around the object if an object is detected. These proposals are then passed to the classification network for further processing.

The classification network is responsible for assigning a class label to each proposal generated by the RPN. It takes the proposed region of the image and extracts features using a CNN, similar to the CNN used for image classification. The extracted features are then fed into one or more fully connected layers for classification. The final output is a list of bounding boxes around objects along with their corresponding class labels.

Refer to the following figure for object classification vs. detection with neural networks:

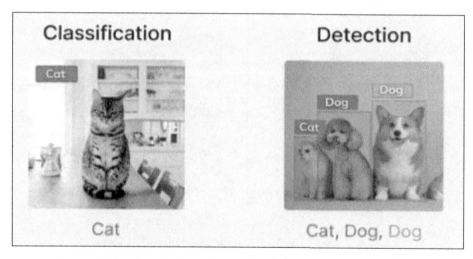

Figure 9.9: *Object classification vs. detection with neural networks*

The training of an object detection network involves a process known as joint training, which involves optimizing the parameters of both the RPN and the classification network. The loss function used for object detection is typically a combination of the cross-entropy loss for classification and a localization loss for the bounding box predictions.

There are several popular object detection networks in use today, including Faster R-CNN, **YOLO (You Only Look Once)**, and **SSD (Single Shot Detector)**. These networks differ in their architecture and the trade-offs they make between speed and accuracy.

Once the object detection network is trained, it can be used to detect objects in new images. The performance of the network is evaluated using metrics such as **mean average precision (mAP)**, which measures the accuracy of both object detection and classification.

Face detection and recognition with neural networks

Face detection and recognition are two related but distinct computer vision tasks that involve detecting and recognizing human faces in images or video streams.

Face detection is the process of locating the presence of human faces in images or videos. It is typically achieved using machine learning algorithms that are trained on large datasets of labeled images. Face detection is a challenging problem due to the variability of human faces, including variations in pose, expression, lighting, and occlusions.

There are many face detection algorithms available, but one of the most popular and effective methods is the Viola-Jones algorithm. This algorithm uses Haar cascades, which are a type of classifier that can detect the presence of specific features in an image. The Viola-Jones algorithm works by scanning the image with a sliding window and applying the Haar cascades to each sub-image to detect the presence of faces.

Once the faces are detected, the next step is to recognize them. Face recognition is the process of identifying a person based on their facial features. It is also typically achieved using machine learning algorithms that are trained on labeled datasets. Face recognition is a challenging problem due to the variability of facial features and the need to handle differences in lighting, pose, and expression.

There are several approaches to face recognition, including feature-based methods and deep learning-based methods. Feature-based methods extract features from the face, such as the distance between the eyes or the shape of the nose, and use these features to identify the person. Deep learning-based methods use neural networks to learn the features directly from the images.

One popular deep learning-based method for face recognition is the FaceNet model, which uses a convolutional neural network to extract a high-dimensional feature vector from the face image. The feature vector is then compared to a database of known faces to identify the person.

Another popular approach to face recognition is the use of Eigenfaces, which are a set of principal components of the face images that capture the variability in the dataset. The Eigenfaces can be used to represent each face as a linear combination of these principal components, and the similarity between two faces can be computed as the distance between their respective Eigenface representations.

In recent years, deep learning-based methods have become state-of-the-art for face detection and recognition. These methods are able to achieve high accuracy on large-scale datasets, and they can handle a wide range of variations in the input data.

One of the key challenges in face detection and recognition is privacy and security concerns. The use of facial recognition technology has raised concerns about the potential for misuse, including the possibility of mass surveillance and violation of personal privacy. To address these concerns, several countries have introduced regulations governing the use of facial recognition technology.

In conclusion, face detection and recognition are important computer vision tasks that have a wide range of applications, from security and surveillance to social media and entertainment. While there are many challenges associated with these tasks, advances in machine learning and deep learning have enabled significant progress in recent years, and these methods are likely to continue to improve in the future.

However, it is important to address the ethical and legal concerns associated with the use of facial recognition technology and to ensure that it is used in a responsible and transparent manner.

Semantic segmentation in neural networks

Semantic segmentation is a task in computer vision that involves assigning a label to each pixel in an image, thereby dividing the image into regions or segments that correspond to meaningful objects or parts of objects. This task is achieved using a type of neural network called a semantic segmentation network, which is specifically designed to work with image data.

The architecture of a semantic segmentation network is similar to that of a convolutional neural network (CNN), with additional layers that are responsible for producing a dense output of predicted labels for each pixel in the input image. The network typically consists of an encoder, which extracts features from the input image using convolutional and pooling layers, and a decoder, which upsamples the feature maps and produces a dense output of predicted labels.

The encoder part of the network is typically based on a pre-trained CNN such as VGG or ResNet, which has been trained on a large dataset of images for image classification or object detection tasks. The decoder part of the network uses a series of upsampling layers to increase the spatial resolution of the feature maps and produce a dense output of predicted labels for each pixel in the input image.

Refer to the following figure for semantic segmentation in neural networks:

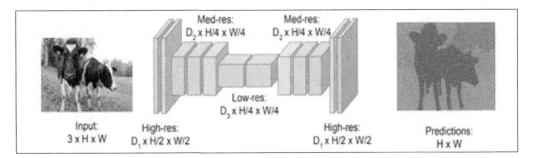

Figure 9.10: Semantic segmentation in neural networks

The training of a semantic segmentation network involves a process known as backpropagation, which involves calculating the gradient of the loss function with respect to the parameters of the network and using this gradient to update the parameters via stochastic gradient descent. The loss function used for semantic segmentation is typically cross-entropy loss, which compares the predicted label for each pixel with the true label and penalizes the network for incorrect predictions.

Once the semantic segmentation network is trained, it can be used to segment new images into meaningful objects or parts of objects. The performance of the network is evaluated using metrics such as **mean intersection over union (mIoU)**, which measures the similarity between the predicted segmentation and the ground truth segmentation for a set of images.

There are several popular semantic segmentation networks in use today, including U-Net, SegNet, and DeepLab. These networks differ in their architecture and the trade-offs they make between speed and accuracy.

Generative adversarial networks

Generative adversarial networks (GANs) are a type of deep learning model that can generate new data that is similar to a given dataset. The basic idea behind GANs is to have two neural networks trained together: a generator network and a discriminator network.

The generator network takes as input a random noise vector and produces a new sample that is similar to the training data. The discriminator network takes as input a sample from either the training data or the generator network and tries to classify it as real (from the training data) or fake (from the generator network). The two networks are trained together in a game-like setting, where the generator network tries to fool the discriminator network and the discriminator network tries to distinguish between real and fake samples.

During training, the generator network learns to produce samples that are increasingly difficult for the discriminator network to distinguish from real samples. At the same time, the discriminator network becomes better at distinguishing between real and fake samples. The training process continues until the generator network produces samples that are indistinguishable from real samples.

GANs have been used to generate a wide variety of data types, including images, music, and text. In the case of image generation, the generator network typically produces an image by generating pixel values for each pixel in the image. The discriminator network then tries to classify the image as real or fake. The two networks are trained together in a way that encourages the generator network to produce realistic images.

GANs have also been used for other tasks, such as image-to-image translation and style transfer. In these tasks, the generator network takes as input an image from one domain (for example, a photograph) and produces an image in a different domain (for example, a painting). The discriminator network is trained to distinguish between images from the two domains, and the generator network is trained to produce images that are difficult for the discriminator network to classify.

GANs are a powerful tool for generating new data that is similar to a given dataset. However, they can be difficult to train and require careful tuning of hyperparameters. There are also several variants of GANs, including conditional GANs and cycle-consistent GANs, which are designed to address specific challenges in GAN training.

Integration of OpenCV with Robotics

OpenCV can be used in conjunction with robotics to provide computer vision capabilities to robots. This integration can be used for a variety of tasks, such as object recognition, navigation, and obstacle avoidance. In this section, we will explore the different ways in which OpenCV can be integrated with robotics:

Object recognition: One of the primary applications of computer vision in robotics is object recognition. Robots need to be able to recognize objects in their environment so that they can interact with them appropriately. OpenCV provides a number of algorithms for object recognition, including feature detection and matching, Haar cascades, and deep learning-based approaches such as YOLO and SSD.

Navigation: Navigation is another important application of computer vision in robotics. Robots need to be able to navigate through their environment to reach their destination or complete a task. OpenCV can be used to provide visual feedback to the robot, which can help it navigate through complex environments. This can be achieved using techniques such as optical flow, stereo vision, and **SLAM (Simultaneous Localization and Mapping)**.

Obstacle avoidance: Obstacle avoidance is another important application of computer vision in robotics. Robots need to be able to detect and avoid obstacles in their environment to avoid collisions and navigate safely. OpenCV can be used to provide obstacle detection and tracking capabilities to the robot. This can be achieved using techniques such as background subtraction, edge detection, and contour detection.

Robot control: Once the robot has detected an object, navigated to it, and avoided any obstacles in its path, it needs to be able to interact with the object. OpenCV can be used to provide visual feedback to the robot to help it manipulate objects. This can be achieved using techniques such as object tracking and motion detection.

Integration with robot operating systems (ROS): Robot operating system (ROS) is an open-source framework for building robot applications. OpenCV can be integrated with ROS to provide computer vision capabilities to robots. This integration allows robots to receive visual feedback from their environment and make decisions based on that feedback.

In conclusion, the integration of OpenCV with robotics can provide a wide range of computer vision capabilities to robots, including object recognition, navigation, obstacle avoidance, robot control, and integration with **Robot Operating Systems (ROS)**. This integration can help robots operate more effectively and safely in complex environments.

Iris Dataset in TensorFlow

The iris dataset is popular in machine learning and data science. It consists of 150 samples of iris flowers, with 50 samples for each of three different species: Setosa, Versicolor, and Virginica. Each sample contains 4 features: the length and width of the sepals and petals, measured in centimeters.

TensorFlow is a popular open-source library for machine learning and deep learning. It provides a wide range of tools and functions for building and training machine learning models.

Here's an example of how the Iris dataset can be used with TensorFlow:

NOTE: Use Google Colab for this exercise.

Load the data: The first step is to load the Iris dataset into TensorFlow. This can be done using the `tf.keras.datasets` module, which provides a number of commonly used datasets.

1. **Preprocess** the data: After loading the data, it's important to preprocess it to ensure that it's in a suitable format for training the machine learning model. This may involve scaling the feature values to a common range, encoding the class labels as numerical values, and splitting the data into training and testing sets.

2. **Build the model**: Once the data has been preprocessed, the next step is to build a machine-learning model using TensorFlow. This can be done using the `tf.keras` module, which provides a high-level API for building and training deep learning models.

3. **Train the model**: After building the model, we can train it on the training data using the fit method. This involves specifying the number of epochs (iterations over the training data), the batch size (number of samples to process at once), and the validation data (to monitor the model's performance on unseen data).

4. **Evaluate the model**: After training the model, we can evaluate its performance on the test data using the evaluate method. This will return the loss and accuracy of the model on the test data.

```
import tensorflow as tf
from sklearn.datasets import load_iris
from sklearn.model_selection import train_test_split

# Load the iris dataset
iris_data = load_iris()
```

Refer to the following figure for the Iris dataset in TensorFlow:

Figure 9.11: *Iris dataset in TensorFlow*

```python
# Split the dataset into features (X) and labels (y)
X = iris_data.data
y = iris_data.target

# Split the data into training and testing sets
x_train, x_test, y_train, y_test = train_test_split(X, y, test_size=0.2, random_state=42)

(x_train, y_train), (x_test, y_test) = tf.keras.datasets.iris.load_data()

# Scale the feature values to a common range
x_train_scaled = (x_train - x_train.min(axis=0)) / (x_train.max(axis=0) - x_train.min(axis=0))
x_test_scaled = (x_test - x_train.min(axis=0)) / (x_train.max(axis=0) - x_train.min(axis=0))

# Encode the class labels as numerical values
y_train_encoded = tf.keras.utils.to_categorical(y_train)
y_test_encoded = tf.keras.utils.to_categorical(y_test)

model = tf.keras.Sequential([
    tf.keras.layers.Input(shape=(4,)),
    tf.keras.layers.Dense(16, activation='relu'),
    tf.keras.layers.Dense(3, activation='softmax')
])

model.compile(optimizer='adam',
              loss='categorical_crossentropy',
              metrics=['accuracy'])

history = model.fit(x_train_scaled, y_train_encoded,
                    epochs=100,
                    batch_size=16,
                    validation_data=(x_test_scaled, y_test_encoded))

loss, accuracy = model.evaluate(x_test_scaled, y_test_encoded)
print('Test loss:', loss)
print('Test accuracy:', accuracy)
```

Refer to the following figure for the Iris dataset model training and results:

```
Epoch 95/100
8/8 [==============================] - 0s 6ms/step - loss: 0.4234 - accuracy: 0.8833 - val_loss: 0.4006 - val_accuracy: 0.8667
Epoch 96/100
8/8 [==============================] - 0s 9ms/step - loss: 0.4207 - accuracy: 0.8917 - val_loss: 0.3977 - val_accuracy: 0.8667
Epoch 97/100
8/8 [==============================] - 0s 9ms/step - loss: 0.4182 - accuracy: 0.8917 - val_loss: 0.3953 - val_accuracy: 0.8667
Epoch 98/100
8/8 [==============================] - 0s 9ms/step - loss: 0.4161 - accuracy: 0.9000 - val_loss: 0.3934 - val_accuracy: 0.9000
Epoch 99/100
8/8 [==============================] - 0s 6ms/step - loss: 0.4137 - accuracy: 0.8917 - val_loss: 0.3909 - val_accuracy: 0.9000
Epoch 100/100
8/8 [==============================] - 0s 6ms/step - loss: 0.4111 - accuracy: 0.8917 - val_loss: 0.3879 - val_accuracy: 0.8667
1/1 [==============================] - 0s 28ms/step - loss: 0.3879 - accuracy: 0.8667
Test loss: 0.38791307806096869
Test accuracy: 0.8666666746139526
```

Figure 9.12: *Iris dataset model training and results*

In this code, we first import the necessary libraries, including TensorFlow and the Iris dataset from scikit-learn. We then split the dataset into training and testing sets using the `train_test_split` function.

Next, we define the model architecture using a sequential model with two dense layers, one with 16 units and ReLU activation, and another with three units and softmax activation. We then compile the model with the Adam optimizer and sparse categorical cross-entropy loss function.

We then train the model using the `fit` function, passing in the training data and specifying the number of epochs and validation split. Finally, we evaluate the model on the test set using the evaluate function and print the test accuracy.

This is just a basic example of how the Iris dataset can be used with TensorFlow. There are many other techniques and algorithms that can be used to improve the accuracy and performance of the model, such as regularization, dropout, and hyperparameter tuning.

Fashion-MNIST in TensorFlow

Fashion-MNIST is a dataset consisting of 70,000 grayscale images of 28x28 pixels, each representing one of ten different clothing categories. It was created as a more challenging alternative to the classic MNIST dataset, which consists of handwritten digits.

TensorFlow is a popular open-source machine learning framework that provides tools for building and training neural networks. It includes a variety of pre-built models and datasets, including Fashion-MNIST, which can be easily accessed and used for experimenting with different machine-learning techniques.

Using TensorFlow, you can load the Fashion-MNIST dataset and train a neural network to classify the clothing images into their respective categories. This involves defining the structure of the neural network, specifying the loss

Introduction to Deep Learning with OpenCV

function and optimization algorithm, and training the model using the training data.

Once the model is trained, you can evaluate its performance on a separate test set of images to see how well it generalizes to new data. TensorFlow also provides tools for visualizing the results and analyzing the performance of the model.

Here's an example code for training a Fashion-MNIST model using TensorFlow:

> **NOTE:** Use Google Colab for this exercise.

```
## Import necessary libraries
import tensorflow as tf
from tensorflow import keras
from tensorflow.keras import layers
import matplotlib.pyplot as plt

# Load the Fashion-MNIST dataset
(x_train, y_train), (x_test, y_test) = keras.datasets.fashion_mnist.load_data()

# visualize the loaded data
plt.figure(figsize=(10, 10))
for i in range(5):
    plt.subplot(1, 5, i + 1)
    plt.xticks([])
    plt.yticks([])
    plt.grid(False)
    plt.imshow(x_train[i], cmap=plt.cm.binary)
    plt.xlabel(class_names[y_train[i]])
plt.show()
```

Refer to the following figure for sample images from Fashion-MNIST:

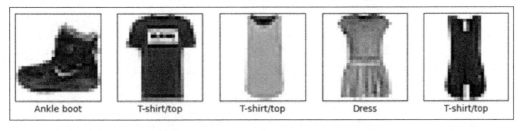

Figure 9.13: Sample images from Fashion-MNIST

```python
# Normalize the pixel values to between 0 and 1
x_train = x_train.astype('float32') / 255.0
x_test = x_test.astype('float32') / 255.0

# Define the model architecture
model = keras.Sequential([
    layers.Flatten(input_shape=(28, 28)),
    layers.Dense(128, activation='relu'),
    layers.Dense(10)
])

# Compile the model with categorical cross entropy loss and Adam optimizer
model.compile(optimizer='adam',
              loss=tf.keras.losses.
              SparseCategoricalCrossentropy(from_logits=True),
              metrics=['accuracy'])

# Train the model for a specified number of epochs
model.fit(x_train, y_train, epochs=10, validation_data=(x_test, y_test))

# Evaluate the model on the test set
test_loss, test_acc = model.evaluate(x_test, y_test, verbose=2)
print('\nTest accuracy:', test_acc)
```

Refer to the following figure for model training for Fashion-MNIST:

```
Epoch 1/10
1875/1875 [==============================] - 9s 5ms/step - loss: 0.4979 - accuracy: 0.8235 - val_loss: 0.4491 - val_accuracy: 0.8390
Epoch 2/10
1875/1875 [==============================] - 8s 4ms/step - loss: 0.3742 - accuracy: 0.8647 - val_loss: 0.3763 - val_accuracy: 0.8642
Epoch 3/10
1875/1875 [==============================] - 8s 4ms/step - loss: 0.3348 - accuracy: 0.8778 - val_loss: 0.3884 - val_accuracy: 0.8651
Epoch 4/10
1875/1875 [==============================] - 8s 4ms/step - loss: 0.3125 - accuracy: 0.8858 - val_loss: 0.3457 - val_accuracy: 0.8751
Epoch 5/10
1875/1875 [==============================] - 8s 4ms/step - loss: 0.2946 - accuracy: 0.8910 - val_loss: 0.3727 - val_accuracy: 0.8688
Epoch 6/10
1875/1875 [==============================] - 7s 4ms/step - loss: 0.2791 - accuracy: 0.8959 - val_loss: 0.3521 - val_accuracy: 0.8710
Epoch 7/10
1875/1875 [==============================] - 8s 4ms/step - loss: 0.2684 - accuracy: 0.8999 - val_loss: 0.3449 - val_accuracy: 0.8770
Epoch 8/10
1875/1875 [==============================] - 7s 4ms/step - loss: 0.2564 - accuracy: 0.9053 - val_loss: 0.3412 - val_accuracy: 0.8817
Epoch 9/10
1875/1875 [==============================] - 8s 4ms/step - loss: 0.2479 - accuracy: 0.9075 - val_loss: 0.3262 - val_accuracy: 0.8846
Epoch 10/10
1875/1875 [==============================] - 9s 5ms/step - loss: 0.2383 - accuracy: 0.9123 - val_loss: 0.3521 - val_accuracy: 0.8759
313/313 - 0s - loss: 0.3521 - accuracy: 0.8759 - 476ms/epoch - 2ms/step

Test accuracy: 0.8758999705314636
```

Figure 9.14: *Model training for Fashion-MNIST*

```
# Make predictions on the test set
y_pred = model.predict(x_test)

# Get the class with the highest probability for each prediction
y_pred_classes = np.argmax(y_pred, axis=1)

# Define the class names for Fashion-MNIST
class_names = ['T-shirt/top', 'Trouser', 'Pullover', 'Dress', 'Coat',
               'Sandal', 'Shirt', 'Sneaker', 'Bag', 'Ankle boot']

# Plot a sample of the test set with their predicted and true labels
figure, axes = plt.subplots(nrows=5, ncols=5, figsize=(12,12))
for i, ax in enumerate(axes.flat):
    ax.imshow(x_test[i], cmap='gray')
    ax.set_title(f"True: {class_names[y_test[i]]}\nPredicted: {class_names[y_pred_classes[i]]}")
    ax.axis('off')
plt.show()
```

Refer to the following figure for the Fashion-MNIST result:

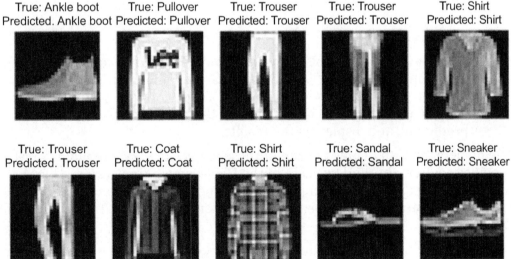

Figure 9.15: *TensorFlow Fashion-MNIST result*

Digit Recognition Training Using TensorFlow

Digit recognition requires a detailed explanation of various concepts and techniques, including image processing, machine learning, deep learning, and computer vision. However, I can provide an overview of the general approach and steps involved in implementing a Digit recognition system using Tensorflow and OpenCV. Here's a general outline of the approach:

1. **Data acquisition and preparation**: The first step is to obtain a dataset of handwritten digits, such as the MNIST dataset, and prepare it for training the model. This may involve resizing, normalization, and other preprocessing steps to ensure that the images are in a suitable format for processing.

2. **Training the model**: The next step is to train a deep learning model using TensorFlow, such as a CNN, on the prepared dataset. This involves defining the architecture of the model, specifying the hyperparameters, and running the training process on the data.

3. **Model evaluation**: After training the model, it is important to evaluate its performance on a separate test dataset to measure its accuracy and other metrics. This can help identify any issues or areas for improvement in the model.

4. **Integration with OpenCV**: Once the model is trained and evaluated, it can be integrated with OpenCV to create a complete Digit Recognition system. This involves using OpenCV to capture and preprocess images of handwritten digits, feeding them into the trained model for prediction, and displaying the results.

The implementation details of each of these steps can vary depending on the specific requirements and use case of the Digit Recognition system. However, with the preceding general approach, it is possible to create an accurate and robust system for recognizing handwritten digits using Tensorflow and OpenCV.

Digit recognition is a common problem in computer vision that involves identifying handwritten digits (0-9) from images. TensorFlow is an open-source machine learning library developed by Google that can be used to solve this problem. In this explanation, we will use the popular MNIST dataset, which consists of 70,000 grayscale images of handwritten digits, each with a size of 28x28 pixels.

Introduction to Deep Learning with OpenCV

To implement digit recognition in TensorFlow, follow these steps:

> **NOTE: Use Google Colab for this exercise.**

```
## Import necessary libraries
import tensorflow as tf
from tensorflow.keras import layers, models
import numpy as np
import matplotlib.pyplot as plt

## Load and preprocess the MNIST dataset
mnist = tf.keras.datasets.mnist (train_images, train_labels), (test_images,    test_labels) = mnist.load_data()

## Normalize the pixel values to the range [0, 1]
train_images = train_images / 255.0
test_images = test_images / 255.0

## Create the model
model = models.Sequential([
    layers.InputLayer(input_shape=(28, 28, 1)),
    layers.Conv2D(32, kernel_size=(3, 3), activation='relu'),
    layers.MaxPooling2D(pool_size=(2, 2)),
    layers.Conv2D(64, kernel_size=(3, 3), activation='relu'),
    layers.MaxPooling2D(pool_size=(2, 2)),
    layers.Flatten(),
    layers.Dense(128, activation='relu'),
    layers.Dense(10, activation='softmax')
])

model.summary()

##Compile the model
model.compile(optimizer='adam',
              loss=tf.keras.losses.
              SparseCategoricalCrossentropy(from_logits=True),
              metrics=['accuracy'])

## train the model
train_images = np.expand_dims(train_images, axis=-1)
test_images = np.expand_dims(test_images, axis=-1)
```

```
history = model.fit(train_images, train_labels, epochs=10,
validation_data=(test_images, test_labels))

## evaluate the model
test_loss, test_acc = model.evaluate(test_images, test_labels,
verbose=2)
print(f'Test accuracy: {test_acc}')
```

Refer to the following figure for training digit recognition in TensorFlow:

```
1875/1875 [==============================] - 74s 39ms/step - loss: 0.1287 - accuracy: 0.9609 - val_loss: 0.0461
Epoch 2/10
1875/1875 [==============================] - 74s 39ms/step - loss: 0.0428 - accuracy: 0.9867 - val_loss: 0.0320
Epoch 3/10
1875/1875 [==============================] - 68s 36ms/step - loss: 0.0280 - accuracy: 0.9911 - val_loss: 0.0370
Epoch 4/10
1875/1875 [==============================] - 70s 37ms/step - loss: 0.0213 - accuracy: 0.9935 - val_loss: 0.0271
Epoch 5/10
1875/1875 [==============================] - 70s 38ms/step - loss: 0.0161 - accuracy: 0.9947 - val_loss: 0.0275
Epoch 6/10
1875/1875 [==============================] - 70s 37ms/step - loss: 0.0123 - accuracy: 0.9959 - val_loss: 0.0309
Epoch 7/10
1875/1875 [==============================] - 72s 38ms/step - loss: 0.0105 - accuracy: 0.9966 - val_loss: 0.0309
Epoch 8/10
1875/1875 [==============================] - 69s 37ms/step - loss: 0.0083 - accuracy: 0.9973 - val_loss: 0.0342
Epoch 9/10
1875/1875 [==============================] - 67s 36ms/step - loss: 0.0060 - accuracy: 0.9980 - val_loss: 0.0322
Epoch 10/10
1875/1875 [==============================] - 77s 41ms/step - loss: 0.0064 - accuracy: 0.9980 - val_loss: 0.0329
313/313 - 3s - loss: 0.0329 - accuracy: 0.9921 - 3s/epoch - 10ms/step
Test accuracy: 0.9921000003814697
```

Figure 9.16: *Training digit recognition in TensorFlow*

```
## visualize predictions
predictions = model.predict(test_images)

def plot_image(predictions_array, true_label, img):
    plt.grid(False)
    plt.xticks([])
    plt.yticks([])
    plt.imshow(img, cmap=plt.cm.binary)

    predicted_label = np.argmax(predictions_array)

    if predicted_label == true_label:
        color = 'blue'
    else:
        color = 'red'
        plt.xlabel(f"{predicted_label} ({100 * np.max(predictions_
        array):.2f}%) {true_label}", color=color)
```

Introduction to Deep Learning with OpenCV

```
num_rows = 5
num_cols = 3
num_images = num_rows * num_cols

plt.figure(figsize=(2 * 2 * num_cols, 2 * num_rows))
for i in range(num_images):
    plt.subplot(num_rows, 2 * num_cols, 2 * i + 1)
    plot_image(predictions[i], test_labels[i], test_images[i, :, :, 0])

plt.show()

# Save the trained model
model.save('model.h5')
```

Refer to the following figure for the prediction value in digit recognition:

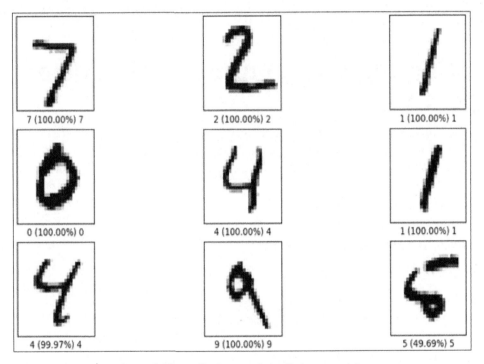

Figure 9.17: Prediction result in digit recognition

NOTE: Download the model.h5 file for future purposes.

In this code, the MNIST dataset is loaded using the `mnist.load_data()` function and the pixel values are normalized to be between 0 and 1.

The architecture of the model is defined using a Sequential model, which consists of a Flatten layer to convert the 2D input images to a 1D array, a Dense layer with 128 units and ReLU activation function, a Dropout layer to prevent overfitting and a final Dense layer with 10 units for the 10 possible digit classes.

The `loss` function is defined as `SparseCategoricalCrossentropy`, and the Adam optimizer is used for optimization. The model is compiled using the `compile()` function and trained on the training set using the `fit()` function. The trained model is evaluated on the test set using the `evaluate()` function and saved using the `save()` function.

Note that this is just a simple example code, and there may be additional considerations such as hyperparameter tuning, cross-validation, and other techniques to improve the performance of the Digit Recognition model.

This code will create a simple CNN model for digit recognition in TensorFlow, train it on the MNIST dataset, and visualize its predictions. The model should achieve an accuracy of around 98-99% on the test set.

Testing Digit Recognition Model Using OpenCV

Here's a sample code for implementing Digit Recognition in TensorFlow with OpenCV. This code assumes that you already have a trained TensorFlow model for digit recognition, and focuses on the integration with OpenCV for capturing and processing input images:

```
import tensorflow as tf
import numpy as np
import matplotlib.pyplot as plt
import matplotlib.image as img

# Load the pre-trained model
model = tf.keras.models.load_model('model.h5')

# Load an example digit image
digit_img = plt.imread('six.jpg')
img = img.imread('six.jpg')

# Preprocess the image
digit_img = tf.image.rgb_to_grayscale(digit_img)
digit_img = tf.image.resize(digit_img, [28, 28])
```

```
    digit_img = np.expand_dims(digit_img, axis=0)
    # Make a prediction
    digit_pred = model.predict(digit_img)

    # Get the predicted digit
    digit = np.argmax(digit_pred)

    # Print the predicted digit
    print(f"Predicted digit: {digit}")
    imgplot = plt.imshow(img)
    plt.show()
```

Refer to the following figure for testing the prediction value in digit recognition using an image:

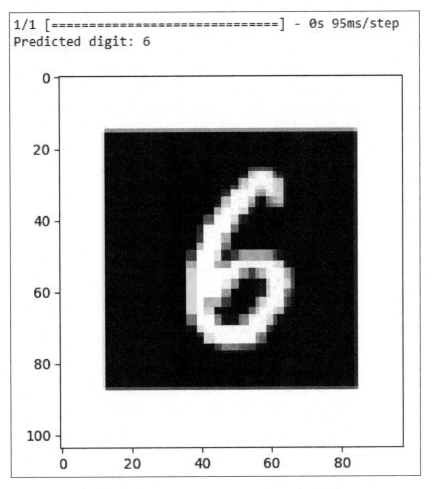

Figure 9.18: Testing prediction in digit recognition

In this code, the `preprocess_image()` function takes an input image, resizes it to the required size, converts it to grayscale, normalizes the pixel values, and reshapes it to match the input shape of the model. The `capture_and_process()` function captures frames from the default camera device, preprocesses them using the `preprocess_image()` function, feeds them into the trained model for prediction, maps the predicted labels to their corresponding digits using a dictionary, and displays the predicted digits on the processed images using the `cv2.putText()` function.

Note that this is just a simple example code, and there may be additional preprocessing steps, error handling, and other considerations that need to be addressed depending on the specific requirements and use case of the Digit Recognition system.

Dog Versus Cat Classification in TensorFlow with OpenCV

Dog versus cat classification is a common problem in computer vision and machine learning. It refers to the task of developing an algorithm that can correctly classify an image as either a dog or a cat. This problem is often used as a benchmark for evaluating the performance of various machine-learning models and algorithms.

The classification problem typically involves training a machine-learning model on a large dataset of labeled images of dogs and cats. The model is then tested on a separate set of images to evaluate its accuracy in correctly identifying the animal in the image. The accuracy of the model can be improved by adjusting various parameters and features of the model, or by using more advanced machine learning techniques such as deep learning.

There are several challenges associated with the dog vs. cat classification problem. For example, dogs and cats can have similar color patterns and fur textures, making it difficult for a machine-learning model to distinguish between the two. In addition, the position and orientation of the animal in the image can also affect the accuracy of the classification.

Overall, the dog vs. cat classification problem is an important area of research in computer vision and machine learning, with many practical applications in areas such as animal behavior monitoring, wildlife conservation, and pet identification.

Here's an example code for training a dog vs. cat classification using TensorFlow:

```
import tensorflow as tf
```

```
from tensorflow.keras.preprocessing.image import ImageDataGenerator

# load the data
!git clone https://github.com/laxmimerit/dog-cat-full-dataset.git
valid_data_dir = '/content/dog-cat-full-dataset/data/test'
train_data_dir = '/content/dog-cat-full-dataset/data/train'
```

Refer to the following figure for load the Dog vs. cat classification dataset:

```
Cloning into 'dog-cat-full-dataset'...
remote: Enumerating objects: 25027, done.
remote: Total 25027 (delta 0), reused 0 (delta 0), pack-reused 25027
Receiving objects: 100% (25027/25027), 541.62 MiB | 34.93 MiB/s, done.
Resolving deltas: 100% (5/5), done.
Updating files: 100% (25001/25001), done.
Found 20000 images belonging to 2 classes.
Found 5000 images belonging to 2 classes.
```

Figure 9.19: Load the Dog vs. cat classification dataset

```
# Define the image size and batch size
img_size = 224
batch_size = 32

# Create an instance of the ImageDataGenerator class for data
augmentation
train_datagen = ImageDataGenerator(
    rescale=1./255,
    rotation_range=20,
    zoom_range=0.2,
    horizontal_flip=True
)

# Create generators for the training and validation datasets
train_generator = train_datagen.flow_from_directory(
    train_data_dir,
    target_size=(img_size, img_size),
    batch_size=batch_size,
    class_mode='binary'
)
validation_generator = train_datagen.flow_from_directory(
    valid_data_dir,
```

```python
        target_size=(img_size, img_size),
        batch_size=batch_size,
        class_mode='binary'
)

# Define the architecture of the model
model = tf.keras.models.Sequential([
    tf.keras.layers.Conv2D(32, (3, 3), activation='relu', input_shape=(img_size, img_size, 3)),
    tf.keras.layers.MaxPooling2D((2, 2)),
    tf.keras.layers.Conv2D(64, (3, 3), activation='relu'),
    tf.keras.layers.MaxPooling2D((2, 2)),
    tf.keras.layers.Conv2D(128, (3, 3), activation='relu'),
    tf.keras.layers.MaxPooling2D((2, 2)),
    tf.keras.layers.Flatten(),
    tf.keras.layers.Dense(128, activation='relu'),
    tf.keras.layers.Dropout(0.5),
    tf.keras.layers.Dense(1, activation='sigmoid')
])

# Define the loss function and optimizer
loss_fn = tf.keras.losses.BinaryCrossentropy()
optimizer = tf.keras.optimizers.Adam()

# Compile the model
model.compile(optimizer=optimizer,
              loss=loss_fn,
              metrics=['accuracy'])

# Train the model on the training set
model.fit(train_generator,
        steps_per_epoch=train_generator.samples//batch_size,
        epochs=10,
        validation_data=validation_generator,
        validation_steps=validation_generator.samples//batch_size)

# Save the trained model
model.save('model.h5')
```

Refer to the following figure for train the Dog versus cat classification model:

```
Epoch 1/5
1000/1000 [==============================] - 404s 404ms/step - loss: 0.6789 - accuracy: 0.6014 - val_loss: 0.5671
Epoch 2/5
1000/1000 [==============================] - 396s 396ms/step - loss: 0.6064 - accuracy: 0.6839 - val_loss: 0.5907
Epoch 3/5
1000/1000 [==============================] - 392s 392ms/step - loss: 0.5669 - accuracy: 0.7124 - val_loss: 0.5182
Epoch 4/5
1000/1000 [==============================] - 402s 402ms/step - loss: 0.5435 - accuracy: 0.7365 - val_loss: 0.5559
Epoch 5/5
1000/1000 [==============================] - 399s 399ms/step - loss: 0.5245 - accuracy: 0.7444 - val_loss: 0.4981
```

Figure 9.20: Train the dog vs. cat classification model

In this code, the training and validation datasets are loaded using the `ImageDataGenerator` class with data augmentation techniques such as rescaling, rotation, zooming, and flipping. The generators are created for the training and validation datasets using the `flow_from_directory()` function, which reads the images from their respective directories and resizes them to the specified size. The architecture of the model is defined using a Sequential model, which consists of several convolutional layers, pooling layers, a flatten layer, and two dense layers.

The loss function is defined as `BinaryCrossentropy`, and the Adam optimizer is used for optimization. The model is compiled using the `compile()` function and trained on the training set using the `fit()` function with the generators. The trained model is saved using the `save()` function.

Dog versus cat classification with OpenCV

To perform dog versus cat classification with OpenCV, we can use a combination of image processing techniques and machine learning algorithms. Here's a basic outline of the steps involved:

Collect and preprocess the data: The first step is to collect a large dataset of labeled images of dogs and cats. The images should be preprocessed to remove any noise and standardize the size and color of the images.

1. **Extract features**: The next step is to extract relevant features from the images. This can be done using various techniques such as **histograms of oriented gradients (HOG)**, **local binary patterns (LBP)**, or color histograms.

2. **Train the model**: Once the features have been extracted, we can use a machine learning algorithm such as **support vector machines (SVM)** or random forests to train the model on the labeled dataset.

3. **Test the model**: After the model has been trained, we can test it on a separate set of images to evaluate its accuracy in correctly classifying dogs and cats.

Here's an example code snippet using OpenCV in Python to perform dog versus cat classification:

```
import cv2
import numpy as np
import tensorflow as tf

# Load the saved model
model = tf.keras.models.load_model('model.h5')

## Define the function to preprocess the image
def preprocess(img):
    img = cv2.resize(img, (256, 256))
    img = img / 255.0
    img = np.expand_dims(img, axis=0)


    # Make predictions
    prediction = model.predict(img)
    if prediction[0] > 0.7:
        return('Dog')
    else:
        return('Cat')

# Load the test image using OpenCV
img = cv2.imread('kitten.jpg')
# Preprocess the image
label = preprocess(img)

# Display the test image with the predicted label
cv2.putText(img, label, (10,30), cv2.FONT_HERSHEY_SIMPLEX, 1, (0,255,0), 2)

cv2.imshow('Test Image', resized_img)
cv2.waitKey(0)
cv2.destroyAllWindows()
```

Refer to the following figure for dog prediction using OpenCV:

Figure 9.21: Dog prediction using OpenCV

Refer to the following figure for cat prediction using OpenCV:

Figure 9.22: Cat prediction using OpenCV

In this code, the saved model is loaded using the `load_model()` function from TensorFlow. The labels for dog and cat are defined as a list. The test image is loaded using OpenCV's `imread()` function and resized to the size of the input images used in the model. The color of the image is converted from BGR to RGB and normalized by dividing each pixel by 255. The model is used to predict the class of the test image using the `predict()` function from TensorFlow.

The predicted label is obtained by finding the index of the maximum value in the predicted array and using it to get the corresponding label from the list. The predicted label is displayed on the test image using the `putText()` function from OpenCV. Finally, the test image with the predicted label is displayed using the `imshow()` function, and the window is closed using the `waitKey()` and `destroyAllWindows()` functions.

Conclusion

In this chapter, we have discussed the essential introduction to machine learning, deep learning concepts and their architectures, activation functions and optimization techniques. We will also discuss deep learning projects which are Fashion data sets, Digit resignation and cat vs. dog classifications training and testing using OpenCV, TensorFlow and Python programming languages.

In the next chapter, we will discuss advanced deep learning projects along with their real-time project explanation using OpenCV and Tensorflow.

Points to Remember

Use Google Colab (https://colab.research.google.com/) for the above deep-learning project training.

Install TensorFlow if working on a local machine using the following command:

```
! pip install tensorflow
```

References

OpenCV Deep Learning Overview

https://github.com/opencv/opencv/wiki/Deep-Learning-in-OpenCV

https://learnopencv.com/deep-learning-with-opencvs-dnn-module-a-definitive-guide/

CHAPTER 10

Advance Deep Learning Projects with OpenCV

Introduction

In this chapter, we will cover advanced deep-learning projects and their detailed code explanations. We will also discuss face recognition, emotion detection and content-based image retrieval projects using TensorFlow, OpenCV and Python programming languages.

Structure

In this chapter, we will cover the following topics:

- Introduction to YOLO detection
- YOLO v3 object detection using TensorFlow
- YOLO v5 custom dataset using TensorFlow
- Face recognition using TensorFlow with OpenCV
- Real-time age prediction using TensorFlow
- Emotion detection using TensorFlow
- Content-based image retrieval using TensorFlow

Introduction to YOLO

You Only Look Once (YOLO) is a real-time object detection algorithm that uses deep learning to recognize objects in images and videos. Unlike other object detection algorithms that perform detection in multiple stages, YOLO performs detection in a single stage, making it much faster than other methods.

The YOLO algorithm divides the input image into a grid of cells and predicts the bounding box and class probabilities for each cell. The bounding box coordinates are relative to the coordinates of the cell, which means that a single object can be detected in multiple cells.

Here are the main components of the YOLO algorithm:

Input: YOLO takes an input image or video and resizes it to a fixed size.

- **Deep learning model**: YOLO uses a deep convolutional neural network (CNN) as its backbone architecture. The network is trained on a large dataset of labeled images to learn how to recognize objects.
- **Bounding box prediction**: The YOLO algorithm predicts the bounding boxes for each object in the input image. Each bounding box is represented by five values: x, y, w, h, and confidence score. The (x, y) coordinates represent the center of the box, while w and h represent the width and height of the box, respectively. The confidence score represents how confident the algorithm is that there is an object in the box.

Refer to the following figure for Bounding box prediction in YOLO:

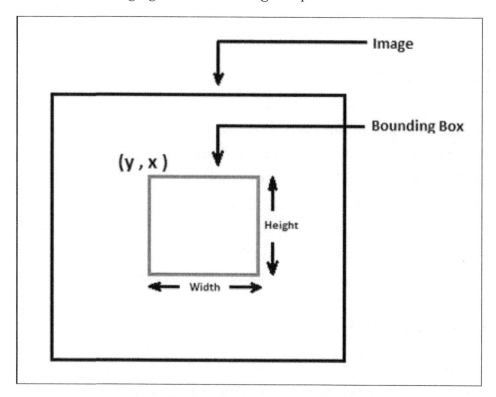

Figure 10.1: *Bounding box prediction in YOLO*

Non-maximum suppression: Non-maximum suppression (NMS) is a post-processing step used in object detection algorithms to eliminate duplicate detections of the same object. It works by selecting the detection with the highest confidence score and suppressing all other overlapping detections that have a lower score. This is done by defining a threshold for the IoU between the bounding boxes of the detections. If the IoU between two bounding boxes is greater than the threshold, the detection with the lower score is suppressed. This process is repeated until all the remaining detections have an IoU below the threshold.

Since multiple bounding boxes may be predicted for a single object, non-maximum suppression is used to remove the redundant boxes. Non-maximum suppression compares the confidence scores of overlapping boxes and keeps the box with the highest score while suppressing the others.

Refer to the following figure for Non-maximum suppression in YOLO:

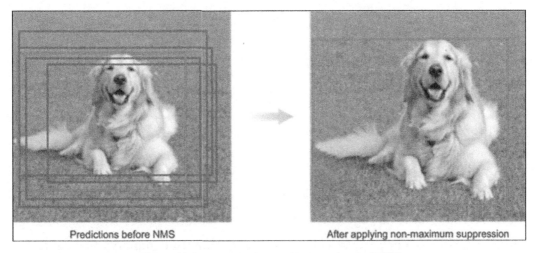

Figure 10.2: Non-Maximum Suppression in YOLO

Intersection over Union (IoU): it is a measurement of the overlap between two bounding boxes. It is calculated as the ratio of the intersection area between the two bounding boxes and the union area of the two bounding boxes. In object detection tasks, IoU is used as a metric to evaluate the performance of the model by comparing the predicted bounding boxes with the ground truth bounding boxes. A commonly used threshold for IoU is 0.5, which means that a predicted bounding box is considered a true positive if its IoU with the ground truth bounding box is greater than or equal to 0.5.

Refer to the following figure for Intersection over Union in YOLO:

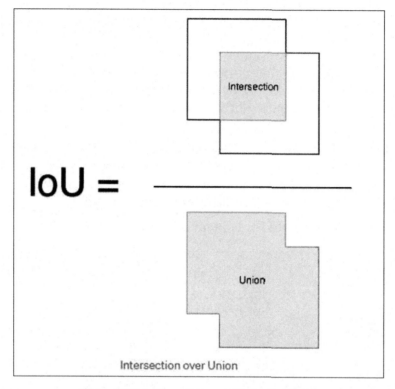

Figure 10.3: *Intersection over Union in YOLO*

Output: The final output of the YOLO algorithm is a list of bounding boxes and their corresponding class probabilities.

YOLO has several advantages over other object detection algorithms, including:

Speed: YOLO can perform object detection in real-time, making it suitable for applications where speed is important.

- **Accuracy:** YOLO has high accuracy in object detection, especially for large and small objects.
- **Flexibility:** YOLO can detect objects of different sizes, shapes, and orientations, making it suitable for a wide range of applications.
- **Simplicity:** YOLO performs object detection in a single stage, making it easier to implement and modify compared to other methods.

Refer to the following figure for YOLO architecture:

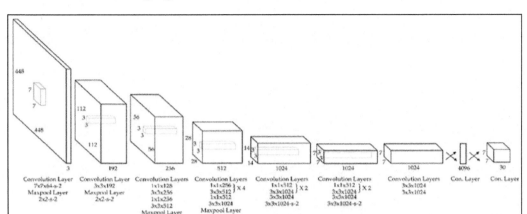

Figure 10.4: *Image of YOLO architecture*

Overall, YOLO is a powerful object detection algorithm that has many practical applications in computer vision, including object detection, object tracking, and self-driving cars.

YOLO Versions

There have been several versions of YOLO, each with its own improvements and modifications. Here are brief explanations of the different versions of YOLO:

YOLO v1: The first version of YOLO was released in 2015. It divides the input image into a grid and each grid cell predicts the class and bounding box of the object that lies within it. However, this version suffered from accuracy issues due to its inability to handle objects of different sizes.

- **YOLO v2:** Released in 2016, YOLO v2 addressed the issues with the previous version by adding anchor boxes to the model architecture. Anchor boxes are pre-defined boxes of different sizes and aspect ratios that the model uses to predict the bounding box coordinates for objects of different sizes.

- **YOLO v3:** Released in 2018, YOLO v3 improved upon the previous versions by introducing a few new concepts such as multi-scale detection, feature pyramid networks, and more. The model architecture was redesigned to be deeper and more complex, resulting in improved accuracy.

- **YOLO v4:** Released in 2020, YOLO v4 is currently the state-of-the-art version of YOLO. It introduced several new features such as the use of CSPDarknet53 as the backbone network, spatial pyramid pooling (SPP), and improved anchor box selection. YOLO v4 is known for its impressive speed and accuracy in object detection tasks.

YOLO v3 Object Detection Using TensorFlow

YOLO v3 (You Only Look Once version 3) is a real-time object detection algorithm developed by Joseph Redmon and his team in 2018. It is an improvement over YOLOv2, and it uses a single neural network for both object detection and classification tasks. YOLO v3 uses a fully convolutional network to predict the bounding boxes and the class probabilities of objects in an image.

YOLO v3 is based on the Darknet framework and is trained on the COCO dataset, which contains 80 object categories. The network uses anchor boxes to detect objects of different sizes, and it uses skip connections to improve the accuracy of the predictions.

Refer to the following figure for 80 classes available under COCO's pre-trained weights:

```
'person', 'bicycle', 'car', 'motorcycle', 'airplane', 'bus', 'train', 'truck',
'boat', 'traffic light', 'fire hydrant', 'stop sign', 'parking meter', 'bench',
'bird', 'cat', 'dog', 'horse', 'sheep', 'cow', 'elephant', 'bear', 'zebra',
'giraffe', 'backpack', 'umbrella', 'handbag', 'tie', 'suitcase', 'frisbee',
'skis', 'snowboard', 'sports ball', 'kite', 'baseball bat', 'baseball glove',
'skateboard', 'surfboard', 'tennis racket', 'bottle', 'wine glass', 'cup', 'fork',
'knife', 'spoon', 'bowl', 'banana', 'apple', 'sandwich', 'orange', 'broccoli',
'carrot', 'hot dog', 'pizza', 'donut', 'cake', 'chair', 'couch', 'potted plant',
'bed', 'dining table', 'toilet', 'tv', 'laptop', 'mouse', 'remote', 'keyboard',
'cell phone', 'microwave', 'oven', 'toaster', 'sink', 'refrigerator', 'book',
'clock', 'vase', 'scissors', 'teddy bear', 'hair drier', 'toothbrush'
```

Figure 10.5: Classes available under COCO's pre-trained weights

YOLO v3 has three different versions: YOLOv3, YOLOv3-SPP, and YOLOv3-Tiny. The YOLOv3-SPP (Spatial Pyramid Pooling) version includes spatial pyramid pooling, which allows the network to better capture objects at different scales. The YOLOv3-Tiny version is a smaller and faster version of the network that sacrifices some accuracy for speed.

YOLO v3 also introduced some improvements over YOLOv2, including:

Better accuracy: YOLO v3 uses a more complex network architecture and incorporates skip connections, which improves the accuracy of the predictions.

- **Multi-scale predictions**: YOLO v3 uses anchor boxes of different sizes to detect objects at different scales, which improves the accuracy of the predictions.
- **Improved non-maximum suppression**: YOLO v3 uses a more sophisticated non-maximum suppression algorithm, which helps to eliminate duplicate detections.
- **Improved training**: YOLO v3 uses a technique called label smoothing to improve the generalization of the network and reduce overfitting.

Here's an example of how to perform YOLO v3 object detection in OpenCV:

Download the **yolov3.weights**, and **yolov3.cfg** files from the following website:

https://pjreddie.com/darknet/yolo/

YOLO v3 object detection OpenCV code:

```
import cv2
import numpy as np

## load YOLO3 weights and cfg file
net = cv2.dnn.readNet("yolov3.weights","yolov3.cfg")

## load the class values
classes = []
with open("coco.names","r") as f:
    classes = [line.strip() for line in f.readlines()]
#print(classes)

## get the convolution layer
layer_names = net.getLayerNames()
outputlayers = [layer_names[i - 1] for i in net.getUnconnectedOutLayers()]

colors= np.random.uniform(0,255,size=(len(classes),3))
```

```python
#loading image or video
cap=cv2.VideoCapture("dog.mp4") #0 for 1st webcam
font = cv2.FONT_HERSHEY_SIMPLEX

# Get the width and height of the video frames
width = int(cap.get(cv2.CAP_PROP_FRAME_WIDTH))
height = int(cap.get(cv2.CAP_PROP_FRAME_HEIGHT))

# Define the codec and create VideoWriter object
fourcc = cv2.VideoWriter_fourcc(*'mp4v')
vids = cv2.VideoWriter('yolo.mp4', fourcc, 30, (width, height))

while True:
    ret,frame= cap.read() # read the frame
    if not ret: break
    height,width,channels = frame.shape

    #detecting objects, blob conversion which is basically
    extracting features from image
    blob = cv2.dnn.
    blobFromImage(frame,0.00392,(320,320),(0,0,0),True,crop=False)
    #reduce 416 to 320
    net.setInput(blob)
    outs = net.forward(outputlayers)

    #Showing info on screen/ get confidence score of algorithm in
    detecting an object in blob
    class_ids=[]
    confidences=[]
    boxes=[]
    for out in outs:
        for detection in out:
            scores = detection[5:]
            class_id = np.argmax(scores)
            confidence = scores[class_id]
            if confidence > 0.3:

                #object detected
                center_x= int(detection[0]*width)
                center_y= int(detection[1]*height)
```

```
                w = int(detection[2]*width)
                h = int(detection[3]*height)

                #rectangle co-ordinaters
                x=int(center_x - w/2)
                y=int(center_y - h/2)

                boxes.append([x,y,w,h]) #put all rectangle areas
                confidences.append(float(confidence)) #how
                confidence was that object detected and show that
                percentage
                class_ids.append(class_id) #name of the object tha
                was detected

    # any box having value less than 0.6- that will be removed
    indexes = cv2.dnn.NMSBoxes(boxes,confidences,0.4,0.6)

    # put the text values on the frame
    for i in range(len(boxes)):
        if i in indexes:
            x,y,w,h = boxes[i]
            label = str(classes[class_ids[i]])
            confidence= confidences[i]
            color = colors[class_ids[i]]
            cv2.rectangle(frame,(x,y),(x+w,y+h),color,2)
            cv2.putText(frame,label+"
            "+str(round(confidence,2)),(x,y+30),font,1,(255,255,255),2)

    #writing the frame
    vids.write(frame)
    #wait 1ms the loop will start again and we will process the next
    frame
    cv2.imshow("Video",frame)
    if cv2.waitKey(25) & 0xFF == ord('q'): #Q key stops the process
        break;

# break the loop
cap.release()
vids.release()
cv2.destroyAllWindows()
```

Refer to the following figure for object detection using YOLO v3 using TensorFlow:

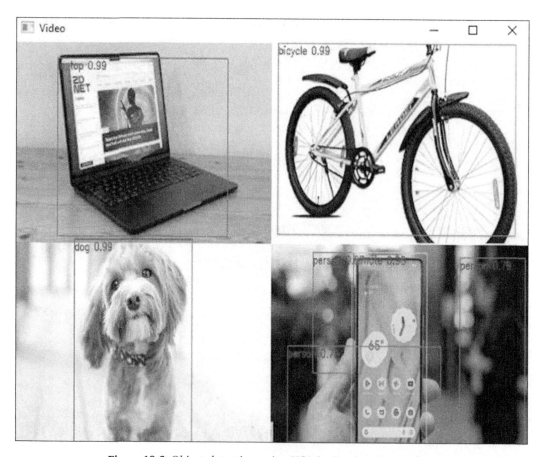

Figure 10.6: Object detection using YOLO v3 using TensorFlow

Overall, YOLO v3 is a powerful object detection algorithm that can detect objects in real-time with high accuracy.

YOLO v5 and Custom Dataset Using TensorFlow

YOLOv5 is an updated version of the YOLO (You Only Look Once) object detection algorithm, which is a popular deep learning-based method for real-time object detection. YOLOv5 improves upon its predecessors by introducing a more efficient and accurate architecture, with a focus on using modern deep learning techniques like Scaled-YOLO and Mish activation functions.

To use YOLOv5 with a custom dataset, we need to follow these steps:

Collect and prepare the dataset: Collect a dataset of images and label each object in the image with a bounding box and corresponding class label. This can be done manually or using annotation tools like LabelImg or RectLabel.

1. **Organize the dataset:** Organize the dataset into a format compatible with YOLOv5. Each image should be in JPEG or PNG format and have a corresponding text file containing the object labels in the YOLO format.

2. **Train the model:** Train the YOLOv5 model on the prepared dataset using a deep learning framework like PyTorch or TensorFlow. During training, the model will learn to detect objects based on the annotated labels in the training dataset.

3. **Evaluate the model:** Evaluate the performance of the trained model on a test dataset to measure its accuracy, precision, recall, and other metrics.

4. **Fine-tune the model:** Fine-tune the YOLOv5 model based on the evaluation results, by adjusting its hyperparameters, architecture, or training process, to achieve better performance on the custom dataset.

5. **Deploy the model:** Deploy the trained YOLOv5 model in a real-world application or system, where it can detect objects in real-time images or videos.

Here is an example of how to perform YOLO v5 and a custom dataset using TensorFlow:

1. Go to Google Colab and create a new notebook.

   https://colab.research.google.com/

2. Change the Runtime type to GPU as a hardware accelerator by following the steps.

   Click Runtime → Change Runtime type → select GPU in hardware accelerator dropdown → click Save.

3. Clone the yolov5 repository by using the following code:

   `! git clone` https://github.com/ultralytics/yolov5.git

4. Install YOLO v5 Dependencies in the Colab notebook:

   `! pip install -U -r requirements.txt`

   ```
   import torch
   import os
   ```

```python
from iPython.display import Image, clear_output
# from utils.google_utils import gdrive_download
clear_output()
%cd /content/yolov5/
```

5. Download the custom (fish images) data set that you are interested in (using the Roboflow api):

```
# https://public.roboflow.com/

!curl -L "https://public.roboflow.com/ds/lujgbDXgkE?key=CgA5u2f1oB" > roboflow.zip; unzip roboflow.zip; rm roboflow.zip

# Create the custom model configuration file

#extracting information from the roboflow file

%cat /content/yolov5/data.yaml
```

6. Define the number of classes based on data.yaml:

```python
import yaml
with open("data.yaml", 'r') as stream:
    num_classes = str(yaml.safe_load(stream)['nc'])
```

```
%cat /content/yolov5/models/yolov5s.yaml
```

7. Customize iPython write file so we can write variables:

```python
from IPython.core.magic import register_line_cell_magic

@register_line_cell_magic
def writetemplate(line, cell):
    with open(line, 'w') as f:
        f.write(cell.format(**globals()))
```

```
%%writetemplate /content/yolov5/models/custom_yolov5s.yaml

# parameters
nc: {num_classes}  # number of classes
depth_multiple: 0.33  # model depth multiple
width_multiple: 0.50  # layer channel multiple
```

```yaml
# anchors
anchors:
  - [10,13, 16,30, 33,23]  # P3/8
  - [30,61, 62,45, 59,119]  # P4/16
  - [116,90, 156,198, 373,326]  # P5/32

# YOLOv5 backbone
backbone:
  # [from, number, module, args]
  [[-1, 1, Focus, [64, 3]],  # 0-P1/2
   [-1, 1, Conv, [128, 3, 2]],  # 1-P2/4
   [-1, 3, BottleneckCSP, [128]],
   [-1, 1, Conv, [256, 3, 2]],  # 3-P3/8
   [-1, 9, BottleneckCSP, [256]],
   [-1, 1, Conv, [512, 3, 2]],  # 5-P4/16
   [-1, 9, BottleneckCSP, [512]],
   [-1, 1, Conv, [1024, 3, 2]],  # 7-P5/32
   [-1, 1, SPP, [1024, [5, 9, 13]]],
   [-1, 3, BottleneckCSP, [1024, False]],  # 9
  ]

# YOLOv5 head
head:
  [[-1, 1, Conv, [512, 1, 1]],
   [-1, 1, nn.Upsample, [None, 2, 'nearest']],
   [[-1, 6], 1, Concat, [1]],  # cat backbone P4
   [-1, 3, BottleneckCSP, [512, False]],  # 13

   [-1, 1, Conv, [256, 1, 1]],
   [-1, 1, nn.Upsample, [None, 2, 'nearest']],
   [[-1, 4], 1, Concat, [1]],  # cat backbone P3
   [-1, 3, BottleneckCSP, [256, False]],  # 17 (P3/8-small)
```

```
   [-1, 1, Conv, [256, 3, 2]],
   [[-1, 14], 1, Concat, [1]],  # cat head P4
   [-1, 3, BottleneckCSP, [512, False]],  # 20 (P4/16-medium)

   [-1, 1, Conv, [512, 3, 2]],
   [[-1, 10], 1, Concat, [1]],  # cat head P5
   [-1, 3, BottleneckCSP, [1024, False]],  # 23 (P5/32-large)

   [[17, 20, 23], 1, Detect, [nc, anchors]],  # Detect(P3, P4, P5)
  ]
```

8. Train yolov5 on the custom images using the custom configuration file:

   ```
   # train yolov5s on custom data for 100 epochs
   # time its performance
   %%time
   %cd /content/yolov5/
   ```

   ```
   !python train.py --img 416 --batch 16 --epochs 100 --data ./
   data.yaml --cfg ./models/custom_yolov5s.yaml --weights '' --name
   yolov5s_results  --cache
   ```

9. Run yolov5 detection on images:

   ```
   # run yolov5 detection on images.

   # copy the location of the weights file and replace it in the
   following code

   !python detect.py --weights /content/yolov5/runs/train/yolov5s_
   results/weights/best.pt --img 416 --conf 0.4 --source ./test/
   images

   import glob
   from IPython.display import Image, display
   for imageName in glob.glob('/content/yolov5/runs/detect/exp3/*.
   jpg'):
      display(Image(filename=imageName))
       print("\n")
   ```

Refer to the following figure for YOLO v5 object detection using a custom dataset:

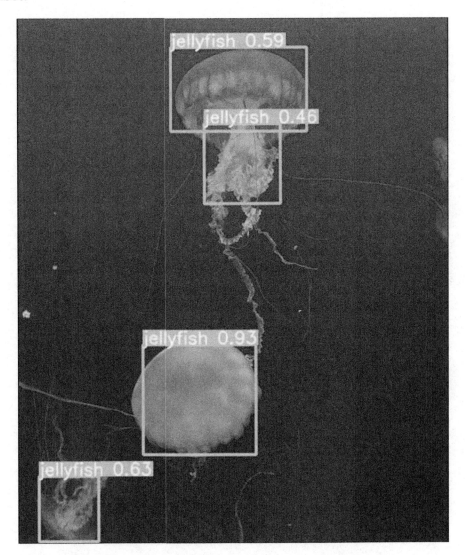

Figure 10.7: *YOLO v5 custom dataset object detection using image*

10. Run yolov5 detection on video:

```
# copy the location of the weights file and replace it in the
following code

!python detect.py --weights runs/train/yolov5s_results4/weights/
best.pt --img 416 --conf 0.5 --source ../aquarium.mp4
```

Refer to the following figure for YOLO v5 custom dataset object detection using video:

Figure 10.8: *YOLO v5 custom dataset object detection using video*

Overall, YOLOv5 is a powerful and efficient object detection algorithm that can be used with a custom dataset to detect objects in real-world scenarios.

Face Recognition Using TensorFlow with OpenCV

Face recognition is an essential field in computer vision that automatically identifies an individual from a digital image or a video frame. It has various applications in security, surveillance, human-computer interaction, and entertainment.

There are several approaches to face recognition, including traditional computer vision techniques, machine learning-based methods, and deep learning-based techniques. Here, we will focus on the theory behind conventional and machine learning-based methods.

Traditional computer vision-based face recognition methods typically involve the following steps:

Face detection: In this step, the algorithm identifies the regions in the image that are likely to contain faces. This can be done using techniques such as Haar cascades or HOG-based detectors.

1. **Feature extraction:** Once the faces have been detected, the algorithm extracts feature from the face region that can be used to represent the face. These features can include geometric features such as the location of the eyes, nose, and mouth, or texture-based features such as the histogram of oriented gradients (HOG) or local binary patterns (LBP).
2. **Feature matching:** In this step, the algorithm compares the extracted features of the input face with those of the faces in the database to find the best match. This can be done using techniques such as the Euclidean distance or cosine similarity.

Machine learning-based face recognition methods typically involve the following steps:

Data collection: In this step, a dataset of face images is collected. This dataset should be diverse and contain images of people of different ages, genders, ethnicities, and lighting conditions.

1. **Feature extraction:** Similar to traditional methods, features are extracted from the face region. However, in machine learning-based methods, the choice of features is often learned automatically using techniques such as principal component analysis (PCA) or linear discriminant analysis (LDA).
2. **Training:** In this step, a classifier is trained using the extracted features and the corresponding labels (that is, the names of the people in the

images). Popular classifiers for face recognition include support vector machines (SVMs), k-nearest neighbors (KNN), and neural networks.

3. **Testing**: In this step, the trained classifier is tested on a new set of face images to evaluate its performance. The performance can be measured using metrics such as accuracy, precision, recall, and F1 score.

There are several challenges associated with face recognition, including variations in pose, expression, illumination, and occlusion. To overcome these challenges, researchers have developed various techniques such as 3D face modeling, active appearance models, and deep neural networks.

In summary, face recognition is an essential field in computer vision with several applications. Traditional computer vision-based methods involve face detection, feature extraction, and feature matching, while machine learning-based methods involve data collection, feature extraction, training, and testing. The choice of approach depends on the specific application and the available resources.

FaceNet Architecture

FaceNet is a deep learning model for face recognition developed by researchers at Google. It is based on a Siamese neural network architecture, which learns a high-dimensional feature representation of faces that can be used for face verification and identification.

Refer to the following figure for Siamese neural network architecture:

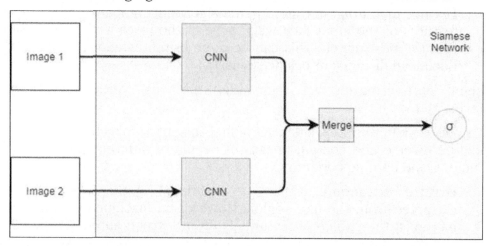

Figure 10.9: Image of Siamese neural network architecture

The main idea behind FaceNet is to learn a mapping function that takes an input face image and maps it to a high-dimensional feature space, where the

Advance Deep Learning Projects with OpenCV

distance between two feature vectors corresponds to the similarity between the two faces. This is achieved by training a Siamese neural network, which consists of two identical subnetworks that share the same parameters.

During training, pairs of face images are fed into the Siamese network, and the output feature vectors are compared using a contrastive loss function, which encourages similar faces to have similar feature vectors and dissimilar faces to have dissimilar feature vectors. The network is trained to minimize this loss function using backpropagation and stochastic gradient descent.

Once the FaceNet model has been trained, it can be used for face recognition by comparing the feature vectors of two faces and computing their distance using a distance metric such as Euclidean distance or cosine similarity. If the distance between the two feature vectors is below a certain threshold, the faces are considered to be the same person. One of the key advantages of FaceNet is its ability to generalize well to new faces, even those that are not present in the training dataset. This is due to the use of a large-scale dataset of faces for training, which allows the network to learn a general representation of faces that is robust to variations in pose, lighting, and other factors.

Refer to the following figure for FaceNet neural network architecture.

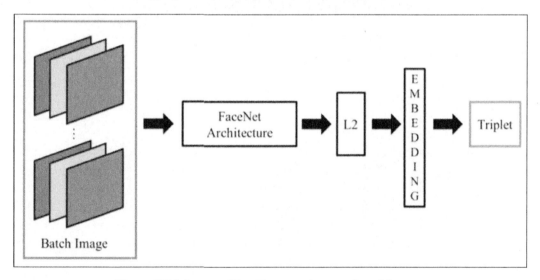

Figure 10.10: *Image of FaceNet neural network architecture*

FaceNet has been shown to achieve state-of-the-art performance on several face recognition benchmarks, including **LFW (Labeled Faces in the Wild)** and MegaFace. It has also been used in practical applications such as Google Photos and the Nest Hello video doorbell.

Here's an example of how to perform Face recognition using TensorFlow with OpenCV:

1. Download the facenet_keras.h5 files from the following website: https://www.kaggle.com/datasets/rmamun/kerasfaceneth5.

2. Refer to the following figure for the Face recognition code folder and architecture:

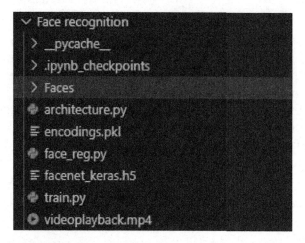

Figure 10.11: Face recognition code folder and architecture

3. Refer to the following figure for Under the Faces, folder keeps the datasets:

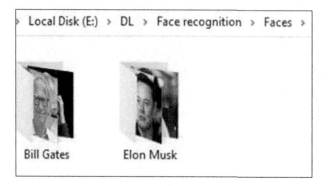

Figure 10.12: Test image for Face recognition folder

4. Install the following packages.

   ```
   ! pip install mtcnn
   ```

5. Download the required architecture.py file following the GitHub profile:

   https://github.com/mugeshraja06/Practical-Machine-Learning-With-Open-CV/blob/main/Chapter%2010/architecture.py

6. Create the train.py file and paste the following code:

```
from architecture import *
import os
import cv2
import mtcnn
import pickle
import numpy as np
from sklearn.preprocessing import Normalizer
from tensorflow.models import load_model

face_data = 'Faces/'
required_shape = (160,160)
face_encoder = InceptionResNetV2()
path = "/Face recognition/facenet_keras.h5"
face_encoder.load_weights(path)
face_detector = mtcnn.MTCNN()
encodes = []
encoding_dict = dict()
l2_normalizer = Normalizer('l2')

import cv2
import numpy as np
import mtcnn
from architecture import *
from sklearn.preprocessing import Normalizer
from scipy.spatial.distance import cosine
from keras.models import load_model
import pickle
```

7. Train the dataset using the **train.py** file and test the code using the **face_reg.py** file using the following code:

```
l2_normalizer = Normalizer('l2')

def normalize(img):
    mean, std = img.mean(), img.std()
    return (img - mean) / std

confidence_t=0.99
recognition_t=0.5
required_size = (160,160)
```

```python
def get_face(img, box):
    x1, y1, width, height = box
    x1, y1 = abs(x1), abs(y1)
    x2, y2 = x1 + width, y1 + height
    face = img[y1:y2, x1:x2]
    return face, (x1, y1), (x2, y2)

def get_encode(face_encoder, face, size):
    face = normalize(face)
    face = cv2.resize(face, size)
    encode = face_encoder.predict(np.expand_dims(face, axis=0))[0]
    return encode

def load_pickle(path):
    with open(path, 'rb') as f:
        encoding_dict = pickle.load(f)
    return encoding_dict

def detect(img ,detector,encoder,encoding_dict):
    img_rgb = cv2.cvtColor(img, cv2.COLOR_BGR2RGB)
    results = detector.detect_faces(img_rgb)
    for res in results:
        if res['confidence'] < confidence_t:
            continue
        face, pt_1, pt_2 = get_face(img_rgb, res['box'])
        encode = get_encode(encoder, face, required_size)
        encode = l2_normalizer.transform(encode.reshape(1, -1))[0]
        name = 'unknown'

        distance = float("inf")
        for db_name, db_encode in encoding_dict.items():
            dist = cosine(db_encode, encode)
            if dist < recognition_t and dist < distance:
                name = db_name
                distance = dist
```

```python
            if name == 'unknown':
                cv2.rectangle(img, pt_1, pt_2, (0, 0, 255), 2)
                cv2.putText(img, name, pt_1, cv2.FONT_HERSHEY_SIMPLEX,
                    1, (0, 0, 255), 1)
            else:
                cv2.rectangle(img, pt_1, pt_2, (0, 255, 0), 2)
                cv2.putText(img, name , (pt_1[0], pt_1[1] - 5), cv2.
                FONT_HERSHEY_SIMPLEX, 1,
                            (0, 0, 255), 2)

        return img

if __name__ == "__main__":
    required_shape = (160,160)
    face_encoder = InceptionResNetV2()
    path_m = "facenet_keras.h5"
    face_encoder.load_weights(path_m)
    encodings_path = 'encodings.pkl'
    face_detector = mtcnn.MTCNN()
    encoding_dict = load_pickle(encodings_path)

    cap = cv2.VideoCapture("videoplayback.mp4")

    while cap.isOpened():
        ret,frame = cap.read()

        if not ret:
            print("CAM NOT OPEND")
            break

        frame= detect(frame , face_detector , face_encoder ,
        encoding_dict)

        cv2.imshow("frame", frame)

        if cv2.waitKey(1) & 0xFF == ord('q'):
            break
```

Refer to the following figure for the output of the face recognition code:

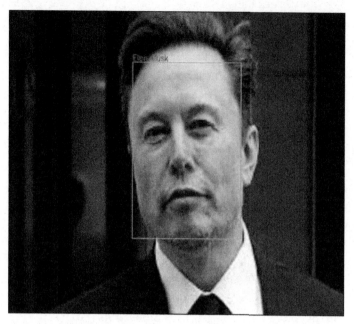

Figure 10.13: Output of face recognition code

Refer to the following figure for the output of the face recognition code:

Figure 10.14: Output of face recognition code

Real-time Age Prediction Using TensorFlow and RESNET 50_CNN

Real-time age prediction using TensorFlow involves training a deep learning model on a dataset of images labeled with age information and then using the trained model to predict the ages of new images in real-time. Here's an overview of the main steps involved:

1. **Data preparation:** The first step is to prepare a dataset of images labeled with age information. This can be done by manually labeling the images with age information or by using an existing dataset that has been labeled. The dataset should be split into training and validation sets.

2. **Model training:** The next step is to train a deep-learning model on the labeled images. One popular approach is to use a convolutional neural network (CNN) with multiple layers, such as VGG or ResNet. The model should be trained on the training set using a loss function that compares the predicted ages to the actual ages in the labeled images. The model should be validated on the validation set to ensure that it is not overfitting.

3. Model deployment: Once the model has been trained and validated, it can be deployed for real-time age prediction. This involves using the trained model to predict the ages of new images in real-time. One common approach is to use a webcam to capture images in real time, and then use the trained model to predict the ages of the captured images.

4. Display output: Finally, the predicted ages can be displayed as an overlay on top of the captured images, or as a separate output window.

Overall, real-time age prediction using TensorFlow requires expertise in deep learning and computer vision, as well as access to a labeled dataset and a webcam. While the specific implementation details may vary depending on the application, the underlying principles and techniques are similar.

RESNET 50_CNN

ResNet-50 is a type of convolutional neural network (CNN) that is used for image classification and object detection tasks. It was introduced by Microsoft

Research in 2015 and has since become a popular architecture for deep learning models.

Here's an overview of the main components of the ResNet-50 CNN:

Convolutional layers: The first layer of the ResNet-50 CNN is a convolutional layer that processes the input image. The CNN has a total of 50 layers, with additional convolutional layers added at different stages of the network.

- **Residual blocks:** The ResNet-50 CNN uses a special type of block known as a residual block, which allows the network to learn more complex features by skipping over some layers. Each residual block consists of two or more convolutional layers, followed by a skip connection that adds the input of the block to its output. This allows the network to learn residual functions, which are the differences between the input and output of each block.

  Refer to the following figure for ResNet-50 CNN residual block:

  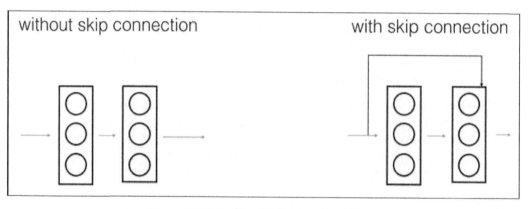

  Figure 10.15: ResNet-50 CNN residual block

- **Pooling layers:** The ResNet-50 CNN uses pooling layers to downsample the feature maps produced by the convolutional layers. This helps to reduce the dimensionality of the feature maps and extract more meaningful features.

Refer to the following figure for Pooling layers in CNN:

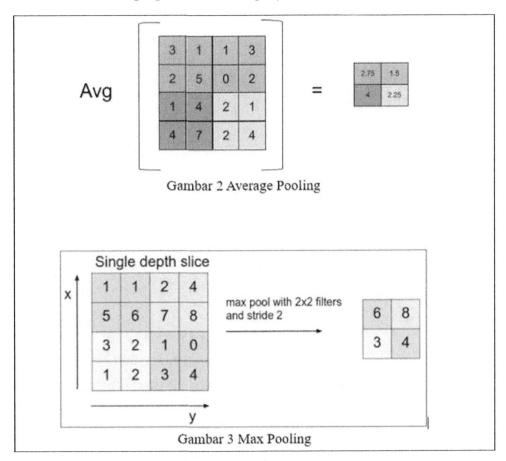

Gambar 2 Average Pooling

Gambar 3 Max Pooling

Figure 10.16: *Pooling layers in CNN*

- **Fully connected layers:** The final layers of the ResNet-50 CNN are fully connected layers that perform the classification or detection task. The output of the CNN is a probability distribution over the possible classes or objects.

Refer to the following figure for the fully connected layer in CNN:

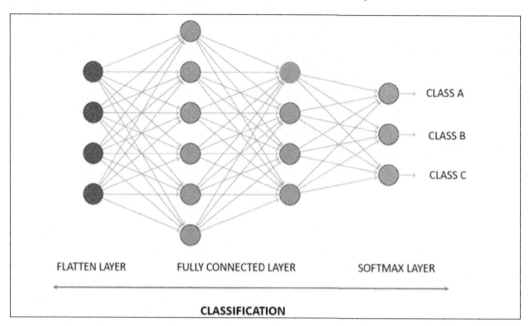

Figure 10.17: Fully connected layer in CNN

Here's an overview of the key innovations of the ResNet-50 CNN:

- **Residual connections:** The key innovation of ResNet is the use of residual connections, which allow the network to learn residual functions that capture the difference between the input and output of each block. This helps to overcome the problem of vanishing gradients, which can occur in deep neural networks with many layers.

- **Pretraining:** ResNet-50 is often pre-trained on large datasets such as ImageNet, which contains millions of labeled images. Pretraining allows the network to learn general features that can be transferred to new tasks, such as fine-tuning the network on a smaller dataset for a specific classification or detection task.

- **Transfer learning:** ResNet-50 is often used as part of a transfer learning pipeline, where the pre-trained network is used as a feature extractor for a new task. This involves freezing the weights of the ResNet-50 layers and training a new classifier or detection head on top of the feature maps produced by the ResNet-50 layers.

- **Applications:** ResNet-50 has been used for a wide range of applications in computer vision, including image classification, object detection, facial recognition, and medical image analysis. Its ability to learn

complex features makes it particularly useful for tasks that require high accuracy and robustness.
- **Variations:** There are several variations of the ResNet architecture, including ResNet-101, ResNet-152, and ResNeXt. These variations add more layers and more complex structures to the ResNet architecture, allowing for even higher accuracy and better performance on complex tasks.

Here's an example of how to perform Real-time age prediction using TensorFlow with images and OpenCV:

1. Download the age-model.h5 files from the following website:

    https://www.kaggle.com/datasets/mugeshraja/real-time-age-prediction

2. Load the `age-model.h5` files and run the following code and load the `haarcascade_frontalface_default.xml` file:

```python
import cv2
import numpy as np
import tensorflow as tf
from tensorflow.keras.models import load_model

# Load the pre-trained ResNet-50 model
model = load_model('age-model.h5')
# Load the Haar Cascade classifier for face detection
face_cascade = cv2.CascadeClassifier('haarcascade_frontalface_default.xml')

def predict_age(image):
    # Preprocess the image
    image = cv2.imread(image)
    image = cv2.resize(image, (224, 224))
    image = np.expand_dims(image, axis=0)

    # Use the fully connected layer to predict the age of the person in the image
    age =round(model.predict(image)[0][0])
    return age

predict_age("image.jpg")
```

Here's an example of how to perform Real-time age prediction using TensorFlow with videos and OpenCV:

```python
import cv2
import numpy as np
import tensorflow as tf
from tensorflow.keras.models import load_model

# Load the pre-trained ResNet-50 model
model = load_model('age-model.h5')
# Load the Haar Cascade classifier for face detection
face_cascade = cv2.CascadeClassifier('haarcascade_frontalface_default.xml')

# Define a function to predict the age of a person from an image
def predict_age(image):
    # Preprocess the image
    image = cv2.resize(image, (224, 224))
    image = np.expand_dims(image, axis=0)

    # Use the ResNet-50 model to extract features from the image
    age =round(model.predict(image)[0][0])

    return age

# Define a function to capture video from the default camera and
predict the age of the person in each frame
def real_time_age_prediction():
    cap = cv2.VideoCapture("videoplayback.mp4")
    while True:
        ret, frame = cap.read()

        # Predict the age of the person in the frame
        age = predict_age(frame)

        # Display the age on the frame
        cv2.putText(frame, str(age), (50, 50), cv2.FONT_HERSHEY_SIMPLEX, 1, (0, 0, 255), 2)

        # Convert the image to grayscale for face detection
        gray = cv2.cvtColor(frame, cv2.COLOR_BGR2GRAY)

        # Detect faces in the grayscale image using the Haar Cascade classifier
```

```
        faces = face_cascade.detectMultiScale(gray, scaleFactor=1.1,
        minNeighbors=5)

        # Draw rectangles around the detected faces
        for (x, y, w, h) in faces:
            cv2.rectangle(frame, (x, y), (x+w, y+h), (0, 255, 0), 2)

        # Display the resulting frame
        cv2.imshow('frame', frame)
        if cv2.waitKey(1) & 0xFF == ord('q'):
            break

    # Release the capture and destroy the window
    cap.release()
    cv2.destroyAllWindows()

# Call the function for real-time age prediction
real_time_age_prediction()
```

Refer to the following figure for Real-time age prediction with videos and OpenCV:

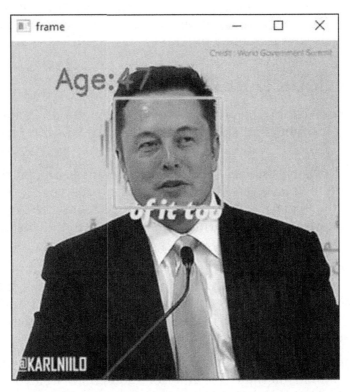

Figure 10.18: *Real-time age prediction using TensorFlow*

Overall, the ResNet-50 CNN is a deep neural network that is able to learn complex features and perform accurate classification and detection tasks. Its use of residual blocks allows it to overcome the problem of vanishing gradients, which can occur in deep neural networks with many layers. The ResNet-50 CNN has been used for a wide range of applications, including image classification, object detection, and facial recognition.

Facial Expression Recognition Using TensorFlow

Emotion detection is the process of identifying human emotions from images, videos, or audio signals. It has various applications, including marketing, psychology, security, and healthcare. Emotion detection can be used to analyze customer feedback, recognize mental health problems, or detect potential security threats, among other things. In this section, we will explain the theory behind emotion detection.

Emotions are complex psychological states that are composed of various components, including physiological, cognitive, and behavioral aspects. Emotions can be positive, such as joy, love, and excitement, or negative, such as fear, anger, and sadness. Emotions are subjective experiences that vary across individuals, cultures, and contexts.

Emotion detection methods

Emotion detection can be performed using various methods, including machine learning, deep learning, and signal processing. Some of the commonly used methods are:

Facial expression analysis: Facial expression analysis is a popular method for emotion detection. It involves analyzing facial features, such as the shape and movement of the eyebrows, mouth, and eyes, to recognize emotions. Facial expression analysis can be performed using rule-based or machine-learning approaches.

- **Speech analysis:** Speech analysis is another method for emotion detection. It involves analyzing the acoustic features of speech signals, such as pitch, intensity, and duration, to recognize emotions. Speech analysis can be performed using signal processing or machine learning techniques.
- **Physiological signals analysis:** Physiological signals analysis is a less common method for emotion detection. It involves analyzing physiological signals, such as heart rate, skin conductance, and

respiration, to recognize emotions. Physiological signals analysis can be performed using signal processing or machine learning techniques.

- **Multimodal analysis:** Multimodal analysis is a combination of multiple methods, such as facial expression analysis, speech analysis, and physiological signals analysis, to improve emotion detection accuracy. Multimodal analysis can be performed using machine learning or deep learning techniques.
- **Emotion recognition datasets:** Emotion recognition datasets are essential for developing and evaluating emotion detection algorithms.

Facial expression recognition is a computer vision task that involves detecting and recognizing the emotions or expressions on a person's face. TensorFlow is a popular open-source machine-learning library that can be used to build and train models for facial expression recognition.

To build a facial expression recognition model using TensorFlow, the following steps are typically involved:

1. **Data collection:** Collect a dataset of images of faces with different expressions, such as happiness, sadness, anger, and surprise.
2. **Data preprocessing:** Preprocess the images by resizing them to a uniform size, normalizing the pixel values, and augmenting the dataset by applying transformations such as rotation, flipping, and zooming to create more diverse images.
3. **Model architecture:** Design the neural network architecture, which typically consists of several convolutional layers followed by pooling layers, and a few fully connected layers for classification.
4. **Model training:** Train the model using the training dataset, by minimizing a loss function such as cross-entropy, and optimizing the model parameters using an optimizer such as stochastic gradient descent.
5. **Model evaluation:** Evaluate the performance of the model on a validation dataset, by measuring metrics such as accuracy, precision, recall, and F1 score.
6. **Model deployment:** Deploy the model in a production environment, by integrating it with a web or mobile app, or an edge device such as a camera.

TensorFlow provides a high-level API called Keras, which simplifies the process of building and training deep learning models. Keras includes pre-trained models for facial expression recognition, such as the VGGFace and ResNet models, which can be fine-tuned on custom datasets for improved performance.

Here's an example of how to perform Real-time age prediction using TensorFlow with OpenCV:

1. Download the emotion dataset files from the following website: https://www.kaggle.com/datasets/jonathanoheix/face-expression-recognition-dataset

2. Refer to the following figure for Under the Emotion folder keeps the datasets:

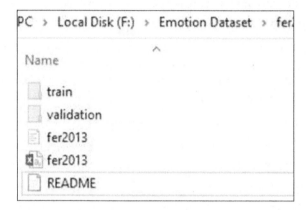

Figure 10.19: Train and Validation dataset under emotion folder

3. Refer to the following figure to Keep the following five Emotions (neutral, happiness, sadness, anger, and surprise) under the Train and validation:

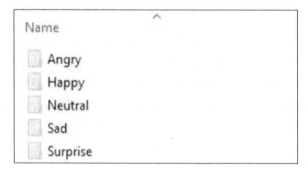

Figure 10.20: All emotion folders under the train and validation folder

4. Train the emotion and save the model using the following code:

```
import tensorflow as tf
from tensorflow import keras
from tensorflow.keras.preprocessing.image import ImageDataGenerator
from tensorflow.keras.models import Sequential
```

```python
from tensorflow.keras.layers import
Dense,Dropout,Activation,Flatten,BatchNormalization
from tensorflow.keras.layers import Conv2D,MaxPooling2D
import os

print(tf.__version__)

from tensorflow.keras.optimizers import Adam
from tensorflow.keras.callbacks import ModelCheckpoint,
EarlyStopping, ReduceLROnPlateau

## assign the image size and class
num_classes = 5   # ['Angry','Happy','Neutral','Sad','Surprise']
img_rows,img_cols = 48,48
batch_size = 32

## give the path to training and validation datasets
train_data_dir = 'Emotion Dataset\\fer2013\\train'
validation_data_dir = 'Emotion Dataset\\fer2013\\validation'

## split the data
train_datagen = ImageDataGenerator(rescale=1./255,rotation_
range=30,shear_range=0.3,
                                    zoom_range=0.3,width_shift_
                                    range=0.4,
                                    height_shift_range=0.4,horizontal_
                                    flip=True,fill_mode='nearest')

validation_datagen = ImageDataGenerator(rescale=1./255)

train_generator = train_datagen.flow_from_directory(train_data_
dir,color_mode='grayscale',

target_size=(img_rows,img_cols),batch_size=batch_size,

class_mode='categorical',shuffle=True)

validation_generator = validation_datagen.flow_from_
directory(validation_data_dir,color_mode='grayscale',
                                    target_size=(img_rows,img_
                                    cols),batch_size=batch_size,
                                    class_
                                    mode='categorical',shuffle=True)

## build the model
model = Sequential()
```

```python
model.add(Conv2D(32,(3,3),padding='same',kernel_initializer='he_normal',input_shape=(img_rows,img_cols,1)))
model.add(Activation('elu'))
model.add(BatchNormalization())
model.add(Conv2D(32,(3,3),padding='same',kernel_initializer='he_normal',input_shape=(img_rows,img_cols,1)))
model.add(Activation('elu'))
model.add(BatchNormalization())
model.add(MaxPooling2D(pool_size=(2,2)))
model.add(Dropout(0.2))

model.add(Conv2D(64,(3,3),padding='same',kernel_initializer='he_normal'))
model.add(Activation('elu'))
model.add(BatchNormalization())
model.add(Conv2D(64,(3,3),padding='same',kernel_initializer='he_normal'))
model.add(Activation('elu'))
model.add(BatchNormalization())
model.add(MaxPooling2D(pool_size=(2,2)))
model.add(Dropout(0.2))

model.add(Conv2D(128,(3,3),padding='same',kernel_initializer='he_normal'))
model.add(Activation('elu'))
model.add(BatchNormalization())
model.add(Conv2D(128,(3,3),padding='same',kernel_initializer='he_normal'))
model.add(Activation('elu'))
model.add(BatchNormalization())
model.add(MaxPooling2D(pool_size=(2,2)))
model.add(Dropout(0.2))

model.add(Conv2D(256,(3,3),padding='same',kernel_initializer='he_normal'))
model.add(Activation('elu'))
model.add(BatchNormalization())
model.add(Conv2D(256,(3,3),padding='same',kernel_initializer='he_normal'))
model.add(Activation('elu'))
model.add(BatchNormalization())
model.add(MaxPooling2D(pool_size=(2,2)))
```

```
model.add(Dropout(0.2))

model.add(Flatten())
model.add(Dense(64,kernel_initializer='he_normal'))
model.add(Activation('elu'))
model.add(BatchNormalization())
model.add(Dropout(0.5))

model.add(Dense(64,kernel_initializer='he_normal'))
model.add(Activation('elu'))
model.add(BatchNormalization())
model.add(Dropout(0.5))

model.add(Dense(num_classes,kernel_initializer='he_normal'))
model.add(Activation('softmax'))

print(model.summary())
```

Refer to the following figure for the emotion recognition model:

Layer (type)	Output Shape	Param #
conv2d (Conv2D)	(None, 48, 48, 32)	320
activation (Activation)	(None, 48, 48, 32)	0
batch_normalization (BatchNo	(None, 48, 48, 32)	128
conv2d_1 (Conv2D)	(None, 48, 48, 32)	9248
activation_1 (Activation)	(None, 48, 48, 32)	0
batch_normalization_1 (Batch	(None, 48, 48, 32)	128
max_pooling2d (MaxPooling2D)	(None, 24, 24, 32)	0
dropout (Dropout)	(None, 24, 24, 32)	0
conv2d_2 (Conv2D)	(None, 24, 24, 64)	18496
activation_2 (Activation)	(None, 24, 24, 64)	0
batch_normalization_2 (Batch	(None, 24, 24, 64)	256

Model: "sequential"

Figure 10.21: Emotion recognition model

```python
## Save the Model
    checkpoint = ModelCheckpoint('Emotion_model.h5',
                      monitor='val_loss',
                      mode='min',
                      save_best_only=True,
                      verbose=1)

earlystop = EarlyStopping(monitor='val_loss',
                    min_delta=0,
                    patience=3,
                    verbose=1,
                    restore_best_weights=True
                    )

reduce_lr = ReduceLROnPlateau(monitor='val_loss',
                        factor=0.2,
                        patience=3,
                        verbose=1,
                        min_delta=0.0001)

callbacks = [earlystop,checkpoint,reduce_lr]

## Compile the CNN Model
    model.compile(loss='categorical_crossentropy',
          optimizer = Adam(lr=0.001),
          metrics=['accuracy'])

nb_train_samples = 24176
    nb_validation_samples = 3006
    epochs=25

history=model.fit_generator(
            train_generator,
            steps_per_epoch=nb_train_samples//batch_size,
            epochs=epochs,
            callbacks=callbacks,
            validation_data=validation_generator,
            validation_steps=nb_validation_samples//batch_
            size)
```

Refer to the following figure for Training the emotion recognition model:

```
Epoch 1/25
754/755 [============================>.] - ETA: 6s - loss: 1.8282 - accuracy: 0.2451
Epoch 00001: val_loss improved from inf to 1.55999, saving model to Emotion_model1.h5
755/755 [=============================] - 4958s 7s/step - loss: 1.8280 - accuracy: 0.2450 - val_loss: 1.5600 - val_accuracy: 0.2903
Epoch 2/25
754/755 [============================>.] - ETA: 38s - loss: 1.5733 - accuracy: 0.2837
Epoch 00002: val_loss improved from 1.55999 to 1.53648, saving model to Emotion_model1.h5
755/755 [=============================] - 2926s 39s/step - loss: 1.5732 - accuracy: 0.2838 - val_loss: 1.5365 - val_accuracy: 0.3088
Epoch 3/25
754/755 [============================>.] - ETA: 1s - loss: 1.5421 - accuracy: 0.3033
Epoch 00003: val_loss improved from 1.53648 to 1.51408, saving model to Emotion_model1.h5
755/755 [=============================] - 1244s 2s/step - loss: 1.5422 - accuracy: 0.3032 - val_loss: 1.5141 - val_accuracy: 0.3320
Epoch 4/25
754/755 [============================>.] - ETA: 1s - loss: 1.5186 - accuracy: 0.3224
Epoch 00004: val_loss did not improve from 1.51408
755/755 [=============================] - 1235s 2s/step - loss: 1.5185 - accuracy: 0.3225 - val_loss: 1.5238 - val_accuracy: 0.3575
Epoch 5/25
754/755 [============================>.] - ETA: 1s - loss: 1.4522 - accuracy: 0.3576
Epoch 00005: val_loss did not improve from 1.51408
755/755 [=============================] - 1408s 2s/step - loss: 1.4521 - accuracy: 0.3576 - val_loss: 1.7786 - val_accuracy: 0.4012
Epoch 6/25
754/755 [============================>.] - ETA: 1s - loss: 1.3624 - accuracy: 0.4223
Epoch 00006: val_loss improved from 1.51408 to 1.33077, saving model to Emotion_model1.h5
755/755 [=============================] - 1237s 2s/step - loss: 1.3626 - accuracy: 0.4222 - val_loss: 1.3308 - val_accuracy: 0.5148
```

Figure 10.22: *Training the emotion recognition model*

```python
## Plot the Train and Validation Accuracy_Loss
    import numpy as np
    import pandas as pd
    import matplotlib.pyplot as plt

def plot_learningCurve(history):
        # Plot training & validation accuracy values
    epoch_range = range(1, 12)
    plt.plot(epoch_range, history.history['accuracy'])
    plt.plot(epoch_range, history.history['val_accuracy'])
    plt.title('Model accuracy')
    plt.ylabel('Accuracy')
   plt.xlabel('Epoch')
    plt.legend(['Train', 'Val'], loc='upper left')
    plt.show()

  # Plot training & validation loss values
    plt.plot(epoch_range, history.history['loss'])
    plt.plot(epoch_range, history.history['val_loss'])
    plt.title('Model loss')
        plt.ylabel('Loss')
    plt.xlabel('Epoch')
    plt.legend(['Train', 'Val'], loc='upper left')
```

```
        plt.show()

plot_learningCurve(history)
```

Refer to the following figure for Model loss and accuracy for facial expression recognition:

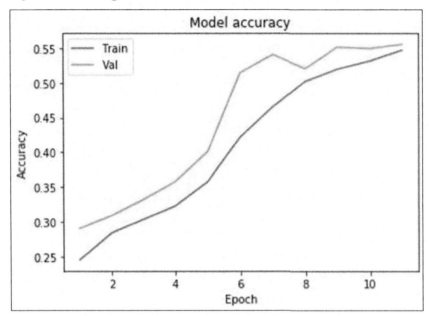

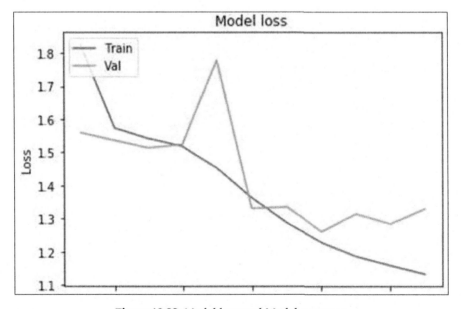

Figure 10.23: *Model loss and Model accuracy*

5. Download the **aarcascade_frontalface_default.xml** file and test the emotion model using the following code:

```
import cv2
import numpy as np

print(cv2.__version__)

import datetime
from tensorflow.keras.models import load_model
from tensorflow.keras.preprocessing.image import img_to_array
from tensorflow.keras.preprocessing import image
face_classifier = cv2.CascadeClassifier('haarcascade_frontalface_default.xml')
classifier =load_model('Emotion_model.h5')

class_labels = ['Angry','Happy','Neutral','Sad','Surprise']

cap = cv2.VideoCapture(0);

print(cap.get(cv2.CAP_PROP_FRAME_WIDTH))
print(cap.get(cv2.CAP_PROP_FRAME_HEIGHT))

# Define the codec and create VideoWriter object
fourcc =cv2.VideoWriter_fourcc(*'MJPG')
out =cv2.VideoWriter('output.avi', fourcc, 20.0 ,(640, 480))

while True:
    # Grab a single frame of video
    ret, frame = cap.read()
    labels = []
    gray = cv2.cvtColor(frame,cv2.COLOR_BGR2GRAY)
    faces = face_classifier.detectMultiScale(gray,1.3,5)

     font = cv2.FONT_HERSHEY_SIMPLEX

    text = 'Width:' + str(cap.get(3)) + "Height:" + str(cap.get(4))
    datet = str(datetime.datetime.now())
```

```python
        txt = cv2.putText(frame , datet, (10, 50),font, 1 ,
        (0,255,255) , 2, cv2.LINE_AA)

    for (x,y,w,h) in faces:
        cv2.rectangle(frame,(x,y),(x+w,y+h),(255,0,0),2)
        roi_gray = gray[y:y+h,x:x+w]
        roi_gray = cv2.resize(roi_gray,(48,48),interpolation=cv2.
        INTER_AREA)
    # rect,face,image = face_detector(frame)

        if np.sum([roi_gray])!=0:
            roi = roi_gray.astype('float')/255.0
            roi = img_to_array(roi)
            roi = np.expand_dims(roi,axis=0)

    # make a prediction on the ROI, then lookup the class
            preds = classifier.predict(roi)[0]
            label=class_labels[preds.argmax()]
            label_position = (x,y)
            cv2.putText(frame,label,label_
            position,font,2,(0,255,0),3)
        else:
            cv2.putText(frame,'No Face
            Found',(20,60),font,2,(0,255,0),3)

    cv2.imshow('Emotion Detector',frame)

    out.write(frame)

    if cv2.waitKey(1) & 0xFF == ord('q'):
        break
cap.release()
out.release()
cv2.destroyAllWindows()
```

Refer to the following figure for Happy emotion in Facial expression recognition:

Figure 10.24: Happy Emotion in Facial expression recognition

Refer to the following figure for Neutral emotion in Facial expression recognition:

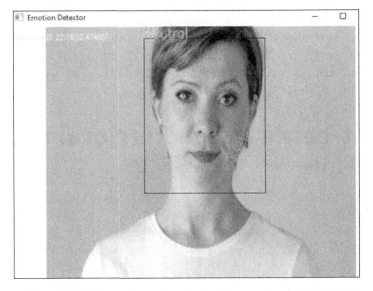

Figure 10.25: Neutral emotion in Facial expression recognition

Refer to the following figure for Angry emotion in Facial expression recognition:

Figure 10.26: Angry emotion in facial expression recognition

Emotion detection is an exciting research field with many applications. It involves identifying human emotions from various sources, including facial expressions, speech signals, and physiological signals. Emotion detection can be performed using machine learning, deep learning, or signal processing techniques. Emotion recognition datasets are essential for developing and evaluating emotion detection algorithms.

Content-based Image Retrieval Using TensorFlow

Content-based image retrieval (CBIR) is a technique that involves searching and retrieving images from a large database based on their visual content. In other words, it is a method of searching for images by similarity in their visual features like color, texture, shape, and other visual cues, rather than relying on textual information or tags.

CBIR is becoming an essential tool in various applications, including multimedia retrieval, medical diagnosis, and remote sensing. It has many real-world applications such as reverse image search, image similarity search, and visual search engines.

Refer to the following figure for content-based image retrieval using TensorFlow:

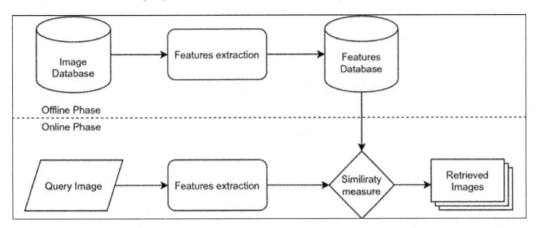

Figure 10.27: Content-based image Retrieval architecture

TensorFlow, one of the most popular deep learning frameworks, has a lot of tools to build a CBIR system. The main steps in creating a CBIR system using TensorFlow are:

1. Data preparation: The first step in CBIR is to prepare the data. The images in the dataset need to be preprocessed and converted into a format suitable for analysis. This step includes data cleaning, normalization, and resizing.

2. Feature extraction: In this step, the relevant features of each image are extracted using a deep learning model. Popular feature extraction models include VGG, ResNet, and Inception.

3. Indexing: Once the features are extracted, an indexing system is created to store and retrieve the image features efficiently. Various techniques like k-means clustering, PCA, and LSH can be used to index the features.

4. Query processing: This step involves comparing the query image's features with the indexed features to retrieve the most similar images.

Here's an overview of how to build a CBIR system using TensorFlow:

1. Data preparation:
    a. Collect the images and organize them into a dataset.
    b. Preprocess the images by cleaning, resizing, and normalizing them.
2. Feature extraction:
    a. Choose a pre-trained deep-learning model for feature extraction. Extract the features for each image in the dataset.

b. Store the extracted features in a file.

3. Indexing:

    a. Choose an indexing method that suits the dataset size and the feature vector length.

    b. Create an index that stores the feature vectors for fast search.

4. Query processing:

    a. Extract features from the query image.

    b. Search the index for the images that match the query features.

    c. Rank the retrieved images by similarity and return the top results.

Here's an example of how to perform Content-based image retrieval using TensorFlow with OpenCV:

1. Download the emotion dataset files from the following website. https://www.kaggle.com/datasets/mugeshraja/unsupervised-image-retrieval-datasets

2. Go to Google Colab and create a new notebook.

    https://colab.research.google.com/

3. Refer to the following figure to load the dataset.zip file in Google Colab using the upload option:

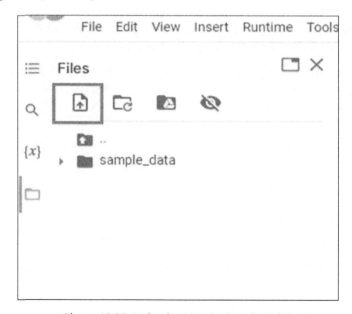

Figure 10.28: Upload option in Google Colab

4. Change the Runtime type to GPU as a hardware accelerator by following the steps.

   Click **Runtime** → **Change Runtime type** → **select** GPU in hardware accelerator dropdown → click **Save**.

5. Run the following code to perform CBIR:

   ```
   from zipfile import ZipFile
   import cv2

   import numpy as np
   import tensorflow as tf
   from tensorflow.keras.layers import Input, Conv2D, MaxPooling2D, UpSampling2D
   from tensorflow.keras.models import Model
   from tensorflow.keras.models import load_model
   import matplotlib.pyplot as plt
   %matplotlib inline
   from glob import glob
   import cv2, os
   import numpy as np
   import matplotlib.pyplot as plt
   import keras
   from keras.preprocessing import image
   ```

6. Unzip the file:

   ```
   file_name = "/dataset.zip"

   with ZipFile(file_name, 'r') as zip:
       zip.extractall()
       print('done')

   # display the image
   img = cv2.imread('/dataset/1001.jpg', -1)
   from google.colab.patches import cv2_imshow
   cv2_imshow(img)
   ```

Refer to the following figure for a sample image from the dataset:

Figure 10.29: Sample image from the dataset

7. Load the images:

```
path = '/dataset'

img_dataset = []
def load_img():
    img_path = os.path.join(path, "*")
    for im in glob(img_path):
        img  = cv2.imread(im)
        data = cv2.cvtColor(img, cv2.COLOR_BGR2GRAY)
        data = cv2.resize(data, (512, 512))
        data = image.img_to_array(data)
        img_dataset.append(data)
    print('All images loaded')
load_img()
# All images loaded
print('Number of the Images: {}'.format(len(img_dataset)))

## display the random images
import random
plt.figure(figsize=(12,8))
```

```
for i in range(5):
    plt.subplot(1, 5, i+1)
    img = image.array_to_img(random.choice(img_dataset))
    plt.imshow(img)
    plt.axis('off')

plt.show()
```
Refer to the following figure for sample images in training datasets:

Figure 10.30: Sample images in training datasets

8. Split the data:

```
end =round(len(img_dataset) * 0.95)

X_train =img_dataset[:end]
X_test  =img_dataset[end:]
print(len(X_train) ,len(X_test))

## Normalize the data
X_train = np.asarray(X_train) / 255
X_test = np.asarray(X_test) / 255

## Reshape the data to have 1 channel
print(X_train.shape, X_test.shape)

X_train = np.reshape(X_train, (-1, 512, 512, 1))
X_test = np.reshape(X_test, (-1, 512, 512, 1))
print(X_train.shape, X_test.shape)
```

9. Create the autoencoder:

```
input_img = Input(shape=(512,512,1))
x = Conv2D(32,(3,3), activation='relu', padding='same')(input_img)
x = MaxPooling2D((2,2), padding='same')(x)
```

```python
x = Conv2D(16,(3,3), activation='relu', padding='same')(x)
x = MaxPooling2D((2,2), padding='same')(x)
x = Conv2D(8,(3,3), activation='relu', padding='same')(x)
x = MaxPooling2D((2,2), padding='same')(x)
x = Conv2D(4,(3,3), activation='relu', padding='same')(x)
x = MaxPooling2D((2,2), padding='same')(x)
x = Conv2D(2,(3,3), activation='relu', padding='same')(x)
encoded = MaxPooling2D((2,2), padding='same', name='encoder')(x)

x = Conv2D(2, (3, 3), activation='relu', padding='same')(encoded)
x = UpSampling2D((2, 2))(x)
x = Conv2D(4, (3, 3), activation='relu', padding='same')(x)
x = UpSampling2D((2, 2))(x)
x = Conv2D(8, (3, 3), activation='relu', padding='same')(x)
x = UpSampling2D((2, 2))(x)
x = Conv2D(16, (3, 3), activation='relu', padding='same')(x)
x = UpSampling2D((2, 2))(x)
x = Conv2D(32, (3, 3), activation='relu', padding='same')(x)
x = UpSampling2D((2, 2))(x)
decoded = Conv2D(1, (3, 3), activation='sigmoid', padding='same')(x)

autoencoder = Model(input_img, decoded)
autoencoder.compile(optimizer='adam', loss='mse')
autoencoder.summary()
```

10. Train and save the model:

    ```python
    autoencoder.fit(X_train, X_train, epochs=4, batch_size=16, callbacks=None );
    autoencoder.save('autoencoder.h5')


    # Create the encoder part
    # The encoder part is the first half of the autoencoder,
    i.e. the part that will encode the input into a latent
    space representation. In this case, the dimension of this
    representation is

    autoencoder =Model('/content/autoencoder.h5')
    encoder = Model(inputs=autoencoder.input, outputs=autoencoder.get_layer('encoder').output)
    ```

```python
encoder.save('encoder.h5')
encoder =Model('/content/encoder.h5')

# Load the query image
# We take a query image from the test set

query = X_test[8]
plt.imshow(query.reshape(512,512), cmap='gray');

# Encode the test images and the query image
X_test.shape
# We remove the query image from the test set (the set in which
we will search for close images)

X_test = np.delete(X_test, 8, axis=0)
X_test.shape

# Encode the query image and the test set
codes = encoder.predict(X_test)
query_code = encoder.predict(query.reshape(1,512,512,1))
codes.shape

query_code.shape

a=1
for i in query_code[0].shape:
    a = a*i
print(a)
```

11. Find the closest images:

    ```python
    # We will find the 9 closest images
    from sklearn.neighbors import NearestNeighbors

    n_neigh = 9
    codes = codes.reshape(-1, a); print(codes.shape)
    query_code = query_code.reshape(1, a); print(query_code.shape)

    # Fit the KNN to the test set
    nbrs = NearestNeighbors(n_neighbors=n_neigh).fit(codes)
    distances, indices = nbrs.kneighbors(np.array(query_code))
    ```

```
closest_images = X_test[indices]
closest_images = closest_images.reshape(-1,512,512,1);
print(closest_images.shape)
```

12. Get the closest images:

    ```
    plt.imshow(query.reshape(512,512), cmap='gray');
    ```

Refer to the following figure to get the closest images:

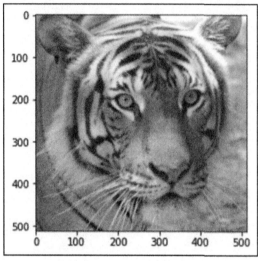

Figure 10.31: *Test the closest images*

```
plt.figure(figsize=(20, 6))
for i in range(n_neigh):
    # display original
    ax = plt.subplot(1, n_neigh, i+1)
    plt.imshow(closest_images[i].reshape(512, 512))
    plt.gray()
    ax.get_xaxis().set_visible(False)
    ax.get_yaxis().set_visible(False)

plt.show()
```

Refer to the following figure for getting the closest images in the CBIR model:

Figure 10.32: *Results from the CBIR model*

Building a CBIR system requires knowledge of deep learning, computer vision, and information retrieval. The choice of pre-trained models, indexing methods, and feature representations can significantly impact the performance of the system.

Conclusion

In this chapter, we have discussed YOLO architecture and its types along with their object detection code and YOLO v5 custom data training explanations. We will also discuss detailed theory and code explanation of face recognition, real-time age detection, emotion detection and content-based image retrieval projects using TensorFlow, OpenCV and Python programming languages.

In the next chapter, we will discuss the deployment of OpenCV projects and the integration of web applications using OpenCV and Python.

Points to Remember

- Use Google Colab (https://colab.research.google.com/) for the above deep-leaving project training.
- Install TensorFlow if working on a local machine using the following command:

    ```
    ! pip install tensorflow
    ```

- Download the `haarcascades.xml` file from Haar Cascade GitHub.

    https://github.com/opencv/opencv/tree/master/data/haarcascades

References

- OpenCV Deep Learning Overview

    https://github.com/opencv/opencv/wiki/Deep-Learning-in-OpenCV

    https://learnopencv.com/deep-learning-with-opencvs-dnn-module-a-definitive-guide/

CHAPTER 11

Deployment of OpenCV Projects

Introduction

In this chapter, we will cover the introduction to the deployment of OpenCV projects using GCP and Microsoft Azure. We will also discuss the integration of deep learning projects with web applications using Flask, OpenCV and Python programming languages.

Structure

In this chapter, we will cover the following topics:

- Introduction to deploying OpenCV projects
- Integrating OpenCV with web applications
- Integrating dog vs. cat classification project and flask

Introduction to Deploying OpenCV Projects

Deploying an OpenCV project refers to the process of making a computer vision application available for use by end-users or integrating it with other systems. Deploying an OpenCV project can be challenging due to the various dependencies involved, such as different hardware, operating systems, libraries, and environments.

The deployment process typically involves creating an executable file, building an installer, or containerizing the application. The following are the general steps involved in deploying an OpenCV project:

1. **Identify the target environment:** Before deploying an OpenCV project, you need to identify the target environment, including the hardware, operating system, and dependencies required to run the application.

2. **Prepare the environment:** Once you have identified the target environment, you need to prepare it by installing the necessary dependencies and libraries required by the OpenCV project.

3. **Build the application:** After preparing the environment, you need to build the OpenCV project to create an executable file, which can be run on the target environment.

4. **Test the application:** After building the application, you need to test it to ensure it works as expected in the target environment.

5. **Create an installer or container:** Once you have tested the application, you can create an installer or containerize the application to make it available for use by end-users or integrate it with other systems.

6. **Monitor the application:** Monitor the deployed project to detect and address any errors or issues that may arise. Perform regular maintenance and updates to keep the deployed project up-to-date and secure.

There are various tools and platforms available for deploying OpenCV projects, including Docker, PyInstaller, and CMake:

- **Docker:** Docker is an open-source containerization platform that allows you to package an OpenCV application and its dependencies into a single container, which can be run on any platform. Docker containers are lightweight, portable, and provide a consistent runtime environment.

- **PyInstaller:** PyInstaller is a cross-platform packaging tool that allows you to package an OpenCV application and its dependencies into a single executable file, which can be run on any platform without requiring any installation or configuration.

- **CMake:** CMake is a cross-platform build system that allows you to automate the build process of an OpenCV project. CMake generates build files for various platforms and environments, which can be used to build the application.

In summary, deploying an OpenCV project requires identifying the target environment, preparing the environment, building the application, testing it, and creating an installer or container. There are various tools and platforms available for deploying OpenCV projects, including Docker, PyInstaller, and CMake.

Deploying OpenCV projects in Azure

Deploying OpenCV projects in Azure can be done in various ways depending on the requirements and resources available. Here is a general guide on how to deploy OpenCV projects in Azure:

1. **Create an Azure account:** Create an Azure account (https://azure.microsoft.com/en-in) and log in to the Azure portal.

   Refer to the following figure for the Azure home page:

   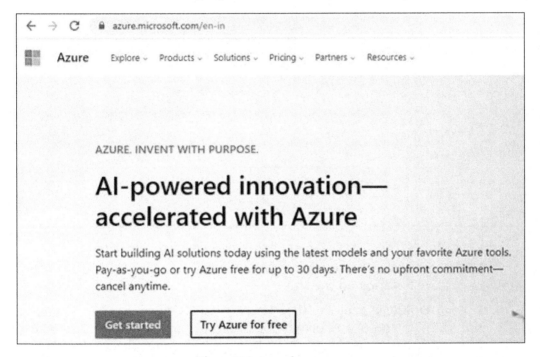

   Figure 11.1: Azure home page

2. **Set up a VM instance:** Create a virtual machine (VM) to host the OpenCV project. You can choose from a variety of VM options available in Azure, depending on the project's resource requirements.

Refer to the following figure for creating a page of an Azure virtual machine:

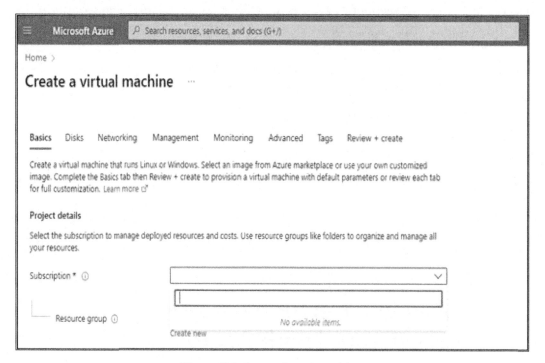

Figure 11.2: *Azure virtual machine*

3. **Install necessary software and libraries:** Install OpenCV and any other necessary libraries on the VM.

4. **Upload OpenCV project files:** Upload your OpenCV project code to the VM. You can use Azure's built-in file transfer tools, such as Azure Storage Explorer or the Azure CLI, to transfer your files to the VM. Set up a web server on the VM to host the OpenCV project. You can use Apache, Nginx, or another web server of your choice.

5. **Configure OpenCV project:** Configure the webserver to run the OpenCV project. This can be done by creating a configuration file for the web server that points to the OpenCV project's main file.

6. **Scale the OpenCV project:** Open the appropriate ports on the VM to allow incoming traffic to the web server. Test the OpenCV project by accessing the web server's public IP address or domain name. Set up SSL encryption to secure traffic to the OpenCV project. (Optional).

7. **Monitoring and logging:** Monitor the project's performance and make any necessary adjustments to the VM's resources or the project's configuration to optimize its performance.

Refer to the following figure for enabling a page of Azure monitoring:

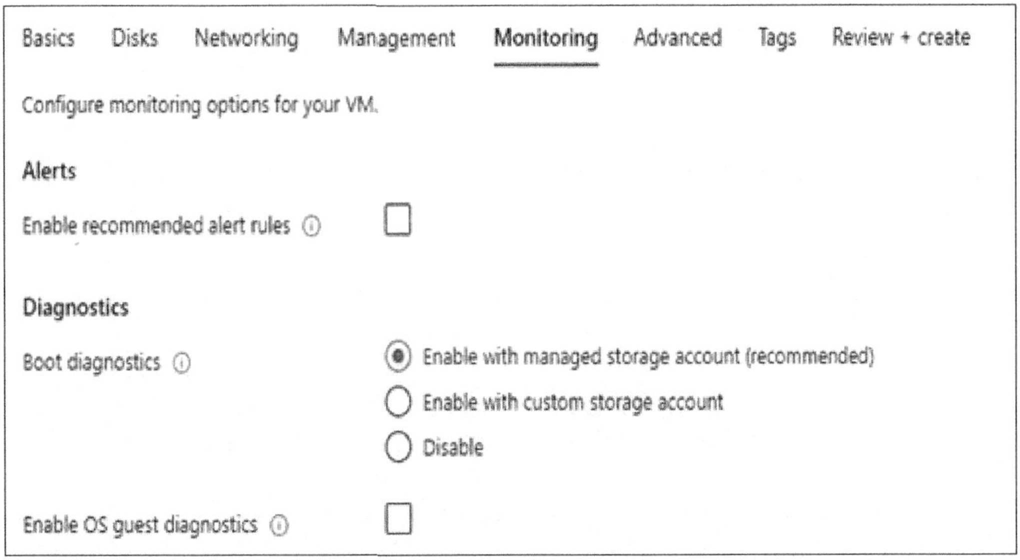

Figure 11.3: *Azure monitoring page*

These are the general steps involved in deploying OpenCV projects in Azure. However, the specific details may vary depending on the project's requirements and the resources available in Azure.

Deploying OpenCV projects in Azure

Deploying OpenCV projects in Google Cloud Platform (GCP) involves several steps, including creating a GCP account, setting up a virtual machine (VM) instance, installing necessary software and libraries, and deploying the OpenCV project on the VM. Here is a step-by-step guide on how to deploy OpenCV projects in GCP:

1. **Create a GCP account:** If you do not already have a GCP account, create one by visiting the GCP website (https://console.cloud.google.com/) and following the prompts to create an account.

   Refer to the following figure for the GCP home page:

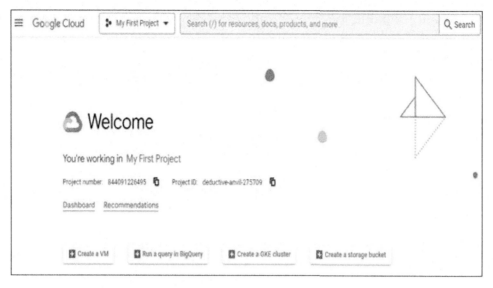

Figure 11.4: GCP home page

2. **Set up a VM instance:** After creating your GCP account, create a VM instance by navigating to the Compute Engine section of the GCP console and clicking on "**Create instance**." Choose the operating system, machine type, and other specifications for the VM as per your requirement.

Refer to the following figure for creating a page of a GCP virtual machine.

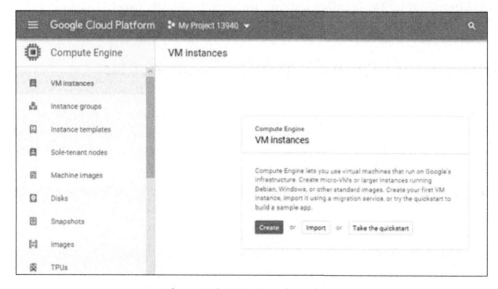

Figure 11.5: GCP virtual machine

3. **Install necessary software and libraries:** Once the VM instance is created, install the necessary software and libraries required for the OpenCV project. This can be done by logging into the VM instance and running commands to install the required packages.

4. **Upload OpenCV project files:** Upload the OpenCV project files to the VM instance. This can be done by using the command-line interface or by using a web-based file manager.

5. **Test the OpenCV project:** Once the OpenCV project files are uploaded to the VM instance, test the project to ensure it is working correctly. This can be done by running the project on the VM instance and verifying the output.

6. **Deploy the OpenCV project:** After testing the project, deploy it on the VM instance so that it can be accessed from outside the instance. This can be done by configuring the firewall rules and exposing the required ports.

7. **Scale the OpenCV project:** If required, scale the OpenCV project by creating additional VM instances and configuring them to work together. If you're using Kubernetes Engine or App Engine, you can scale your application to handle more traffic by adding more nodes or instances.

8. **Monitoring and logging:** GCP provides several tools for monitoring and logging your OpenCV projects, such as Cloud Monitoring and Cloud Logging. These tools can help you identify and troubleshoot issues with your application.

Refer to the following figure for enabling a page of GCP monitoring:

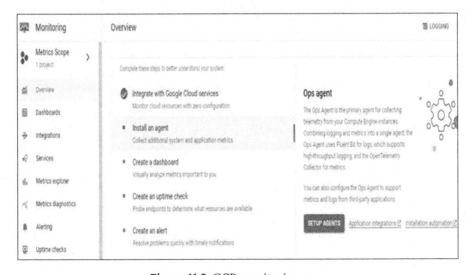

Figure 11.6: GCP monitoring page

Overall, deploying an OpenCV project on GCP requires some initial setup and configuration, but GCP provides a robust platform for running and scaling your applications.

Integrating OpenCV with web applications

It is a powerful way to bring computer vision capabilities to the web. OpenCV provides a wide range of computer vision tools, while web applications offer a convenient platform for users to interact with these tools.

There are several ways to integrate OpenCV with web applications, including:

Using web frameworks: Web frameworks like Flask, Django, and Ruby on Rails allow developers to build web applications with Python, Ruby, or other programming languages. OpenCV can be integrated with these frameworks to build web applications that incorporate computer vision capabilities.

- **Using APIs:** APIs provide a way to expose OpenCV functionality to web applications. Developers can build APIs using OpenCV and use them to integrate computer vision capabilities into web applications.
- **Using JavaScript libraries:** JavaScript libraries like OpenCV.js provide a way to use OpenCV functionality directly in web browsers. Developers can use these libraries to build web applications that incorporate computer vision capabilities.

When integrating OpenCV with web applications, there are several considerations to keep in mind. These include:

Performance: Computer vision algorithms can be computationally intensive, and web applications must be able to handle this workload. Optimizing algorithms for performance is key to building fast and responsive web applications.

- **Security:** Web applications that incorporate computer vision capabilities must be designed with security in mind. User data and images must be handled carefully to ensure that they are not compromised.
- **Usability:** Web applications must be easy to use and intuitive for users. Careful design of user interfaces and workflows is essential to building applications that users can understand and use effectively.

Overall, integrating OpenCV with web applications provides an exciting opportunity to bring computer vision capabilities to the web.

With careful attention to performance, security, and usability, developers can build powerful and effective applications that help users to solve real-world problems.

Integrating dog vs. cat classification project and flask

Deploying an OpenCV project using Flask involves creating a web application that can take input images, process them using OpenCV, and display the output to the user on a web page. Here's a step-by-step guide on how to do this:

1. **Install Flask:** Flask is a web application framework for Python. To install it, use the command **! pip install flask** in the command line.
2. **Create a new Flask app:** Create a new Python file and import Flask at the top:

    ```
    from flask import Flask
    app = Flask(__name__)
    ```

To deploy the dog vs cat project using Flask, you can follow these general steps:

Train your model and save it to disk in a format that can be loaded by your Flask app (for example, .h5 file for Keras models).

1. Write a Flask app that loads the model and defines routes for handling incoming requests. Define a route for uploading an image file to classify.
2. Preprocess the image (for example, resize, convert to RGB) and pass it through the model for classification.
3. Return the classification result (for example, "dog" or "cat") to the user.

Here is some example code that demonstrates these steps:

Step 1: Create a Flask App:

```
from flask import Flask, request, render_template
import os
import cv2
from keras.models import load_model
import numpy as np
app = Flask(__name__)
```

Step 2: Load the trained model:

```
## Load the trained model
model = load_model('dog_vs_cat.h5')
```

Step 3: Define the function to preprocess the image:

```
## Define the function to preprocess the image
def preprocess(img):
    img = cv2.resize(img, (256, 256))
```

```
        img = img / 255.0
        img = np.expand_dims(img, axis=0)
        return img
```

Step 4: Define the prediction function.

```
## Define the prediction function
@app.route('/predict', methods=['POST'])
def predict():
    # Get the file from the request
    file = request.files['image']
    # Save the file to the uploads folder
    file.save(os.path.join('uploads', file.filename))
    # Read the image
    img = cv2.imread(os.path.join('uploads', file.filename))
    # Preprocess the image
    img = preprocess(img)
    # Make predictions
    prediction = model.predict(img)
    if prediction[0] > 0.7:
        return 'Dog'
    else:
        return 'Cat'
```

Step 5: Define the function to render the index.html template:

```
## Define the function to render the index.html template
@app.route('/')
def index():
    return render_template('index.html')
```

Step 6: Define the main function:

```
## Define the main function
if __name__ == '__main__':
    app.run(debug=True)
```

Step 7: Create a templates folder and add an **index.html** file with the following content:

```
<!DOCTYPE html>
<html>
<head>
```

```
        <title>Dog vs Cat Classifier</title>
    </head>
    <body>
        <h1>Dog vs Cat Classifier</h1>
        <form method="POST" action="/predict" enctype="multipart/form-data">
            <input type="file" name="image">
            <br><br>
            <input type="submit" value="Predict">
        </form>
    </body>
</html>
```

Step 8: Create an uploads folder inside the app folder.

Refer to the following figure for py and HTML file arrangement in Dog vs Cat classification:

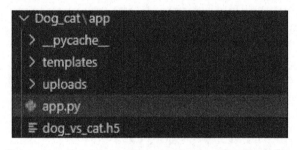

Figure 11.7: Overview of Dog vs Cat classification folder

Step 9: Navigate to the app folder:

```
E:\DL\Dog_cat\app
```

Step 10: Run the Flask app using the following command in Linux:

```
$ export FLASK_APP=app.py
$ flask run
```

Step 11: Run the Flask app using the following command in Windows:

```
$ set FLASK_APP=app.py
$ flask run
```

Refer to the following figure for Dog vs Cat classification code output:

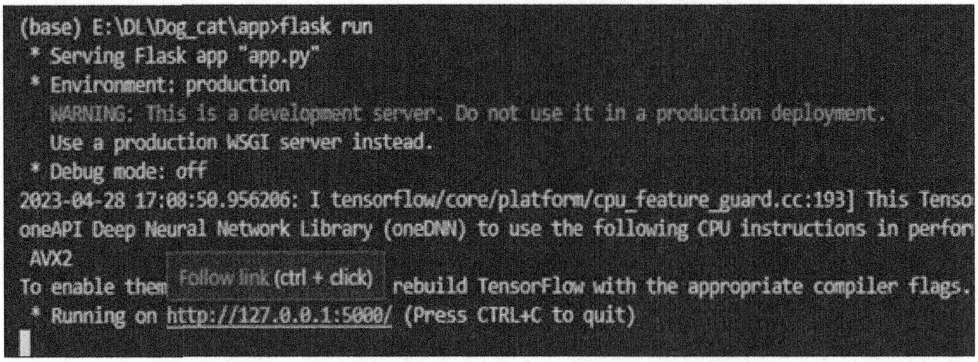

Figure 11.8: Dog vs Cat classification code output

Step 12: Click the following link and upload the dog or cat image.

Link: http://127.0.0.1:5000/

Refer to the following figure for the webpage of Dog vs Cat classification and upload the dog image using choose file button then click **Predict** button.

Figure 11.9: Dog vs Cat classification webpage

Refer to the following figure for Dog vs Cat classification result webpage:

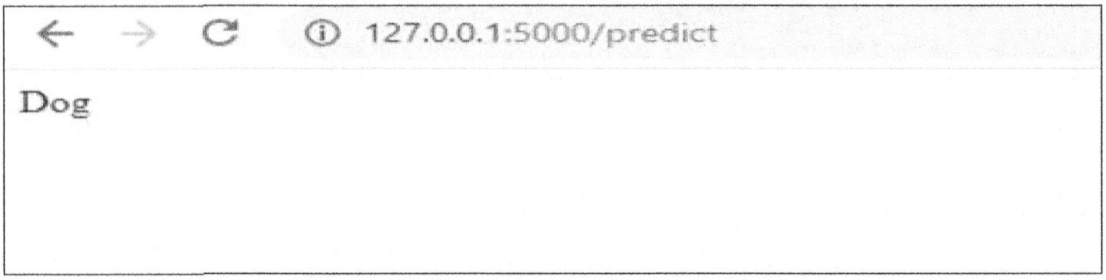

Figure 11.10: Dog vs Cat classification result webpage

In this code, we define a Flask app and load our trained Keras model. We then define two routes: the home route (/) which returns an HTML template with a form for uploading an image, and the predicted route (/predict) which handles the image upload, preprocesses the image, passes it through the model for classification, and returns the classification result as plain text.

The preceding code provides a basic structure for deploying a dog vs cat deep learning project using Flask. However, depending on the specific requirements of your project, you may need to modify the code to suit your needs.

Note that this is just a simple example and there are many other considerations when deploying a machine learning model in production, such as input validation, error handling, and security.

Conclusion

In this chapter, we have discussed an introduction to the deployment of OpenCV projects using GCP and Microsoft Azure and their steps. We have also discussed the installation of Flask and integration of deep learning projects with web applications using Flask, OpenCV and Python programming languages.

Points to Remember

Install Flask if working on a local machine using the following command:

```
! pip install Flask
```

References

Integration of Web application and OpenCV projects.

https://towardsdatascience.com/how-to-deploy-a-pre-trained-keras-model-with-opencv-and-flask-86c9dab76a9c

Deploying OpenCV projects using GCP and Azure.

GCP: https://cloud.google.com/docs

Azure: https://learn.microsoft.com/en-us/azure/azure-portal/

Index

Symbols

1D histogram 111
2D histogram 111

A

activation functions
  about 211
  exponential linear unit (ELU) function 212
  hyperbolic tangent (tanh) function 212
  Leaky ReLU function 212
  rectified linear unit (ReLU) function 212
  sigmoid function 212
  softmax function 212
adaptive learning rate methods 213
adaptive thresholding 99, 100
additive blending 85
Anaconda
  reference link 10
APIs 306
artificial intelligence (AI) 206
artificial neural networks (ANNs)
  about 206, 207
  activation functions 211
  deep learning applications 216
  deep learning frameworks 215
  deep neural networks, training 214, 215
  neural network architecture 211
  neural network optimization techniques 213
augmented reality (AR)
  about 171
  in OpenCV 171-176
autoencoders 209, 210
Azure
  OpenCV project, deploying 301-305

B

background removal 48-50
background subtraction methods
  in OpenCV 151, 152
background subtraction methods, types
  BackgroundSubtractorKNN method 154-156
  BackgroundSubtractorMOG2 method 152-154
  in OpenCV 152
BackgroundSubtractorKNN method 154-156
BackgroundSubtractorMOG2 method 152-154
backpropagation 223
bilateral filter 78
binary thresholding 101, 102
bitwise operations 60-63
Blob Detection 138
box filter 79

C

calib3d module 125
camera calibration with OpenCV 125-129
camera parameters
  setting, in OpenCV 28, 29
CAMShift object tracking method
  with OpenCV 168-171
Canny Edge Detection
  with OpenCV 93-96
Canny Edge Detection Algorithm 90
characters recognition 197
circle detection
  with OpenCV Hough circle transform 123, 124
clustering 205
computer vision

Index

about 1, 2
OpenCV real-time applications 4
computer vision algorithms
  high-level algorithms 2
  low-level algorithms 2
content-based image retrieval (CBIR)
  about 288
  with TensorFlow 288-297
Continuously Adaptive Mean
    Shift (CAMShift) 168
Contours with OpenCV
  drawing 104-107
  finding 104-107
convolutional neural networks
    (CNNs) 208, 211
corner detection
  in OpenCV 137
corner detection, methods
  Blob Detection 138
  FAST Corner Detection 138
  Harris Corner Detection 138
  Scale-Invariant Feature Transform (SIFT) 138
  Shi-Tomasi Corner Detection 138
  Speeded-Up Robust Feature (SURF) 138
corner detection, types
  blob detection 144-146
  FAST corner detection 143, 144
  Harris Corner Detector 139-141
  in OpenCV 139
  scale-invariant feature
      transform (SIFT) 147, 148
  Shi Tomasi Corner Detector 141, 142

D

date and time of videos
  displaying, with OpenCV 29, 31
decision trees 205
deep learning 206
deep learning applications
  autonomous vehicles 216
  healthcare 216
  Natural language processing (NLP) 216
  robotics 217
  speech recognition 216
deep learning in OpenCV
  about 217

face detection, with neural networks 221, 222
face recognition, with neural
    networks 221, 222
image classification, with deep neural
    networks 218, 219
neural networks, in image and video
    analytics 217, 218
object detection, with neural
    networks 219-221
semantic segmentation network 222, 223
deep neural networks
  training 214, 215
Digit Recognition Model
  testing, with OpenCV 236-238
digit recognition training
  with TensorFlow 232-236
dog versus cat classification flask
  integrating 307-311
dog versus cat classification project
  integrating 307-311
dog versus cat classification, with OpenCV
  about 241-244
  in TensorFlow 238-241
dropout 213

E

edge detection
  about 90
  with OpenCV 90
Edge Detection Parameters 90
exponential linear unit (ELU) function 212
eye detection
  in Haar Cascade classifiers 185-188

F

face detection
  with Haar Cascade classifiers 181-185
FaceNet architecture 262-268
face recognition
  with OpenCV 261, 262
  with TensorFlow 261, 262
facial expression recognition
  emotion detection method 276-288
  with TensorFlow 276
Fashion-MNIST in TensorFlow 228-231
FAST Corner Detection 138

Fast Library for Approximate Nearest
        Neighbors (FLANN)
    feature matching 148, 149, 151
feature extraction 261
feature matching
    about 148, 261
    with FLANN 148-151
feedforward neural networks 207
findContours() function 104

G

gaussian filter 77
gaussian pyramids 83
generative adversarial networks
        (GANs) 210, 223, 224
Google Colab
    for OpenCV 11-13
grayscaling 42

H

Haar Cascade classifiers
    about 180, 181
    face detection 181-185
    for eye detection 185-188
    for smile detection 189-193
Harris Corner Detection 138
high-level algorithms 2
Hough Line Transform methods
    Probabilistic Hough Transform 118, 119
    Standard Hough Transform 118
Hough Line Transform theory
    in OpenCV 117, 118
HSV color space
    about 157, 158
    used, for object detection 159-161
    used, for object tracking 161-164
hyperbolic tangent (tanh) function 212

I

image blending
    with OpenCV 85
image cropping 39
image gradients
    with OpenCV 80-82
image histogram 110

image histogram, in OpenCV
    1D histogram 111
    2D histogram 111
    about 110-112
image preprocessing 197
image processing techniques
    about 37, 38
    arguments, adding 45
    background removal 48-50
    grayscaling 42
    image cropping 39
    image resizing 40
    image rotation 40
    images, adding 45
    images, blending with weights 46
    image split 42, 43
    image waitKey() function 38
    merging image 43, 44
    region of interest (ROI) 47
image processing techniques, in OpenCV
    edge detection 38
    feature detection and extraction 38
    image filtering 37
    image segmentation 38
    image thresholding 37
    morphological operation 38
    object detection 38
image pyramids
    about 87, 89
    with OpenCV 83, 84
image resizing 40
image rotation 40
image segmentation
    with OpenCV 177-180
image split 42, 43
images with OpenCV
    blurring 76
    smoothing 76
image thresholding, with OpenCV
    about 97
    adaptive thresholding 99, 100
    binary thresholding 101, 102
    inverted thresholding 103, 104
    otsu's thresholding 100, 101
    simple thresholding 97, 98
image trackbar 65-67

Index

image waitKey() function 38
inverted thresholding 103, 104
iris dataset 225
iris dataset, in TensorFlow
  about 225
  example 226, 228

J

JavaScript libraries 306
Jupyter Notebook 7

K

Keras 215
k-Nearest Neighbors (k-NN)
  classification 204, 205

L

Laplacian of Gaussian (LoG) filter
  about 90
  with OpenCV 92, 93
laplacian pyramids 83
Leaky ReLU function 212
Long Short-Term Memory (LSTM) 209
low-level algorithms 2

M

machine learning (ML) 203, 204
machine learning (ML) types
  about 204-206
  reinforcement learning 204
  unsupervised learning 204
MacOS
  Open-Source Computer Vision Library
    (OpenCV), downloading 10, 11
  Open-Source Computer Vision Library
    (OpenCV), installing 10, 11
Matplotlib, with OpenCV
  about 69
  techniques 69-72
mean average precision (mAP) 221
mean filter 79, 80
mean intersection over union (mIoU) 223
Mean Shift object tracking
  with OpenCV 165-168
median filter 77

merging image 43
mini-batch gradient descent 213
momentum 213
morphological transformations, with OpenCV
  about 72
  closing 75, 76
  dilation 73, 74
  erosion 72, 73
  opening 74, 75
motion detection
  with OpenCV 164
motion tracking
  with OpenCV 164
mouse_callback() function 35
mouse click event 34
mouse event
  examples 53-60
  mouse click event 34
  mouse move event 34
  with OpenCV 33-35
mouse move event 34
multi-layer perceptron (MLP) 211

N

neural network architecture 211
neural network optimization techniques
  about 213
  adaptive learning rate methods 213
  dropout 213
  mini-batch gradient descent 213
  momentum 213
  regularization techniques 213
  stochastic gradient descent (SGD) 213
neural networks 206
neural networks, types
  about 207
  autoencoders 209, 210
  convolutional neural networks (CNNs) 208
  feedforward neural networks 207
  generative adversarial networks (GANs) 210
  recurrent neural networks (RNNs) 209
normalized cross-correlation (NCC) 113

O

object detection
  with HSV color space 159-161

object tracking
  with HSV color space 161-164
OpenCV architecture
  about 5
  core functionality 5
  feature detection and description 6
  high-level GUI 5
  image processing 5
  machine learning 6
  miscellaneous 6
  object detection and recognition 6
  video I/O 5
OpenCV Hough circle transform
  using, in circle detection 123, 124
OpenCV library
  features 6, 7
OpenCV methods
  background subtraction 164
  kalman filter 165
  optical flow 165
  template matching 165
OpenCV project
  deploying 299, 300
  deploying, in Azure 301-305
  tools and platforms 300
OpenCV real-time applications
  examples 4, 5
  in computer vision 4
OpenCV with robotics
  integrating 224, 225
Open-Source Computer Vision Library
    (OpenCV)
  about 2, 3
  augmented reality (AR) 171-176
  background subtraction methods 151, 152
  benefits 3, 4
  camera parameters, setting 28, 29
  CAMShift object tracking method 168-171
  Canny Edge Detection 93-96
  corner detection 137
  Digit Recognition Model, testing 236-238
  downloading, for MacOS 10, 11
  downloading, for Windows 8-10
  edge detection 90
  Google Colab 11-13
  Hough Line Transform theory 117, 118

image blending 85
image gradients 80-82
image pyramids 83, 84
images, displaying 16
image segmentation 177-180
images, reading 15
images, writing 16
installing, for MacOS 10, 11
installing, for Windows 8-10
integrating, with web application 306
Laplacian of Gaussian (LoG) filter 92, 93
Mean Shift object tracking 165-168
motion detection 164
motion tracking 164
mouse events 33-35
Optical Character Recognition
    (OCR) 197-201
Python code editors 7
QR code detection 193-196
Sobel operator 90-92
used, for converting color in images 17
used, for converting color in video 21, 22
used, for detecting simple geometric
    shapes 107-110
used, for displaying date and time
    of videos 29, 31
used, for displaying text on videos 31-33
used, for drawing geometric shapes
    on images 23-27
videos, displaying from camera 18, 19
videos, reading from camera 18, 19
videos, writing from camera 19-21
Open Source Computer Vision (OpenCV) 197
optical character recognition (OCR)
  about 117
  with OpenCV 197-201
otsu's thresholding 100, 101

P

principal component analysis (PCA) 205
Probabilistic Hough Transform (PHT)
  about 118-121
  with OpenCV 121, 122
probability density function (PDF) 165
PyCharm 7
Python code editors

Index

for OpenCV 7
Jupyter Notebook 7
PyCharm 7
Spyder 7
Sublime Text 8
Visual Studio Code 7
PyTorch 215

Q

QR code detection
  with OpenCV 193-196

R

real-time age prediction
  with RESNET 50_CNN 269, 270
  with TensorFlow 269, 270
rectified linear unit (ReLU) function 208, 212
recurrent neural networks (RNNs) 209, 211
region of interest (ROI) 47, 48
region proposal network (RPN) 220
regularization techniques 213
reinforcement learning 204
ResNet-50 CNN
  components 270, 271
  key innovations 272, 273
RESNET 50_CNN 269, 273-276
road lane line detection with OpenCV 131-137
Robot Operating Systems (ROS) 225

S

scale-invariant feature transform (SIFT) 138, 147
semantic segmentation
  about 222
  in network 222
Shi-Tomasi Corner Detection 138
sigmoid function 212
simple geometric shapes
  detecting, with OpenCV 107-110
simple thresholding 97, 98
Simultaneous Localization and Mapping (SLAM) 225
single-layer perceptron
  about 211
  convolutional neural networks (CNNs) 211

multi-layer perceptron (MLP) 211
recurrent neural network (RNNs) 211
Single Shot Detector (SSD) 220
smile detection
  in Haar Cascade classifiers 189-193
Sobel operator
  about 90
  with OpenCV 90-92
softmax function 212
Speeded-Up Robust Feature (SURF) 138
Spyder 7
Standard Hough Transform
  about 118
  with OpenCV 119, 120
stochastic gradient descent (SGD) 213
Sublime Text 8
sum of squared differences (SSD) 113
supervised learning 204
support vector machines (SVMs)
  classification 204, 205

T

template matching
  about 113
  with OpenCV 113-117
template-matching methods
  correlation coefficient 114
  cross-correlation 113
  normalized correlation coefficient 114
  normalized cross-correlation 113
  normalized sum of squared differences 113
  sum of squared differences 113
TensorFlow
  about 215
  digit recognition training 232-236
  using, in content-based image retrieval (CBIR) 288-297
  using, in facial expression recognition 276
  using, in YOLO v3 object detection 250-254
  using, in YOLO v5 custom dataset 254-260
text on videos
  displaying, with OpenCV 31-33
text region detection 197
text segmentation 197
trackbar
  binding 63-65

U

unsupervised learning 204

V

video frame
  pausing 52, 53
  reshaping 50, 51
Visual Studio Code 7

W

warpAffine 41
Watershed algorithm 178
web application
  used, for integrating OpenCV 306
weighted blending 86, 87
Windows
  Open-Source Computer Vision Library
      (OpenCV), downloading 8-10
  Open-Source Computer Vision Library
      (OpenCV), installing 8-10

Y

YOLO algorithm
  about 245
  components 246-248
YOLO architecture 249
YOLO v2 249
YOLO v3 249
YOLO v3 object detection
  with TensorFlow 250, 251, 254
YOLO v4 250
YOLO v5 custom dataset
  with TensorFlow 254-260
YOLO Versions
  about 249
  YOLO v2 249
  YOLO v3 249
  YOLO v4 250
You Only Look Once (YOLO) 220, 245

Printed in Great Britain
by Amazon